# Preface Books

A series of scholarly and critical studies of major writers intended for those needing modern and authoritative guidance through the characteristic difficulties of their work to reach an intelligent understanding and enjoyment of it.

General Editor: MAURICE HUSSEY

A Preface to Wordsworth — JOHN PURKIS
A Preface to Donne — JAMES WINNY
A Preface to Jane Austen — CHRISTOPHER GILLIE
A Preface to Yeats — EDWARD MALINS
A Preface to Pope — I. R. F. GORDON
A Preface to Hardy — MERRYN WILLIAMS
A Preface to James Joyce — SYDNEY BOLT
A Preface to Hopkins — GRAHAM STOREY
A Preface to Conrad — CEDRIC WATTS
A Preface to Lawrence — GĀMINI SALGĀDO
A Preface to Forster — CHRISTOPHER GILLIE
A Preface to Auden — ALLAN RODWAY
A Preface to Dickens — ALLAN GRANT
A Preface to Shelley — PATRICIA HODGART
A Preface to Keats — CEDRIC WATTS
A Preface to George Eliot — JOHN PURKIS

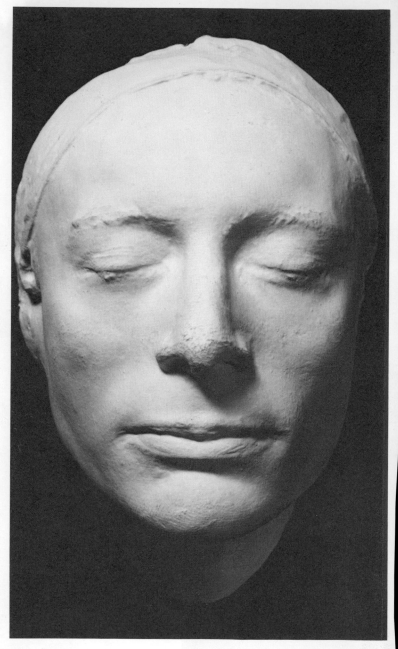

*This frontispiece shows a life-mask of Keats (1816) by Benjamin Haydon.*

# A Preface to Keats

*Cedric Watts*

Longman, London and New York

LONGMAN GROUP LIMITED
*Longman House*
*Burnt Mill, Harlow, Essex CM20 2JE, England*

First published 1985
Produced by Longman Group (F.E.) Ltd.
Printed in Hong Kong.

**Library of Congress Cataloging in Publication Data**

Watts, Cedric Thomas.
  A preface to Keats.

  Bibliography: p.
  Includes indexes.
  Summary: Discusses the life and work of John Keats in
the social and political context of the world and time in
which he lived.
  1. Keats, John, 1795–1821.   2. Poets, English–19th
century – Biography. [1. Keats, John, 1795–1821.
2. Poets, English]   I. Title.
PR4836.W34   1985      821'.7 [B] [92]      84-7194
ISBN 0-582-35368-8
ISBN 0-582-35367-X (pbk.)

*Cover picture: detail from John Millais's 'Lorenzo and Isabella' (1849), a*
*radiant Pre-Raphaelite painting suggested by stanzas 1 and 21 of Keats's*
*'Isabella; or, The Pot of Basil'. The foot jabbing the dog belongs (of course)*
*to one of the murderous brothers.*

CEDRIC WATTS took a first in English and a doctorate at Cambridge, and since 1965 has taught at Sussex University, where he is a Professor of English. He is author of *Conrad's 'Heart of Darkness': A Critical and Contextual Discussion* (Mursia, Milan, 1977), *A Preface to Conrad* (Longman, 1982), *R. B. Cunninghame Graham* (Hall, Boston, 1983) and *The Deceptive Text* (Harvester, 1984), and co-author, with Laurence Davies, of *Cunninghame Graham: A Critical Biography* (Cambridge University Press, 1979). He has edited *Joseph Conrad's Letters to R. B. Cunninghame Graham* (Cambridge University Press, 1969), *The English Novel* (Sussex Books, 1976) and *Selected Writings of Cunninghame Graham* (Associated University Presses, 1981). He is a member of the Keats-Shelley Memorial Association.

# Contents

# List of illustrations

To My Wife

# Foreword

The brevity of life, the creativity that arises from illness, and the belief in the triumph of art are all vividly illuminated in the career of John Keats. The rapidity of his artistic and technical development that arose from these conditions permitted him to fashion an identity still more remarkable for the pressure of other poets of the highest order contending for public response in the early years of the nineteenth century. Cedric Watts here provides for modern readers of Keats an essential service. In addition to a series of close and faithful discussions of the poetry and letters of his subject he shows the importance of placing him within the developing traditions of English poetry as a whole. For Keats this stemmed from Shakespeare and Milton, a poet often too strong for him to withstand, and in the period after his death when his reputation grew, we see a modified tradition flowing towards Hardy, Wilfred Owen and others who were able to make creative use of their study of the Romantic idiom.

Professor Watts offers only a brief segment of quotations with which to document the poet's ideas upon matters outside his concern with art. One does not go to Keats for insight into the history of academic ideas and this study is rendered more economical for this decision. What will most strongly emerge, however, is that the poet's lack of faith, while serving in due course as an encouragement for Victorian and later agnostics, found its own compensation in a renaissance–style preoccupation with ancient mythology and an extension of the range of classical icons in modern English verse. A detailed catalogue of these symbols and allegories is provided in the appendix. It has always been, after all, Keats's awareness of humanity and of the natural life that most readily seizes upon the imagination of his readers, and these qualities, deployed above all in the Odes and the main narratives, inform the most valuable parts of Cedric Watts's alert and sensitive study.

As an afterthought: is there the reader who is most at one with his subject in a particular place? If so, then, he may discover where to follow the paths of the poet. I am thinking not only of the Protestant cemetery in Rome or up on Hampstead Heath, where I myself have mused upon him, but also that the man whose name was 'writ in water' may be pursued into the river meadows of Winchester.

MAURICE HUSSEY
General Editor

# Acknowledgements and editorial notes

All quotations from Keats's poems and plays are from Jack Stillinger's edition, *The Poems of John Keats* (London: Heinemann, 1978). Other editions consulted include H. W. Garrod's *The Poetical Works of John Keats* (Oxford University Press, 1939, revised edition 1958), Miriam Allott's *The Poems of John Keats* (London: Longman, 1970, fourth impression 1977), and John Barnard's *John Keats: The Complete Poems* (Harmondsworth: Penguin, 1973). I have found particularly useful Professor Allott's extensive commentaries on the poems. Quotations from Keats's letters are from *The Letters of John Keats 1814–1821*, edited by Hyder Edward Rollins (two volumes, Cambridge University Press, 1958). When preparing the biographical material, I consulted the writings of Robert Gittings and Timothy Hilton, and W. J. Bate's *John Keats* (London: Oxford University Press, 1967) was particularly useful.

When quoting texts, I have preserved any errors or idiosyncrasies in spelling, punctuation and capitalisation that their editors have preserved, except that in a few cases, in the interests of clarity, I have supplied the corrections which are enclosed in square brackets. Such brackets also enclose any small modification (e.g. initial capitalisation) of a quoted passage to fit the present grammatical context. (The square-bracketed emendations in Keats's letters are mainly Rollins'.) In poems, I have where necessary inserted a grave accent over any otherwise-unsounded syllable that needs to be sounded in order to preserve the metre. In quotations of poetry or prose, a row of three dots represents an ellipsis already present in the material being quoted, whereas a row of five dots ( . . . . . ) represents an omission that I have made.

This book was written between 1981 and 1983.

The author and publisher are grateful to the following for permission to quote copyright material:

its author, Tony Harrison, for an extract from the poem 'A Kumquat for John Keats'; author's agents, Michael B. Yeats & Anne Yeats for the poem 'Ephemera' by W. B. Yeats from *The Collected Poems of W. B. Yeats* pub. Macmillan (London) Ltd., 1963; Faber & Faber Ltd for an extract from the poem 'Burnt Norton' from *Four quartets* by T. S. Eliot.

We are grateful to the following for permission to reproduce photographs, etc.:

British Library, page 39; British Museum, pages 30 and 55; Fitzwilliam Museum, Cambridge, page 124; Guildhall Library, page 66; Keats House, pages 42, 43, 45, 53 and 58; Mansell Collection, page 105; National Gallery, page 143; National Portrait Gallery, pages ii, 15, 22, 47, 57, 70 (courtesy Leslie Gunston) and 163; Tate Gallery, pages 82 and 157; Victoria and Albert Museum, pages 11, 20, 28 and 92.

The painting *Lorenzo and Isabella* by John Millais, 1849, is reproduced on the cover by permission of the Walker Art Gallery, Liverpool.

# Abbreviations

| | |
|---|---|
| A | *The Poems of John Keats*, edited by Miriam Allott. London: Longman, 1970 (4th impression, 1977). |
| B | Walter Jackson Bate: *John Keats*. Oxford University Press, 1963 (corrected paperback edition, 1967). |
| BH | Charles Dickens: *Bleak House*. London: Collins, 1953. |
| BTW | *'Between Two Worlds': Byron's Letters and Journals*, Vol. VII, edited by Leslie A. Marchand. London: John Murray, 1977. |
| CC | Charles and Mary Cowden Clarke: *Recollections of Writers*. London: Sampson Low, Marston, Searle, and Rivington, 1878. |
| CH | *Keats: The Critical Heritage*, edited by G. M. Matthews. London: Routledge and Kegan Paul, 1971. |
| DP | Percy Bysshe Shelley: *A Defence of Poetry*. Oxford: Blackwell, 1972. |
| G | Robert Gittings: *John Keats*. London: Heinemann, 1968. |
| GMH | *The Poems of Gerard Manley Hopkins*, edited by W. H. Gardner and N. H. MacKenzie. Oxford University Press, 1970. |
| GSF | *John Keats: The Odes: A Casebook*, edited by G. S. Fraser. London: Macmillan, 1971. |
| H | Leigh Hunt: *Lord Byron and Some of His Contemporaries*. London: Colburn, 1828. |
| HJ | *The Autobiography and Journals of Benjamin Robert Haydon*, edited by Malcolm Elwin. London: Macdonald, 1950. |
| JHR | *Selected Prose of John Hamilton Reynolds*, edited by Leonidas M. Jones. Cambridge, Mass.: Harvard University Press, 1966. |
| KC | *The Keats Circle: Letters and Papers 1816–1878*, 2 Volumes, edited by Hyder Edward Rollins. Cambridge, Mass.: Harvard University Press, 1948 (2nd edition). |
| L | F. R. Leavis: *Revaluation: Tradition and Development in English Poetry*. London: Chatto and Windus, 1936 (rpt. Peregrine Books, 1964). |
| P | *The Poetical Works of John Keats*, edited by H. W. Garrod. Second edition, Oxford University Press, 1958. |
| R | *The Letters of John Keats 1814–1821*, 2 Volumes, edited by Hyder Edward Rollins. Cambridge University Press, 1958. |
| S | *The Complete Poetical Works of Percy Bysshe Shelley*, edited by Thomas Hutchinson. Oxford University Press, 1929. |

STC     *The Notebooks of Samuel Taylor Coleridge: I: 1794–1804*, edited by Kathleen Coburn. New York: Pantheon Books and Bollingen Foundation, 1957.

TH     *Selected Poems of Thomas Hood*, edited by John Clubbe. Cambridge, Mass.: Harvard University Press, 1970.

WL     *The Letters of William and Dorothy Wordsworth: The Later Years*, Vol. III, edited by Ernest de Selincourt. Oxford University Press, 1939.

WP     *The Poetical Works of Wordsworth*, edited by Thomas Hutchinson, revised by Ernest de Selincourt. Oxford University Press, 1904 (rpt. 1951).

Y     *The Collected Poems of W. B. Yeats.* London: Macmillan, 1963.

# Part One
## *The Writer and His Setting*

# Chronological table

| KEATS'S LIFE | OTHER EVENTS |
|---|---|
| | 1789 French Revolution. |
| | 1793 Reign of Terror: Louis XVI guillotined. France declares war on Britain. |
| | 1793–1800 Repressive measures in England by Pitt's Government. |
| | 1794 Blake: *Songs of Innocence and of Experience.* Paine: *Age of Reason.* Mrs Radcliffe: *Mysteries of Udolpho.* |
| 1795 (31 October) John Keats born at Moorgate. | |
| 1797 Birth of George Keats. | 1797 Coleridge's 'Kubla Khan' written. |
| | 1798 Wordsworth and Coleridge: *Lyrical Ballads.* |
| 1799 Birth of Tom Keats. | 1799 Napoleon becomes First Consul of France. |
| | 1799–1800 Combination Acts. |
| 1800 Birth of Fanny Brawne. | 1800 Volta invents electric battery. |
| 1803 Birth of Fanny (Frances Mary) Keats. John Keats attends school at Enfield. | |

| 1804 | Keats's father dies. His mother re-marries. The Keats children move to their grandparents' home. | 1804 | Napoleon proclaimed Emperor. |
|---|---|---|---|
| 1805 | Grandfather dies. | 1805 | Nelson victorious at Trafalgar. Napoleon defeats Russians and Austrians at Austerlitz. Wordsworth: *The Prelude.* |
| | | 1808 | Goethe: *Faust*, Part I. |
| | | 1809 | Darwin born. Tennyson born. |
| 1810 | Mother dies of tuberculosis. | 1810 | George III becomes increasingly insane. Crabbe: *The Borough.* |
| 1811 | Keats leaves school to become apothecary's apprentice. | 1811 | Prince of Wales becomes Regent. |
| | | 1811–12 | Luddite riots. |
| | | 1812 | Napoleon's retreat from Moscow. Charles Dickens born. Byron: *Childe Harold* (I and II). |
| | | 1813 | Jane Austen: *Pride and Prejudice.* Leigh Hunt begins two-years' prison sentence. |
| 1814 | Early attempts at verse. Death of grandmother. | 1814 | Scott: *Waverley.* Edmund Kean gains fame. |
| 1815 | Poems include sonnet on Leigh Hunt's release from jail. Enters Guy's Hospital as student. | 1815 | Napoleon defeated at Waterloo. End of war between Britain and France. |

| | | | |
|---|---|---|---|
| 1816 | Sonnet 'O Solitude' published. Qualifies as apothecary. Writes 'Chapman's Homer' sonnet. Meets Hunt, Haydon and Reynolds. | 1816 | Shelley: *Alastor*. Hunt: *Story of Rimini*. Coleridge: 'Kubla Khan' and 'Christabel' published. |
| 1817 | Moves to Hampstead. First book, *Poems*, published. Writes *Endymion*. Meets Wordsworth and Lamb at Haydon's 'Immortal Dinner'. | 1817 | Jane Austen dies. Kean acts *Richard III*. *Blackwood's* attacks the 'Cockney School of Poetry'. |
| 1818 | *Endymion* published. Tours Lakes and Scotland. Meets Fanny Brawne. *Quarterly Review* attacks *Endymion*. Begins *Hyperion*. Tom dies (tuberculosis). | 1818 | Hazlitt lectures on poetry. Karl Marx born. |
| 1819 | Writes 'The Eve of St. Agnes', 'La Belle Dame' and the major odes, including 'To Autumn'. Abandons *Hyperion*. Writes *Otho*. Becomes engaged to Fanny Brawne. | 1819 | George Eliot born. 'Peterloo' Massacre. Richard Carlile jailed. Victoria born. |
| | | 1819–24 | Byron: *Don Juan* published. |
| 1820 | (February) Severe haemorrhage. (July) *Lamia* volume published. (September) Sails for Italy with Severn. (October) Arrives at Naples. (November) Arrives in Rome. | 1820 | Birth of Engels. Death of George III. Prince Regent becomes George IV. Shelley writes 'Ode to Liberty' and 'To a Skylark'. |
| 1821 | (23 February) Dies of tuberculosis. | 1821 | Shelley's *Adonais*. Death of Napoleon. |

# 1 Keats's life

His short life was perceived by those who knew him to be of unusual intensity; it insisted on being recorded in many ways, from the attempt to capture his ardent look with pencil or pen to the watchful preservation of this hastiest scrap of verse. . . . .

EDMUND BLUNDEN

## Childhood and schooldays

John Keats's short life began in London on 31 October 1795. He was the first child of parents who had been married just over a year; subsequent children were George (born in 1797), Tom (1799), Edward, who was born in 1801 and died in infancy, and Frances – Fanny – born in 1803. Their father was a lively and energetic ostler at his father-in-law's livery stables, the Swan and Hoop, at Moorgate; and in the course of time he became the manager. However, in April 1804 he fell from his horse while riding down the road, fractured his skull, and died without regaining consciousness. His widow, who subsequently gained the reputation of an alcoholic, rapidly re-married, and the children were taken to the home of their grandparents. John Jennings, the grandfather, soon died, leaving them to the care of his widow, Alice.

Financial provision for the Keats children should have been ample, for John Jennings had prospered in business and left an estate of over £13,000, of which a substantial share – about £8,000 – was designated for the children. (At that time, a working man could live decently on £50 per year.) However, the will was complicated and unclear; it led to disputes within the family; and the lawyers were slow and unhelpful. Richard Abbey, who became the children's guardian, seems to have been mean and grudging. As young men, John Keats and his brother George were often to be short of funds, neither knowing nor having access to their full entitlement. Many years later, in *Bleak House*, Charles Dickens was to portray Chancery as a legal labyrinth in which lawsuits might be pursued for decades by claimants who enriched the lawyers rather than themselves. He had in mind, among other cases, the wrangles over the Keats inheritance. One particular sum reposed in Chancery until 1888, when it was discovered by a solicitor and claimed for Fanny Keats, who was then eighty-five.

The children's mother died in 1810 from tuberculosis – the widespread contagious disease of the lungs which was to claim her sons Tom and John in the course of time. The grandmother seems to have provided a happy home for the children: John Keats later

5

recalled that her house was a place of pets (caged birds, mice and goldfish) and pranks (he filled washtubs with minnows and sticklebacks). From 1803 to 1811 young Keats attended the Reverend John Clarke's School at Enfield, a liberal, progressive boarding school without fagging or flogging, set in rural surroundings; the boys could tend their own garden plots. The pupils were mainly middle-class by background, destined to become artists, lawyers, musicians, writers, and members of the professions generally. Keats was a popular lad: small but lively, with bright eager eyes and a wide mouth quick to grin; generous, pugnacious, friendly and mercurial. There is a story that when an usher at the school, on receiving some impertinence, had boxed brother Tom's ears, John 'rushed up, put himself in the received posture of offence, and . . . . . struck the usher – who could, so to say, have put him into his pocket. His passion at times was almost ungovernable; and his brother George, being considerably the taller and stronger, used frequently to hold him down by main force, laughing when John was "in one of his moods" and was endeavouring to beat him' (CC, 123). Even when mature, Keats was to remain rather boyish, both in temperament and in appearance: fully grown, his maximum height was only 154 cm – scarcely more than five feet.

One schoolfellow, Edward Holmes, recalled that Keats was at first 'noted for his indifference to lessons':

> *his love of books & poetry manifested itself chiefly about a year before he left school.* In all active exercises – he excelled. The generosity & daring of his character – with the extreme beauty & animation of his face made I remember an impression on me – & being some years his junior I was obliged to woo his friendship – in which I succeeded but not till I had fought several battles. This violence & vehemence – this pugnacity and generosity of disposition – in passions of tears or outrageous fits of laughter always in extremes will help to paint Keats in his boyhood. Associated as they were with an extraordinary beauty of person & expression – these qualities captivated the boys, and no one was ever more popular.
>
> (*KC* II, 165)

This extreme attractiveness of personality was later illustrated by the great loyalty of the circle of friends who came to know him and his work. If initially at school Keats was more interested in fights than study, he atoned for this towards the end of his time there: he won a first prize for voluntary translation. This prize was C. H. Kauffman's *Dictionary of Merchandize* . . . . . *For the Use of Counting Houses*, which years later provided him with the striking lines about the deafened pearl-divers in 'Isabella; or, The Pot of Basil'. Another prize was to be Bonnycastle's *Introduction to Astronomy*. From the émigré teacher, the Abbé Béliard, he learned fluency in French, and

6

his translations of Latin led him naturally to reference-books on the Greek and Latin myths: particularly John Lemprière's *Bibliotheca Classica; or, A Classical Dictionary*, which furnished him with an abundance of material for his later works. It was at Clarke's school, too, that he gained liberal political ideas, for the headmaster subscribed to Leigh Hunt's liberal magazine, the *Examiner*, and his son lent copies to Keats. Charles Cowden Clarke, the head's son, claimed that the *Examiner* and Burnet's *History of His Own Time* 'no doubt laid the foundation of his love of civil and religious liberty' (CC, 124).

His happiness at school was marred by the death of his mother, which so upset him that he hid himself in the alcove under the master's desk. He was to say: 'I have never known any unalloy'd Happiness for many days together: the death or sickness of some one has always spoilt my hours' (R II, 123). But he was happy enough to return to read poetry with Cowden Clarke, who wrote:

> [A]t the far end of the pond, beneath the iron railings which divided our premises from the meadows beyond, whence the song of the nightingales in May would reach us in the stillness of the night, there stood a rustic arbour, where John Keats and I used to sit and read Spenser's 'Faery Queene' together, when he had left school, and used to come over from Edmonton, where he was apprenticed to Thomas Hammond the surgeon. On the other side of the house lay a small enclosure which we called 'the drying-ground,' and where was a magnificent old morella cherry-tree against a wall well exposed to the sun. Beyond this, a gate led into a small field, or paddock, of two acres, – the pasture-ground of the two cows that supplied the establishment with fresh and abundant milk.
>
> (B, 11)

Such was the miniature Arcadia into which the mother's death had intruded.

## Apprenticeship as surgeon – and as poet

It was probably in 1811, as W. J. Bate has argued (B, 703–4), rather than in 1810, that Keats left school to begin his apprenticeship as a surgeon with Thomas Hammond. To become a doctor would have entailed expensive study at a university; given the lower-middle-class circumstances of the Keats children, a surgeon's apprenticeship evidently seemed more appropriate. From Hammond, Keats learned a variety of skills, including bone-setting and probably the pulling of teeth, for this was the manual side of the medical profession. After several years as an apprentice, Keats registered as a student at Guy's Hospital in October 1815.

7

He attended lectures (in lecture-rooms sometimes crowded with three hundred students at a time) at Guy's Hospital and St. Thomas's; his courses were on anatomy and physiology, chemistry, and the theory and practice of medicine. Keats's lecture-notes were laborious and occasionally confused, and it is characteristic that alongside his notes on fractures of the nose and jaw he has filled a margin with fanciful flowers. He told Cowden Clarke: 'The other day, for instance, during the lecture, there came a sunbeam in the room, and with it a whole troop of creatures floating in the ray; and I was off with them to Oberon and fairyland' (CC, 132). In stark contrast to 'fairyland' was his training as a 'dresser' – as one who regularly cleans and dresses wounds (which in those days so rapidly became infected) – in addition to pulling teeth, setting bones, and cleaning up after the surgeon had sawn and sliced. This was before the use of effective anaesthetics: patients often had to be held down, shouting in agony, while the students pressed forward for a clear view, and the blood pattered into the sawdust-box under the table.

In July 1816 Keats passed his examinations and became licensed to practice as a surgeon and apothecary, though he had a growing aversion to surgery and its requirements of cool ruthlessness. He had been staying at lodgings near Guy's Hospital, but later in the year he joined his brothers at 76 Cheapside, a bustling contrast to the relatively rural Edmonton where they had formerly lived with their grandmother. Brothers George and Tom were working as clerks in the counting-house of Richard Abbey, the guardian, who was a tea-merchant and respected public figure. Tom was eventually forced to leave because of illness (tuberculosis again) and George because of a quarrel with Abbey's junior partner. Apart from four years at school, sister Fanny lived at the house of Abbey and his wife until she was twenty-one. It was a repressive régime in which she had little pocket-money and less liberty, and was discouraged from visiting her brothers.

Naturally enough, given the dependence of biographers upon the recollections of friends, we know far more about Keats's leisure than about his medical work during these apprentice years. As we have seen, he would frequently walk back to his old school at Edmonton to discuss poetry and particularly the works of Spenser (including 'Epithalamion' and of course *The Faerie Queene*), which he read with excitement:

> He *hoisted* himself up, and looked burly and dominant, as he said, 'what an image that is – "*sea-shouldering whales!*"'
>
> (CC, 126)

Here we recognise at once not a cool appreciation of a *mot juste* but rather that sensuous empathy which is a striking characteristic of Keats as man and writer. 'Empathy' is a jargonish term, often glibly and inappropriately used, but its meaning – 'Capacity for intense sympathetic identification with some object' – is clearly appropriate here, as we see how, when appreciating the muscular rightness of 'sea-shouldering', Keats muscularly enacts the term, looking 'burly and dominant'. He was also particularly moved (to tears, we are told) when Clarke read him the following passage from Shakespeare's *Cymbeline*, in which Imogen says that she would have watched her departing lover, Posthumus,

> till the diminution
> Of space had pointed him sharp as my needle:
> Nay, followed him, till he had melted from
> The smallness of a gnat, to air: and then
> Have turn'd mine eye, and wept.
>
> (Act I, scene iv, lines 18–22)

Again, it is the sensuous exactness here which struck Keats. Years later he was to claim that he could imagine that a billiard ball, as it rolled about, experienced 'a sense of delight from its own roundness, smoothness volubility. & the rapidity of its motion' (KC I, 59).

In a verse letter, Keats subsequently expressed his gratitude to Cowden Clarke for awakening him to poetry:

> Who read for me the sonnet swelling loudly
> Up to its climax and then dying proudly?
> Who found for me the grandeur of the ode,
> Growing, like Atlas, stronger from its load?
> Who let me taste that more than cordial dram,
> The sharp, the rapier-pointed epigram?
> Shew'd me that epic was of all the king,
> Round, vast, and spanning all like Saturn's ring?
>
> ('To Charles Cowden Clarke', lines 60–67)

(That reference to Saturn's ring shows how Keats could apply what he had learned from Bonnycastle's *Introduction to Astronomy*.) Another important friendship was with George Felton Mathew – important because Mathew was an aspiring poet (though little talented), and his enthusiasm mirrored and intensified Keats's. Keats thought of their relationship as 'a brotherhood in song', likening it to the collaborative relationship of the seventeenth-century dramatists Beaumont and Fletcher; while Mathew compared Keats to the young Shakespeare and Milton, and addressed him as

> thou, who delightest in fanciful song,
> And tellest strange tales of the elf, & the fay.
>
> ('To a Poetical Friend')

As Keats found more illustrious company, the friendship cooled; but it had provided an important incentive at a formative time.

9

Keats's first poem, probably written early in 1814, is generally thought to be the 'Imitation of Spenser' – a characteristically selective imitation, for all traces of Spenser's Puritanical allegoric purposes have vanished, leaving instead a description of an idyllically fanciful rural retreat. The stanza-form is Spenserian, and there is a debt to the descriptions of the Isle of Mirth and Bower of Bliss in *The Faerie Queene*, Book II, Cantos vi and xii; but what Spenser presents as a temptation to be overcome, Keats presents as a reverie to be indulged. The attraction to the sensuous, characterised in the following stanza from 'Imitation of Spenser', was to be a source of strength and weakness throughout Keats's poetic career.

> There the king-fisher saw his plumage bright
> Vieing with fish of brilliant dye below;
> Whose silken fins and golden scalès light
> Cast upward, through the waves, a ruby glow:
> There saw the swan his neck of archèd snow,
> And oar'd himself along with majesty;
> Sparkled his jetty eyes; his feet did show
> Beneath the waves like Afric's ebony,
> And on his back a fay reclined voluptuously.

(lines 10–18)

Other early exercises included the sonnet 'To Lord Byron' ('Byron, how sweetly sad thy melody'), invoking the melancholy Byron of *Childe Harold* and the oriental verse-tales; while another sonnet ('As from the darkening gloom a silver dove') offered facile tribute to his dead grandmother. 'Fill for me a brimming bowl', though a slight piece, anticipated much of his later work by its oscillation between a desire for drugged oblivion and a desire to celebrate the world's beauty. The sonnet 'Oh Chatterton!' commends the famed fore-runner and poet-martyr of the Romantic Movement, the astonishingly prolific poet from Bristol who had poisoned himself at the age of seventeen. The sympathy with radicalism that had been nurtured at the Reverend Clarke's school found expression in two further sonnets: 'On Peace' and 'Written on the Day That Mr. Leigh Hunt Left Prison'. Leigh Hunt and his brother John had been fined £500 and sentenced to two years in prison for libelling the Prince Regent by describing him (accurately enough) as a dishonourable libertine. In the 'Lines Written on 29 May', Keats echoes the liberalism of Hunt and Cowden Clarke by celebrating the Whig patriot-heroes Algernon Sidney, Lord William Russell and Sir Henry Vane.

Rather more typical of Keats's early preoccupations, however, were 'Specimen of an Induction to a Poem' (beginning 'Lo! I must tell a tale of chivalry') and 'Calidore: A Fragment', in both of which

*James Gillray: 'A Voluptuary under the Horrors of Digestion': a contemporaneous caricature of George, Prince of Wales, subsequently Prince Regent from 1810 to 1820, who then became King George IV. Whereas Keats's poems strenuously idealised voluptuous hedonism, the Prince Regent's conduct prodigally vulgarised it. (Meanwhile, many people went hungry: in 1819 two indigent women were hanged at Manchester for stealing potatoes from an overturned cart.)*

Keats is clearly influenced by Spenser's *Faerie Queene* and by Leigh Hunt's chivalric *The Story of Rimini*. Already we see the problem that was to haunt Keats throughout his career: he had the ambition to embark on a narrative poem of substantial length but not the resources to complete it. In 'Calidore' the scene-setting is richly elaborate but the narrative direction uncertain: as so often in other poems, Keats is readily distracted from the need to tell a tale by the opportunity to indulge in some sensuous 'luxury'; and it is significant that that very word 'luxury', which Hunt liked, becomes a favourite with Keats as with no other great Romantic poet. The poem's temporal location is a confusion, mixing an idealised mediaeval past of chivalry and tournaments, beautiful damsels and knights in gleaming armour, with the sensibility of a voluptuous romantic of the year 1816. When Calidore helps the ladies down from their horses,

> What a kiss,
> What gentle squeeze he gave each lady's hand!
> How tremblingly their delicate ancles spann'd!
> Into how sweet a trance his soul was gone,
> While whisperings of affection
> Made him delay to let their tender feet
> Come to the earth.....
> He feels a moisture on his cheek, and blesses
> With lips that tremble, and with glistening eye,
> All the soft luxury
> That nestled in his arms.

> (lines 80–86, 90–93)

Calidore's tendency to be rapt 'into how sweet a trance' was one which Keats knew well, perhaps too well: his best verse would eventually be achieved only when he had learned to place and control in a dialectical framework the seductions of reverie and 'soft luxury'.

Keats's distaste for the urban London in which he had to live as a medical student was expressed in his sonnet on Solitude:

> O Solitude! if I must with thee dwell,
>   Let it not be among the jumbled heap
>   Of murky buildings.....

This sonnet was his first published piece; and, fittingly, the editor who had seen its merit was Leigh Hunt, who printed it in the *Examiner* on 5 May 1816. Keats was delighted; it is said that subsequently, to prove to the world that he was a poet, he wore his shirt open at the neck with a black ribbon, and grew his hair long. While Keats had been reading Hunt's work with admiration, Hunt had been listening enthusiastically to the poems by Keats that Cowden Clarke read aloud to him; and soon Keats was invited to Hunt's cottage in the Vale of Health (the euphemistic site of a drained marsh) on Hampstead Heath – "'twill be an Era in my existence', declared Keats excitedly, and he was right.

That 'Era' was heralded by his first major sonnet, 'On First Looking into Chapman's Homer'. In the summer of 1816 John Keats had visited Margate with his brother Tom. While there he sent to George Keats a sonnet, 'Many the wonders I this day have seen', and the verse-letter which begins 'Full many a dreary hour have I past' – the main reason for the dreariness of the hours being that he had striven unsuccessfully to produce some worthy poetry. Nevertheless, the verse-letter characteristically makes the lack of subject into a subject, and the meditation on the poetry that Keats feels he should be producing lasts for 142 lines. To Charles Cowden Clarke he sent a similar complaint:

> Whene'er I venture on the stream of rhyme[:]
> With shatter'd boat, oar snapt, and canvass rent,
> I slowly sail, scarce knowing my intent.....
>
> (lines 16–18)

The inspiration that he sought was provided not by the sea at Margate but by a book in London. He visited Clarke, who had been lent a folio edition of George Chapman's Elizabethan translation of Homer, and the two young men spent the night reading aloud some of the passages that they had previously encountered in Pope's translation. Keats was delighted by Chapman's pithy directness of idiom – he gave 'one of his delighted stares' at the passage which says of the shipwrecked Ulysses, 'the sea had soak'd his heart through' (CC, 130). At dawn Keats left Clarke and walked the two miles from Little Warren Street, where Clarke now lived, over London Bridge to his lodgings at Dean Street (amid 'a beastly place' of 'dirt, turnings and windings'). Rapidly he wrote a sonnet and despatched it to Clarke, who received it by 10 a.m. In those few hours, Keats had completed the first of his famous, world-renowned poems: 'On First Looking into Chapman's Homer'. Here, he had found a distinctive, authoritative tone and imagery. The image of Cortés and his men beholding the Pacific magnifies and transforms the subject, so that the poem celebrates not just the private enlightening encounter with Chapman's volume but rather the human sense of awakening to awe-inspiring beauties and opportunities: it is as though Keats now truly recognises his *own* destiny while celebrating *Everyman's* glimpse of destiny. Hunt said that the sonnet 'terminates with so energetic a calmness, and..... completely announced the new poet taking possession' (H, 248). Yet the poem's error (the confusion of Cortés with Balboa) suggests that even on this peak, Keats's position was not fully secure.

## Friendships

In the autumn of 1816 Keats was still working as a dresser, even though, being twenty-one, he now had the age and qualifications to set up business on his own as a surgeon. His guardian, Abbey, assumed that he would adopt the latter course.

> He communicated his Plans to his Ward but his Surprise was not moderate, to hear in Reply, that he did not intend to be a Surgeon – Not intend to be a Surgeon! why what do you mean to be? I mean to rely upon my Abilities as a Poet – John, you are either Mad or a Fool, to talk in so absurd a Manner. My Mind is made up, said the youngster very quietly. I know that I possess Abilities greater than most Men, and therefore I am determined to gain my Living by exercising them. Seeing nothing could be done Abby [*sic*] called him a Silly Boy, & prophesied a speedy Termination to his inconsiderate Enterprise.
>
> (*KC* I, 307–8)

Keats's resolution had been strengthened by the friendships he had made in 1816. By far the most important was that with Leigh Hunt. Before they met, as we have seen, Keats had been influenced by the liberalism of Hunt's *Examiner*, which offered sharp and lively criticism of the Prince Regent and the Tory Government of Liverpool, Sidmouth and Castlereagh; and the two men had been reading each other's poetry with enjoyment. Their meeting took place early in October 1816 – a meeting between a young hero-worshipper and his controversial, celebrated or notorious hero. Hunt later said:

> I shall never forget the impression made upon me by the exuberant specimens of genuine though young poetry that were laid before me, and the promise of which was seconded by the fine fervid countenance of the writer. We became intimate on the spot, and I found the young poet's heart as warm as his imagination. We read and walked together, and used to write verses of an evening upon a given subject. No imaginative pleasure was left unnoticed by us, or unenjoyed; from the recollection of the bards and patriots of old, to the luxury of a summer rain at our window, or the clicking of the coal in winter-time. Not long afterwards, having the pleasure of entertaining at dinner Mr. Godwin, Mr. Hazlitt, and Mr. Basil Montague, I showed them the verses of my young friend, and they were pronounced to be as extraordinary as I thought them.
>
> (H, 247–8)

An encouraging meeting, then, which brought the recognition and

*Thomas Wageman: 'Leigh Hunt' (drawn in 1815, the year of his release from prison.)*

*Leigh Hunt and his brother John had each been fined £500 and sentenced to two years in jail for describing the Prince Regent as 'a violator of his word, a libertine' who had lived half a century 'without one claim on the gratitude of his country, or the respect of posterity'.*

*Keats wrote:*

> What though, for showing truth to flatter'd state,
>> Kind Hunt was shut in prison, yet has he,
>> In his immortal spirit, been as free
> As the sky-searching lark, and as elate.
> Minion of grandeur, think you he did wait?
>> Think you he nought but prison walls did see,
>> Till, so unwilling, thou unturn'dst the key? . . . . .
>> *('Written on the Day That Mr. Leigh Hunt Left Prison'.)*

15

sympathy vital to Keats's creativity. The reference to William Godwin, the influential libertarian philosopher, to Hazlitt, the critic and essayist, and to Basil Montagu, the barrister, legal authority, and editor of Francis Bacon's works, is a reminder of Leigh Hunt's near-centrality in the cultural life of the period: later he was to join Byron and Shelley at Pisa. The recurrence of that word 'luxury' ('the luxury of a summer rain at our window') shows the common interest of Keats and Hunt in the sensuous apprehension of experience, and the evocative precision of 'the clicking of the coal in winter-time' suggests that the younger poet could have learned valuable lessons in his friendly rivalry with the older.

Hunt's poetry and essays have not stood the test of time; they command relatively little attention now, though they can still offer distinctive pleasures to readers who seek them out, and 'Jenny Kissed Me' is still recalled with affection. Admirers of Keats's major poetry, with its dialectical energy and its salting of scepticism, have sometimes regarded Hunt's influence as a retrograde one which encouraged the escapist, whimsical and dilettantish tendencies; and indeed there was some such encouragement, for Hunt cultivated a pose of blithe hedonism. Nevertheless, for fluency of natural description invigorated by unexpectedly bold phrasing, Hunt's work was a valuable model. That is indicated by the felicitous phrases 'suckle's streaky light' and 'flings of sunshine' in this passage (II, 188–95) from 'The Story of Rimini':

> Various the trees and passing foliage here, –
> Wild pear, and oak, and dusky juniper,
> With briony between in trails of white,
> And ivy, and the suckle's streaky light,
> And moss, warm gleaming with a sudden mark,
> Like flings of sunshine left upon the bark,
> And still the pine, long-haired, and dark, and tall,
> In lordly right, predominant o'er all.
>                 (Hunt: *Poetical Works*. Oxford University Press, 1923, p. 12)

Miriam Allott (A, 36) rightly observes of Keats's 'Calidore': 'The influence of Leigh Hunt's "The Story of Rimini" . . . . . is apparent in the poem's diction, loose heroic couplets and sentimental eroticism, but description is substituted for Hunt's narrative energy'. Keatsian usages which were prompted or encouraged by Hunt's example include adjectives ending in 'y' formed from nouns or verbs ('shadowy', 'bowery', 'silvery'); adverbs formed from present participles ('lingeringly', 'refreshingly', 'tremblingly' – not all as odd as Hunt's 'preparingly'); abstract nouns ending in 'ness' ('clearness', 'calmness', 'dimness'); and the habit of using verbs as nouns ('easy float', 'hasty trip', 'airy feel'). One of Hunt's effects was, as Bate has said (B, 80), 'deliberate sentiment put with easy

16

sprightliness'. Sometimes that 'sprightliness' became an archly colloquial or vulgar quality, as in:

> prepared
> To do her duty, where appeal was barred,
> She had stout notions on the marrying score.
> ('The Story of Rimini', Canto II, lines 26–8)

Keats emulated his master in lines like

> God! she is like a milk-white lamb that bleats.....
> ('Woman! when I behold thee, flippant, vain', line 31)

He also learnt from Hunt the couplet which, instead of having an Augustan poise and emphasis, scampers along with a looser, more casual movement: instead of a stately tread, a soft-slipper shuffle.

If Hunt's poetical reputation is now fading, his personal reputation is distinctly tarnished; and this is largely because of the genius of Charles Dickens. In Dickens' *Bleak House*, Hunt is remorselessly caricatured as Harold Skimpole, the parasitic aesthete who claims to be a mere child in the ways of the world, but who is astute in deflecting to other people the payment of his debts: '"I may have been born to be a benefactor to you, by sometimes giving you an opportunity of assisting me in my little perplexities"' (*BH*, 77). 'His wants were few. Give him the papers, conversation, music, mutton, coffee, landscape, fruit in the season, a few sheets of Bristol-board, and a little claret, and he asked no more' (*BH*, 76). Some parts of the caricature ring true: the foppish aestheticism may remind us of the Hunt who papered his prison-cell to resemble a rose-clad bower and whose essays commended connoisseurship of the pleasures of ices, peaches and strawberries ('The Edens of his fancy have no snake', wrote Arthur Symons); while the dependence of Skimpole on others reminds us that Hunt had a resilient capacity to accumulate debts. But centrally the caricature is wrong: Skimpole is ruthlessly predatory beneath his breezily cheerful exterior, whereas Hunt had shown a courageous political determination in his criticism of the corruptions of the court and the repressiveness of the government, and he was magnanimous in his unflagging encouragement and commendation of Keats. He published Keats's work and proclaimed its merits; and of all the nineteenth-century critics he was the most intelligent appreciator of Keats, as he had a sharp eye for telling details and was able to balance his praise with just qualifications.

History has fully vindicated his prophetic certainty of Keats's future fame; and to him we owe a particularly memorable pen-portrait of Keats:

> He was under the middle height, and his lower limbs were small

in comparison with the upper, but neat and well-turned. His shoulders were very broad for his size: he had a face, in which energy and sensibility were remarkably mixed up, an eager power checked and made patient by ill-health. Every feature was at once strongly cut, and delicately alive. If there was any faulty expression, it was in the mouth, which was not without something of a character of pugnacity. The face was rather long than otherwise; the upper lip projected a little over the under; the chin was bold, the cheeks sunken; the eyes mellow and glowing; large, dark and sensitive. At the recital of a noble action, or a beautiful thought, they would suffuse with tears, and his mouth trembled. In this, there was ill health as well as imagination, for he did not like these betrayals of emotion; and he had great personal as well as moral courage. His hair, of a brown colour, was fine, and hung in natural ringlets. The head was a puzzle for the phrenologists, being remarkably small in the skull; a singularity which he had in common with Lord Byron and Mr. Shelley, none of whose hats I could get on. Mr. Keats was sensible of the disproportion above noticed, between his upper and lower extremities; and he would look at his hand, which was faded, and swollen in the veins, and say it was the hand of a man of fifty.

(H, 245–7)

Keats had hailed Hunt as 'Libertas'; Hunt playfully telescoped 'John Keats' into the nickname 'Junkets'. Frequently Keats made the five-mile walk from Clerkenwell or Cheapside to the fashionable rural village of Hampstead; sometimes he stayed overnight, sleeping on the sofa in Hunt's library. Here he composed much of the poem 'Sleep and Poetry', the closing lines of which give an inventory of the room's pictures – of the patriots Alfred and Kościuszko as well as the poets Sappho and Petrarch. In the sonnet which begins 'Keen, fitful gusts are whisp'ring here and there', Keats declared:

> . . . . . I am brimfull of the friendliness
>    That in a little cottage I have found;
> Of fair-hair'd Milton's eloquent distress,
>    And all his love for gentle Lycid drown'd;
> Of lovely Laura in her light green dress,
>    And faithful Petrarch gloriously crown'd.

Hunt could seem complacent and condescending, since to appear patronising is the occupational hazard of patrons; and Keats later turned against him. Nevertheless, all who value Keats's poetry should value Leigh Hunt, who first printed it, who established Keats's reputation, and who gave the grateful young man the warmest of welcomes to the public realms of literature. In December

1816 Hunt's article 'Young Poets' appeared in the *Examiner*: it praised Keats for his 'ardent grappling with Nature' and claimed that he, Shelley and J. H. Reynolds constituted 'a new school of poetry'. Keats was delighted; a friend of his, Henry Stephens, claimed that this article 'sealed his fate' as a poet.

At one visit to Hunt's, Keats met the painter Benjamin Haydon. If Hunt was chatty, urbane and sceptical, Haydon was passionate, intense and devout. He was thirty years old, two years younger than Hunt, nine years older than Keats; bull-necked, and with a laugh (Hunt said) 'like the trumpets of Jericho'. He believed that he had the God-given mission to bring to English painting a Michelangelesque power and Raphaelite grandeur; so that although portrait-painting might have ensured a steady income for him, he chose to give much of his time to vast canvases, often on religious or patriotic historical subjects. He was to survive Keats by many years, but though he gained enough critical praise to maintain his artistic struggles, his poverty and debts increased. Heartbreak came in April 1846, when his exhibition in London was a failure, while next door General Tom Thumb, a dwarf managed by the impresario Barnum, was a great success. Haydon's Journal (HJ, 644) records:

> 21*st* – Tom Thumb had 12,000 people last week; B. R. Haydon, 133½ (the ½ a little girl). Exquisite taste of the English people! O God! Bless me through the evils of this day.

On May 22 he wrote:

> God forgive me. Amen.
> Finis
> of
> B. R. Haydon.
> "Stretch me no longer on this rough world." – *Lear*.
> End of Twenty-sixth Volume.
>
> (HJ, 650)

Having written this, he shot himself in the head, slashed his throat with a razor, and fell dying before his unfinished and now blood-splashed painting of King Alfred with the first British Jury.

When he met Keats, Haydon had still been full of great hopes that he might re-animate British art. If Hunt encouraged Keats's sensuous, fanciful imagination, Haydon amplified his sense of the importance of a lofty subject treated in some work of massive power. The painter wrote: 'Keats was the only man I ever met with who seemed and looked conscious of high calling, except Wordsworth' (HJ, 297). After dining at Haydon's on 19 November 1816, the young poet wrote to him:

> My dear Sir –
> Last Evening wrought me up, and I cannot forbear sending

*Benjamin Haydon: Self-portrait, 1816. He likened himself to 'a man with air-balloons under his armpits, and ether in his soul'. W. J. Bate remarks: 'Haydon's influence was to be salutary, perhaps necessary, to Keats. Without it Keats could have slipped so easily.....back into the coy idiom, the comfortable corner-poetry, that had been his principal nourishment' (B, 101).*

you the following – Your's unfeignedly John Keats –
    Great Spirits now on Earth are sojourning
      He of the Cloud, the Cataract the Lake
      Who on Helvellyn's summit wide awake
    Catches his freshness from Archangel's wing
    He of the Rose, the Violet, the Spring
      The social Smile, the Chain for freedom's sake:
      And lo! – whose stedfastness would never take
    A Meaner Sound than Raphael's Whispering.
    And other Spirits are there standing apart
      Upon the Forehead of the Age to come;
    These, These will give the World another heart
      And other pulses – hear ye not the hum
    Of mighty Workings in a distant Mart?
    Listen awhile ye Nations, and be dumb.!

                    (R I, 117)

Although Wordsworth (whose self-esteem was too redoubtable to be vitiated by modesty) understandably deemed this sonnet 'vigorously conceived and well expressed' (WL, 1368), it is not one of Keats's best: there is confusion in the imagery of the Spirits that stand on a forehead to provide another heart. Nevertheless, it is an enthusiastic tribute to a romantic triad that stirred Keats's ambitions: Wordsworth the profound, Hunt the genial radical, and Haydon the English Raphael. W. J. Bate has observed: 'To the youth who was always afraid that writing only "short pieces" was a falling off from the great poetry of the past, Haydon, with his titanic canvases and his endless, booming confidence, was a sure stay against triviality' (B, 101). The linkage of Keats with Haydon's vast designs has been given enduring form in the painter's great canvas of Christ's entry into Jerusalem, where young Keats appears (with Wordsworth, Hazlitt and Voltaire) among the spectators. It is a cluttered picture – Haydon never achieved the structural power and lucidity of the masters he admired. Ironically, the work of Haydon's which has most vitality and force today is probably his Journal, that stark, raw, painful exposure of a turbulent romantic soul, impelled and tortured by his dreams of artistic glory.

> O God! It is hard, this struggle of forty-two years; but Thy will, and not mine, be done, if it save the art in the end. O God, bless me through all my pictures, the four remaining, and grant nothing on earth may stop the completion of the six . . . . . Let my imagination keep Columbus before my mind for ever. O God, bless my efforts with success . . . . .

                    (HJ, 648, 649)

A third important friendship made by Keats in 1816 was with John Hamilton Reynolds. Reynolds was then a twenty-two-year-old

*Haydon: 'William Wordsworth' (1818).*

*Both vision and pride are indicated by this portrait. 'Wordsworth.....was dilating upon some question in poetry, when upon Keat's insinuating a confirmatory suggestion to his argument, Mrs. Wordsworth put her hand upon his arm, saying – "Mr. Wordsworth is never interrupted." ' (B, 266)* clerk who was later to become an unsuccessful lawyer, but his early ambitions were literary. By the time Keats met him, he had published three small books of verse (*Safie, an Eastern Tale*; *The Eden of Imagination*; and *An Ode*) and was a contributor of critical essays to the *Champion* and the *Enquirer*. He was witty and good-humoured; and though he is best remembered for his Wordsworthian parody (*Peter Bell. Lyrical Ballad*), his essay on Wordsworth's poetry, published in the *Champion* for 9 December 1815, offered fervent tribute:

> We have never heard the sound of a closing gate on a still summer's evening, or the 'tremulous sob of the complaining owl' breaking the silence of night – without recollecting his descriptions with a thrilling delight. . . . .

The *Lyrical Ballads*, which had 'sought to revive gentle tastes, quiet feelings, and innocent affections', had been 'violently opposed, and, as it would seem, overpowered'; but their reputation was now growing:

> We are convinced that the name of Wordsworth will
> In Fame's eternal volume shine for aye.
>
> (JHR, 26–7)

In due course Reynolds was to be as fervent a champion of Keats's work; and in 1848 he told Keats's first scholarly biographer, Monckton Milnes, that his friend had been 'the most loveable associate, – the deepest Listener to the griefs & disappointments of all around him', and that he had 'the greatest power of poetry in him, of any one since Shakespere' (*KC* II, 173). When Reynolds, who eventually termed himself 'that poor obscure – baffled Thing', died in 1852, on his tombstone at Church Litten were inscribed in large letters the words he had specified: 'THE FRIEND OF KEATS'.

## Further poetic experiments

John Keats was not certain how much he stood to inherit, nor was it clear when the inheritance might be due (Abbey let it be thought that the time might not arise until the youngest Keats, Fanny, had reached twenty-one); but he could expect that it might amount to a modest sufficiency of £50 or £60 per year, thus freeing him from the necessity to work. The friendships he had recently made had heightened his poetic ambitions. Nevertheless, he had misgivings about his poetic vocation. He admired great poets of the past; he wanted to be a great poet himself; but *he had nothing to be a great poet about*. That was his central dilemma. He had no doctrine, no philosophy, no creed. He enjoyed daydreams and sensuous pleasures of an innocent kind, but this was a very inadequate repertoire for one who yearned to be another Homer or Spenser. What is more, he knew it. The nagging sense of inadequacy of a means to this end became increasingly strong as he persevered, and the paucity is clearly apparent in the two lengthy poems that he completed in December 1816.

'I stood tip-toe upon a little hill' begins with what the poet frankly terms 'a posey/Of luxuries', and the sensuous catalogue proceeds: 'a bush of May flowers', 'a lush laburnum', 'filbert hedge', 'clumps of woodbine', 'ardent marigolds', and, more interestingly, the rivulets with pebbly beds,

> Where swarms of minnows show their little heads,
> Staying their wavy bodies 'gainst the streams,
> To taste the luxury of sunny beams
> Temper'd with coolness.

(lines 72–5)

The kinetic imagery here is vivid, and the apt verse-movement of 'Staying their wavy bodies 'gainst the streams' was to be repeated years later in the famous passage of the ode 'To Autumn' which addresses the Autumn-gleaner – 'thou dost keep/Steady thy laden head across a brook'. Then, tiring of such luxuries, the poet turns to an idealised past: the dream-like Arcadian past suggested by Ovid's *Metamorphoses*; and he promises to tell the tale of Cynthia the moon-goddess and Endymion the shepherd. He evokes their wedding-night, which he sees as a time of pagan resurrection, revitalisation and love; but then, abruptly and inconclusively, the poem ceases.

> Was there a Poet born? – but now no more,
> My wand'ring spirit must no further soar. –

The longest and most substantial of Keats's poems to appear by December 1816 was 'Sleep and Poetry', and it was greeted enthusiastically by Haydon and Hunt. Another friend, the scholarly and foresighted Richard Woodhouse, composed in its honour the sonnet 'To Apollo'. 'Sleep and Poetry' again deals with the central problem of the disparity between poetic ambition and resources. The piece opens with an invocation to Sleep, 'Wreather of poppy buds', source of visionary dreams, but then praises as superior 'Poesy' in all its rich variety. The speaker imagines that if he succeeded in being admitted to the realms of poetry, he would wander amid vistas of beauty, pastoral and floral, and perhaps eventually become capable of dealing '[l]ike a strong giant' with 'the events of this wide world' and thus attain immortality – by which he means, it appears, enduring fame on earth. Reference to immortality leads him to reflect on the brevity of life –

> A fragile dew-drop on its perilous way
> From a tree's summit

– but also on life's joyous variety: it is

> A pigeon tumbling in clear summer air;
> A laughing school-boy, without grief or care,
> Riding the springy branches of an elm.

The speaker asks for ten years in which he may complete his career as a poet (Keats was to be granted less than five). First he may enjoy the pleasures of a pastoral realm where he can catch nymphs and

> touch their shoulders white
> Into a pretty shrinking with a bite
> As hard as lips can make it:

but after that he may share the visions of the epic poet, concerned with 'the agonies, the strife/ Of human hearts'. Then, in a telling moment of misgiving (which anticipates Keats's major works):

> The visions all are fled – the car is fled
> Into the light of heaven, and in their stead
> A sense of real things comes doubly strong,
> And, like a muddy stream, would bear along
> My soul to nothingness.....

He next considers the development of English poetry. In the Elizabethan Age and the seventeenth century all was well; but, at the Augustan Age, poetry fell into decline – for the era of the Augustan heroic couplet was the time when poets

> sway'd about upon a rocking horse,
> And thought it Pegasus[;]

and Neoclassicism was 'a poor, decrepid standard'

> Mark'd with most flimsy mottos, and in large
> The name of one Boileau!

At the present time, though some poetry is morbid and decadent, there is a revival: cheering, pleasant verse is available (Keats is thinking of Hunt's work), and the speaker, though aware of his own lack of knowledge, will remain true to his great ideal, looking on the prospect before him as on a great ocean:

> An ocean dim, sprinkled with many an isle,
> Spreads awfully before me.

(Perhaps Keats is recalling a conquistador beholding the Pacific, as in the 'Chapman's Homer' sonnet.) In the meantime, there remain the encouragement and friendship of Hunt, and the inspiration provided by the artefacts at his cottage, where the spirit of Poesy is so strong a presence that she prompts the poet to the writing of these very lines.

The oscillations of 'Sleep and Poetry', the shifts from confidence to diffidence, from affirmation to doubt, anticipate the related (though much compressed and more decisive) patterning of contrasts in the great odes, particularly 'Ode to a Nightingale'. The memorable images include not only those of sensuous vitality but also, for example, the reference to 'Poesy' as 'might half slumbering on its own right arm', which perhaps recalls Michelangelo's depiction of new-made Adam. Nevertheless, there are some clear weaknesses and an element of self-contradiction. Keats dramatises himself as the trembling novice; yet he dares to offer arrogant (and ignorant) criticism of the great Augustan poets. He says that he aspires to deal with the real world; but Dryden, Pope, Swift and Johnson could have told him much about it, and greater attention to the precision of their couplets might have shown him how to reduce the frequent slackness of his own.

The strongest element of self-contradiction occurs when the poet stresses the importance of a poetry which advances beyond the merely fanciful and escapist; for there is no doubt that Keats seems most fluently at ease when dealing with a dreamily sensuous realm. He recognises that a major poet must concern himself with 'the agonies, the strife/ Of human hearts', yet he complains that the 'sense of real things' threatens 'like a muddy stream' to annihilate him. Every time he tries to stride out of his lush Arcadia, his pace slackens and his footsteps strangely lead him circuitously back to it. A tell-tale sign of his dilemma is his recurrent preference for the poeticism 'Poesy' instead of 'Poetry', as the more archaic term lends sanction to the prettily (and merely) poetical.

## Enter Shelley

Keats's shortage of ideas was emphasised when he encountered Percy Bysshe Shelley at Hunt's cottage. Aristocratic in descent, Shelley had received the education available to sons of the wealthy: at Eton College and subsequently at University College, Oxford, from which he had been expelled after contributing to the sceptical pamphlet, *The Necessity of Atheism*. He was widely read in literature and philosophy, passionately dedicated to a variety of heterodox ideas ranging from libertarian anarchism to free love and vegetarianism, and eager to wrangle with anyone on any subject. This advocate of self-sacrificing altruism had callously betrayed his young wife, Harriet, who in despair then drowned herself in the Serpentine. Nevertheless, there was spontaneous generosity in his nature: he lent Hunt £1,500, and Hunt ingratiatingly demonstrated that he was a fellow-sceptic by writing two sonnets entitled 'To Percy Shelley', the first sub-titled 'On the Degrading Notions of Deity'. They denounce the Christian God as 'a phantom, swelled into grim size/ Out of [men's] own passions and bigotries', and extol instead 'the Spirit of Beauty'. Keats, following the lead of Shelley and Hunt, produced the sonnet 'Written in Disgust of Vulgar Superstition', which claims that 'The church bells toll a melancholy round', summoning people to gloom and away from 'fireside joys, and Lydian airs,/ And converse high of those with glory crown'd' – for, to this poet, the glories which have reality are the earthly glories of poetic fame, not the eternal glories of Heaven.

The devout Haydon was once invited to a dinner attended by Shelley, Hunt and Keats. He found himself sitting opposite the ex-Etonian,

> [a] hectic, spare, weakly yet intellectual-looking creature . . . . . carving a bit of broccoli or cabbage on his plate, as if it had been the substantial wing of a chicken . . . . .
>
> In a few minutes Shelley opened the conversation by saying in the most feminine and gentle voice, 'As to that detestable religion, the Christian –' . . . . . I felt exactly like a stag at bay, and resolved to gore without mercy . . . . .
>
> (HJ, 298)

Although there was some reserve between Keats and Shelley (partly, perhaps, on social grounds, and partly because of a sense of poetic rivalry), Shelley wrote magnanimously to Keats shortly before the latter's death, and in *Adonais* was to offer a fine elegiac tribute.

## Poems, *1817*

In March 1817 Keats's first book of verse appeared: *Poems*, published by Charles and James Ollier of Welbeck Street. It was a slim volume containing virtually all the work that Keats could muster, beginning with 'I stood tip-toe' and the earliest minor poems, followed by the verse epistles to Mathew, to George and to Cowden Clarke, then seventeen sonnets, and, at the end, 'Sleep and Poetry'. The title-page bore a motto from Spenser expressing Hunt-like sentiments ('What more felicity can fall to creature,/ Than to enjoy delight with liberty'), and the volume opened with a flattering dedicatory sonnet to Hunt. (One of the two publishers, Charles, produced in turn a sonnet beginning 'Keats I admire thy upward daring Soul,/ Thine eager grasp at immortality'.)

Shelley, though he had advised deferment of the project, had still called on the printer to exhort him to take special care with the

*Joseph Severn: charcoal drawing of John Keats, 1817. It conveys Keats's alert intensity.*

volume; and, when it appeared, Keats's friends were rapturous and his brothers were jubilant, convinced that 'their Brother John . . . . . was to exalt the family name'. Clarke recalled:

> The first volume of Keats's minor muse was launched amid the cheers and fond anticipations of all his circle. Everyone of us expected (and not unreasonably) that it would create a sensation in the literary world; for such a first production (and a considerable portion of it from a minor) has rarely occurred . . . . . Alas! the book might have emerged in Timbuctoo with far stronger chance of fame and approbation. It never passed to a second edition; the first was but a small one, and that was never sold off. The whole community, as if by compact, seemed determined to know nothing about it.
>
> (CC, 140)

Keats sent a copy to Wordsworth, inscribed 'To W. Wordsworth with the Author's sincere Reverence'. After Wordsworth's death, the copy was found with most of its leaves uncut.

George Keats soon wrote to the publishers, evidently to complain that they were not promoting the book with sufficient zeal and that he had a better publishing-house in mind. They replied, in a letter with the brisk precision of a stiletto in the stomach,

> Sir, – We regret that your brother ever requested us to publish his book, or that our opinion of its talent should have led us to acquiesce in undertaking it. We are, however, much obliged to you for relieving us from the unpleasant necessity of declining any further connexion with it, which we must have done, as we think the curiosity is satisfied, and the sale has dropped. By far the greater number of persons who have purchased it from us have found fault with it in such plain terms, that we have in many cases offered to take the book back rather than be annoyed with the ridicule which has, time after time, been showered upon it. In fact, it was only on Saturday last that we were under the mortification of having our own opinion of its merits flatly contradicted by a gentleman, who told us he considered it 'no better than a take in' . . . . .
>
> Your most, &c.<br>C. & J. Ollier<br>(Athenæum, 7.6.1873, p. 725)

Fortunately for Keats, other publishers (John Taylor and James Hessey) liked his work and were willing to support his future endeavours. And if *Poems* had had a poor sale, at least the earliest reviews were quite favourable. Those by friends (Reynolds, G. F. Mathew and Hunt) were predictably laudatory; more reassuringly,

30

the *Monthly Magazine*, the *Eclectic Review* and *Scots Magazine* were generously appreciative, discerning what the *Monthly* termed 'a rapturous glow and intoxication of the fancy'. The hostile reviews were to appear later.

## Incentives to ambition

At the beginning of March 1817, Haydon took Keats to the British Museum to see the Elgin Marbles. Lord Elgin, exploiting the permission of the Turkish authorities in conquered Athens, had removed these often massive fragments of sculpture from the ruins of the Parthenon. Haydon, who campaigned for their purchase by the nation, was fervently enthusiastic about these ancient Greek depictions of gods and heroes, centaurs and horses, scenes of battle and ritual; their forms blending the real and the ideal. Keats wrote two sonnets on the occasion: the first ('On Seeing the Elgin Marbles') begins with a characteristic evocation of a swooning state:

> My spirit is too weak – mortality
>   Weighs heavily on me like unwilling sleep,
>   And each imagined pinnacle and steep
> Of godlike hardship tells me I must die
> Like a sick eagle looking at the sky.

The image of the 'sick eagle' well conveys Keats's recurrent situation – that of the man yearning to attain an ideal, yet earthbound; the poet seeking to soar, but unready or fettered. The companion sonnet assures Haydon that if Keats does manage to produce great work eventually, that work will be dedicated to Haydon, champion of the high art of ancient Greece. The sight of these sculptures lingered in Keats's imagination, providing incentive and imagery for later poems: for example, the reference in 'Ode on a Grecian Urn' to the 'heifer lowing at the skies' in the sacrificial procession may well have been suggested by the horned heifer, head tilted skywards, in the procession shown in one fragment of the Elgin Marbles. Furthermore, the very scale of conception indicated by these relics strengthened his belief – and

*George Cruikshank: 'The Elgin Marbles! or John Bull buying* Stones *at the time his numerous Family want* Bread!!' *(1816).*

*In two sonnets, Keats expressed his rapture on beholding 'these mighty things', the Elgin Marbles. A more popular reaction, however, was anger that at a time when unemployment and rising prices were making starvation a daily reality for the poor, the Government was prepared to pay Lord Elgin £35,000 for these ancient relics taken, in questionable legality, from the Parthenon at Athens.*

31

Haydon's – that great artists are those who produce big works, so that to be a great poet he would have to produce long poems.

Haydon encouraged him: 'My dear Keats go on, don't despair, . . . . . read Shakespeare and trust in Providence' (R I, 135); and Keats's rapid, lively, hop-skip-and-jumping letters of this time hold numerous Shakespearian allusions – for example to *King Lear, The Tempest, Antony and Cleopatra* and *A Midsummer Night's Dream* – so that when he wrote to Haydon on their joint ambitions, the opening of *Love's Labour's Lost* came immediately to mind, and he quoted it thus:

> Let Fame, which all hunt after in their Lives,
> Live register'd upon our brazen tombs,
> And so grace us in the disgrace of death:
> When spite of cormorant devouring time
> The endeavour of this present breath may buy
> That Honor which shall bate his Scythe's keen edge
> And make us heirs of all eternity.

(R I, 140–1)

Aided by loans from his new publishers, Keats travelled widely during the period April to September 1817: to Carisbrooke in the Isle of Wight, to Margate (where brother Tom joined him), to Canterbury (in the hope that 'the Remembrance of Chaucer will set me forward like a Billiard-Ball'), to Bo-Peep, near Hastings (where he flirted with Miss Isabella Jones and wrote her a love-poem), to Oxford, to stay with Benjamin Bailey, and to Stratford-upon-Avon, where he wrote his name on the wall of Shakespeare's birth-place. There were various setbacks and worries: Tom's health was a constant source of concern; the friendship with Hunt was cooling; and in October Keats had to dose himself with mercury to fight a possibly-venereal infection. Nevertheless, he persevered with his main task in this period – the writing of *Endymion*.

## Endymion

This long poem, based on the Greek legend of the shepherd loved by the moon-goddess, was a deliberate test of Keats's powers. He explained:

> *Endymion* . . . . . will be a test, a trial of my Powers of Imagination and chiefly of my invention which is a rare thing indeed – by which I must make 4000 Lines of one bare circumstance and fill them with Poetry; and when I consider that this is a great task, and that when done it will take me but a dozen paces towards the Temple of Fame – it makes me say – God forbid that I should be without such a task! I have heard Hunt say and may be asked –

why endeavour after a long Poem? To which I should answer –
Do not the Lovers of Poetry like to have a little Region to wander
in where they may pick and choose, and in which the images are
so numerous that many are forgotten and found new in a second
Reading: which may be food for a Week's stroll in the Summer?
Do not they like this better than what they can read through
before Mrs Williams comes down stairs? a Morning work at
most. Besides a long Poem is a test of Invention which I take to be
the Polar Star of Poetry, as Fancy is the Sails, and Imagination
the Rudder. Did our great Poets ever write short Pieces?

(R I, 170–1)

Watched by pictures of Shakespeare and Haydon, Keats worked
at *Endymion*, and it was completed in the autumn. It was certainly of
substantial length: four books, of approximately 1,000 lines per
book, the whole in heroic couplets treated with Keats's
now-customary flexibility (free enjambment and much mid-line
stopping). But though the length was substantial, the content was
less so. The narrative is slow, diffuse, wandering, and padded with
predictable set-pieces of pastoral, marine and Arcadian description.
The story, of Endymion's love both for Cynthia and for the Indian
Maid, has an obvious allegorical relationship to Keats's attraction
both to the ideal (or illusory), and to the real (or mundane): the
poem resolves the division by revealing that Cynthia and the Indian
are one and the same. The arbitrariness of this dénouement with its
*dea ex machina* not only renders the narrative's conclusion
unsatisfactory but also suggests that in actuality the problem would
prove stubborn.

## Beauty and 'Negative Capability'

In the autumn in which he completed the first draft of *Endymion*,
Keats wrote two letters which have become almost as famous as his
great odes. He had been reading *Paradise Lost*, Book VIII, lines
452–90, in which Adam sees in sleep the creation of Eve and awakes
to find her, real, in the garden. Keats wrote to Ben Bailey, the
theology student, on 22 November 1817:

> I am certain of nothing but of the holiness of the Heart's
> affections and the truth of Imagination – What the imagination
> seizes as Beauty must be truth – whether it existed before or
> not . . . . . The Imagination may be compared to Adam's dream –
> he awoke and found it truth.

(R I, 184–5)

This conception sounds remarkably like William Blake's idea in *The
Marriage of Heaven and Hell* (1793):

What is now proved was once only imagin'd.....
Every thing possible to be believ'd is an image of truth.....
I asked: 'does a firm perswasion that a thing is so, make it so?'
[Ezekiel] replied: 'All poets believe that it does, & in ages of
imagination this firm perswasion removed mountains.....'
                        (*Poetry and Prose of William Blake.*
         London: Nonesuch, 1956, pp. 184, 186)

But whereas Blake held this irrational view with a mystic's intensity
(and consequently inflicted extensive damage on his poetic
abilities), Keats's idea, which slides between a form of Platonic
mysticism and the simple fact that the poet's imaginings become
tangible pages of poetry, was more tentatively held. In the same
letter, he exclaims: 'O for a Life of Sensations rather than of
Thoughts! – which suggests a rapid reversion from the apparently
profound to the patently hedonistic.

   In the following month, writing to his brothers and reflecting on
the rich variety of life in Shakespeare's plays, Keats formulated the
famous notion of '*Negative Capability*' – 'that is when man is capable
of being in uncertainties, Mysteries, doubts, without any irritable
reaching after fact & reason' (R I, 193). What he has in mind is
clear: Shakespeare is able to dramatise a diversity of attitudes and
temperaments, and his imaginative flexibility is such that in a great
play like *1 Henry IV* or *Hamlet*, characters seem to have remarkable
autonomy; we do not feel that characterisation is being manipulated
in the interests of some propagandist statement. Nevertheless,
Keats's notion of 'Negative Capability' underestimates the often
complex but firm control exerted by Shakespeare's co-ordinating
imagination: a clear and consistent series of moral and political
recommendations emerges from the rich diversities of the various
plays. The 'Negative Capability' idea is a half-truth; for though the
great artist gives life to a wide variety of human possibilities, those
possibilities are purposefully co-ordinated. What is important about
the notion for Keats is that it was an *enabling* half-truth. At a stroke,
it enabled him to convert a liability into an asset. The liability was
his lack of system or doctrine; 'Negative Capability' was a licence to
regard such a lack as a liberation. His dilettantism could be seen as
flexibility; his lack of doctrine could itself become a doctrine. Keats
had often felt that he lacked the raw materials for great art;
'Negative Capability' gave him confidence and implied the dialectical basis for the structures of future poems. He developed the
idea in the following year by declaring (27 October 1818) that the
'poetical character' has 'as much delight in conceiving an Iago as an
Imogen. What shocks the virtuous philosop[h]er, delights the
camelion Poet' (R I, 387). These words may remind us of William
Blake's 'Exuberance is Beauty', but there is no evidence that Keats
knew Blake's work. What is certain is that Keats's ideas in late 1817

and 1818 are indebted to William Hazlitt.

Keats attended Hazlitt's lectures and read his articles with eagerness, applauding his 'depth of Taste' (R I, 203); on 14 September he dined with him, and on 18 October walked with him. Hazlitt's favourite theme was the supreme versatility of Shakespeare's genius. He cited with approval Schlegel's pronouncement on Shakespeare:

> He unites in his genius the utmost elevation and the utmost depth; and the most foreign, and even apparently irreconcilable properties subsist in him peaceably together;

and Hazlitt himself proclaimed:

> He was just like any other man, but that he was like all other men. He was the least of an egotist that it was possible to be. He was nothing in himself; but he was all that the others were, or that they could become..... His genius shone equally on the evil and on the good.....
>     Shakspear's imagination ..... unites the most opposite extremes...... .

> > (*Lectures on the English Poets* [1818].
> > London: Dent, 1910, pp. 47, 53)

In Hazlitt's eloquent tributes to Shakespeare we discover what is probably the main literary source of Keats's celebrated speculations about 'Negative Capability' and the 'poetical character'.

## Social life

It was in the company of Haydon in December 1817 that Keats met William Wordsworth. Keats had been greatly impressed and intermittently influenced by Wordsworth's writings, particularly the Immortality Ode, the Tintern Abbey Lines and *The Excursion*, but he came to have misgivings about the egotism of such works, and he seems to have found their author an aloofly impressive rather than engaging figure. Haydon records that when Keats read to Wordsworth the 'Ode to Pan' (from *Endymion*), 'which he did in his usual half chant, (most touching) walking up & down..... Wordsworth drily said "a Very pretty piece of Paganism["] – this was unfeeling, & unworthy of his high Genius to a young Worshipper like Keats – & Keats felt it *deeply*' (*KC* II, 143–4). The young poet's attitudes to influential figures like Wordsworth resembled his attitude to important texts: frequently the pattern was one of initial enthusiasm followed by attempted emulation and finally by a cooling or revulsion. Within months, Keats was to say of Wordsworth:

> [F]or the sake of a few fine imaginative or domestic passages, are

35

we to be bullied into a certain Philosophy engendered in the
whims of an Egotist.....?

(R I, 223)

At Hunt's, he entered a sonnet-contest on the subject of the River
Nile: his host produced 'It flows through old hush'd Egypt', Shelley
'Month after month the gather'd rains descend', and Keats 'Son of
the old moon-mountains African'. None was particularly successful:
Shelley's 'Ozymandias' shows what could be achieved in a sonnet
with a desert setting; but the incident gives an insight into Hunt's
ability to combine the sociable, the playful and the creative.

On 28 December 1817 took place Haydon's 'Immortal Dinner',
with his huge painting of Christ's Entry into Jerusalem as the
backcloth. Charles Lamb, the poet and essayist, was among the
guests. The painter recalled:

> Wordsworth was in fine cue, and we had a glorious set-to – on
> Homer, Shakespeare, Milton and Virgil. Lamb got exceedingly
> merry and exquisitely witty; and his fun in the midst of
> Wordsworth's solemn intonations of oratory was like the sarcasm
> and wit of the fool in the intervals of Lear's passion.....
>
> He then, in a strain of humour beyond description, abused me
> for putting Newton's head into my picture; 'a fellow,' said he,
> 'who believed nothing unless it was as clear as the three sides of a
> triangle.' And then he and Keats agreed he had destroyed all the
> poetry of the rainbow by reducing it to the prismatic colours. It
> was impossible to resist him, and we all drank 'Newton's health,
> and confusion to mathematics.' It was delightful to see the good
> humour of Wordsworth in giving in to all our frolics without
> affectation and laughing as heartily as the best of us.....
>
> It was indeed an immortal evening. Wordsworth's fine
> intonation as he quoted Milton and Virgil, Keats' eager inspired
> look, Lamb's quaint spark of lambent humour, so speeded the
> stream of conversation, that in my life I never passed a more
> delightful time..... It was a night worthy of the Elizabethan
> age, and my solemn Jerusalem flashing up by the flame of the fire,
> with Christ hanging over us like a vision, all made up a picture
> which will long glow upon
>
> 'that inward eye<br>Which is the bliss of solitude.'
>
> Keats made Ritchie [a guest who intended a journey to
> Timbuctoo] promise he would carry his *Endymion* to the great
> desert of Sahara and fling it into the midst.

(HJ, 317, 319)

Other social pleasures included visits to Drury Lane Theatre,
where the diminutive but mercurial Edmund Kean was playing to

packed houses. Keats delighted in the actor's presentation of Hamlet and Richard III, his ability to enrich the characters with unexpected touches of detail (a gesture here, a laugh there), and in general the 'indescribable gusto' which Keats praised in his review for the *Champion* (21 December 1817). 'Cheer us a little', the reviewer begs Kean, 'in the failure of our days! for romance lives but in books. The goblin is driven from the hearth, and the rainbow is robbed of its mystery' (G, 172) – words anticipating not only what was said of the rainbow at Haydon's banquet, but also the central theme of Keats's 'Lamia', in which the illusion of beauty is dispelled by a sage. During the period of this review, Keats was attending that popular course of lectures at which William Hazlitt extolled the diversity and complexity of Shakespeare's genius. Keats also found time to write a large number of his slighter poems, among them 'In drear nighted December', 'O blush not so', 'Hence Burgundy', the *King Lear* sonnet, 'Four seasons fill' and 'To J. R.'. At Hunt's he saw 'a real authenticated Lock of *Milton's Hair*' which prompted the commemorative ode in which he characteristically yearns to 'grow high-rife/ With old philosophy'. In a letter to Taylor of 24 April 1818, he complained:

> I know nothing I have read nothing and I mean to follow Solomon's directions of 'get Wisdom – get understanding' . . . . . the road lies th[r]ough application study and thought . . . . . I have been hovering for some time between an exquisite sense of the luxurious and a love for Philosophy . . . . . I shall turn all my soul to the latter.
>
> (R I, 271)

Perhaps the most plangent poem of these months was the sonnet to which his early death was to give special poignancy:

> When I have fears that I may cease to be
>   Before my pen has glean'd my teeming brain,
> Before high piled books, in charactry,
>   Hold like rich garners the full ripen'd grain;
> When I behold, upon the night's starr'd face,
>   Huge cloudy symbols of a high romance,
> And think that I may never live to trace
>   Their shadows, with the magic hand of chance;
> And when I feel, fair creature of an hour,
>   That I shall never look upon thee more,
> Never have relish in the fairy power
>   Of unreflecting love; – then on the shore
> Of the wide world I stand alone, and think
> Till love and fame to nothingness do sink.

The girl referred to in the phrase 'fair creature of an hour' has not been identified. What is certain is that Keats's study of Shakespeare's sonnets has strongly influenced this poem. The syntactical structure, using the pattern 'When . . . . . When . . . . . Then' was one which Shakespeare liked (as his sonnets 12 and 15 show), and the tone and imagery of the first quatrain have a Shakespearian quality: Keats's 'rich garners' of 'full ripen'd grain' will remind us of his predecessor's lines: 'Summer's green all girded up in sheaves,/ Borne on the bier with white and bristly beard' (Sonnet 12).

Meanwhile, for Keats, the possibility of further social life and travel was increased when his finances underwent a rapid improvement: Abbey made the very substantial sum of £500 available to him. Keats travelled to Liverpool to say farewell to his brother George, who was embarking with his young wife Georgiana for a new life in North America; and subsequently he proceeded on a walking tour of the Lake District, the north of England and Scotland with his friend Charles Brown – they even included a voyage to Ireland and visited Belfast. The journey was in large part a poetic pilgrimage: Keats and Brown called at Wordsworth's home in the Lake District and were disappointed to find that he was out (supporting a Tory candidate at an election); and in Scotland they visited Burns's cottage, but the custodian 'was a great Bore with his Anecdotes'. Among the more grotesque sights was a squalid old Irishwoman in a sedan chair 'like an ape half starved', puffing her pipe while two ragged girls carried her along. Nevertheless, the journey yielded the hoped-for romantic vistas, chief among them being Fingal's Cave: 'For solemnity and grandeur it far surpasses the finest Cathedrall'. As Keats told a friend: 'I have been *werry* romantic indeed, among these Mountains & Lakes. I have got wet through day after day, eaten oat cake, & drank whiskey, walked up to my knees in Bog, got a sore throat, gone to see Icolmkill & Staffa. . . . . We have been taken for Spectacle venders, Razor sellers, Jewellers, travelling linnen drapers, Spies, Excisemen, & many things else. . . . . Besides riding about 400, we have walked above 600 Miles. . . . .' (R I, 359–60). He returned, brown-faced and shabby, to find Tom's tuberculosis much worse; and, if that were not enough to trouble him, the periodicals' attacks began.

Blackwood's Edinburgh Magazine, *Vol. III (August 1818), p. 519. The opening of J. G. Lockhart's review of* Endymion.
   *The reference to 'the land of Cockaigne' suggests that the term 'The Cockney School of Poetry' was a way not only of sneering at Keats and Hunt as plebeian Londoners but also of associating them, half-punningly, with sensual self-indulgence. Here* Endymion *is described as 'imperturbable drivelling idiocy', and Keats is attacked politically for approving Hunt's 'series of libels against his sovereign'.*

to his succession, the greater seems to be the impulse to hasten the return of similar embarrassments,—a prepossession for which I confess myself unable to account satisfactorily, unless by admitting the force of habit, which we all know " is prodigious and unaccountable."

Should you, Mr Editor, consider this sketch worthy of appearing in print, it may, however slight, afford a cud for rumination to some of your readers, and may perhaps induce me, in a future Number, to consider, a little more at large, a subject which I have only touched                SKIN DEEP.

---

COCKNEY SCHOOL OF POETRY.

## No IV.

———— OF KEATS,
THE MUSES' SON OF PROMISE, AND WHAT
FEATS
HE YET MAY DO, &c.
                    CORNELIUS WEBB.

OF all the manias of this mad age, the most incurable, as well as the most common, seems to be no other than the *Metromanie.* The just celebrity of Robert Burns and Miss Baillie has had the melancholy effect of turning the heads of we know not how many farm-servants and unmarried ladies ; our very footmen compose tragedies, and there is scarcely a superannuated governess in the island that does not leave a roll of lyrics behind her in her band-box. To witness the disease of any human understanding, however feeble, is distressing ; but the spectacle of an able mind reduced to a state of insanity is of course ten times more afflicting. It is with such sorrow as this that we have contemplated the case of Mr John Keats. This young man appears to have received from nature talents of an excellent, perhaps even of a superior order—talents which, devoted to the purposes of any useful profession, must have rendered him a respectable, if not an eminent citizen. His friends, we understand, destined him to the career of medicine, and he was bound apprentice some years ago to a worthy apothecary in town. But all has been undone by a sudden attack of the malady to which we have alluded. Whether Mr John had been sent home with a diuretic or compos-

Vol. III.

ing draught to some patient far gone in the poetical mania, we have not heard. This much is certain, that he has caught the infection, and that thoroughly. For some time we were in hopes, that he might get off with a violent fit or two ; but of late the symptoms are terrible. The phrenzy of the " Poems" was bad enough in its way ; but it did not alarm us half so seriously as the calm, settled, imperturbable drivelling idiocy of " Endymion." We hope, however, that in so young a person, and with a constitution originally so good, even now the disease is not utterly incurable. Time, firm treatment, and rational restraint, do much for many apparently hopeless invalids ; and if Mr Keats should happen, at some interval of reason, to cast his eye upon our pages, he may perhaps be convinced of the existence of his malady, which, in such cases, is often all that is necessary to put the patient in a fair way of being cured.

The readers of the Examiner newspaper were informed, some time ago, by a solemn paragraph, in Mr Hunt's best style, of the appearance of two new stars of glorious magnitude and splendour in the poetical horizon of the land of Cockaigne. One of these turned out, by and by, to be no other than Mr John Keats. This precocious adulation confirmed the wavering apprentice in his desire to quit the gallipots, and at the same time excited in his too susceptible mind a fatal admiration for the character and talents of the most worthless and affected of all the versifiers of our time. One of his first productions was the following sonnet, " *written on the day when Mr Leigh Hunt left prison.*" It will be recollected, that the cause of Hunt's confinement was a series of libels against his sovereign, and that its fruit was the odious and incestuous " Story of Rimini."

" What though, for shewing truth to flattered state,
  *Kind Hunt* was shut in prison, yet has he,
  In his immortal spirit been as free
As the sky-searching lark, and as elate.
Minion of grandeur ! think you he did wait?
  Think you he nought but prison walls did see,
  Till, so unwilling, thou unturn'dst the key ?
Ah, no ! far happier, nobler was his fate !
  *In Spenser's halls* ! he strayed, and bowers fair,
  Culling enchanted flowers ; and he flew

3 U

The attacks began when *Blackwood's Edinburgh Magazine* published the first of a series of articles entitled 'On the Cockney School of Poetry'. By 'the Cockney School' the Tory reviewers, Lockhart and Wilson, meant the Liberal Hunt, Keats and Reynolds; and they claimed that this 'School' was vulgar and indecently sensual. Hunt, they said (recalling the sympathetic treatment of mildly incestuous adultery in 'The Story of Rimini'), was guilty of

> low birth and low habits . . . . . ignorance and vulgarity . . . . . His poetry resembles that of a man who has kept company with kept-mistresses. His muse talks indelicately . . . . .; with her, indecency is a disease, she appears to speak unclean things from perfect inanition . . . . . The author has voluntarily chosen – a subject not of simple seduction alone – one in which his mind seems absolutely to gloat over all the details of adultery and incest.
>
> *(Blackwood's*, II, pp. 39, 40; October 1817)

Eventually it was Keats's turn to be pilloried. *Blackwood's* claimed that the mania for poetising had spread to the commoners – to footmen, governesses, and even a certain medical student. The reviewer mocked the 'Cockney rhymes' of Keats's first volume and *Endymion*, and concluded:

> It is a better and a wiser thing to be a starved apothecary than a starved poet; so back to the shop Mr John, back to 'plasters, pills, and ointment boxes,' &c. But, for Heaven's sake, young Sangrado, be a little more sparing of extenuatives and soporifics in your practice than you have been in your poetry.
>
> (III, p. 524; August 1818)

Of the differences between Hunt and Keats, *Blackwood's* had said:

> Mr Hunt is a small poet, but he is a clever man. Mr Keats is a still smaller poet, and he is only a boy of pretty abilities, which he has done every thing in his power to spoil.
>
> (III, p. 522)

In the *Quarterly Review*, John Wilson Croker claimed that though *Endymion* displayed 'gleams of genius', Keats's poetic characteristics were those of the Cockney School, 'which may be defined to consist of the most incongruous ideas in the most uncouth language' . . . . .

> This author is a copyist of Mr. Hunt; but he is more unintelligible, almost as rugged, twice as diffuse, and ten times more tiresome and absurd than his prototype. . . . .
>
> (XIX, p. 205; dated April 1818 but published in September)

With forensic zeal Croker proceeded to the attack. He noted, justly, that in parts of *Endymion* the sense seems to be forced by the need to complete a rhyme ('moon' compelling the 'shady boon' of trees, 'blooms' inducing the 'grandeur of the dooms' of the dead); and he complained, again sometimes justly, of the Huntian liberties with vocabulary, as when Keats uses nouns as verbs ('turtles passion their voices'), employs adverbs as prefixes ('wine, out-sparkling', 'down-sunken hours'), and coins neologisms ('human serpentry', 'needments' and a 'honey-feel of bliss'). The analyses were intricate, the tone generally contemptuous.

Meanwhile, the *British Critic* had completed the triad of hostility with a review which righteously declared:

> We . . . . . will not disgust our readers by retailing to them the artifices of vicious refinement, by which, under the semblance of 'slippery blisses, twinkling eyes, soft completion of faces, and smooth excess of hands,' he would palm upon the unsuspicious and the innocent[,] imaginations better adapted to the stews [i.e. brothels].
>
> (New Series, IX, p. 652; June 1818)

Friends rallied to Keats's defence: Reynolds, Woodhouse and Taylor emphasised in their articles the redeeming beauties of *Endymion*, and two protests against the injustice of the *Quarterly* appeared in *The Morning Chronicle* in October. The controversy re-echoed: many years later, Matthew Arnold was to say: 'The poem as a whole I could wish to be suppressed and lost'.

Though Keats felt deeply wounded by the reviews, he declared:

> Praise or blame has but a momentary effect on the man whose love of beauty in the abstract makes him a severe critic of his own Works. My own domestic criticism has given me pain without comparison beyond what Blackwood or the Quarterly could possibly inflict. . . . . In Endymion, I leaped headlong into the Sea, and thereby have become better acquainted with the Soundings, the quicksands, & the rocks, than if I had stayed upon the green shore, and piped a silly pipe. . . . .
>
> (R I, 373–4)

## Fanny Brawne

On 1 December, brother Tom died peacefully of consumption. John Keats had long felt particularly close to his brothers, but now two had been taken from him by death and one had emigrated to America. He had nursed Tom during the final weeks, and felt the

*Silhouette of Fanny Brawne at the age of 29. (Copy by Charles Brown of an original by Auguste Edouart.)*

*Keats wrote: 'Her shape is very graceful and so are her movements – her Arms are good [,] her hands badish – her feet tolerable' (R II, 13).*

*Miniature of Fanny Brawne by an unknown artist, 1833 – twelve years after
Keats's death, when she was thirty-three years old. '[Her] Profil is better than
her full face which indeed is not full but pale and thin without showing any
bone' (R II, 13).*

loss keenly. One compensation, however, was provided by his growing interest in an eighteen-year-old girl, Fanny Brawne. Her mother, a widow with a private income, had rented part of Wentworth Place, where Keats's friends Charles and Maria Dilke lived, and it was almost certainly there that he first met Fanny. He described her thus:

> She is about my height – with a fine style of countenance of the lengthen'd sort . . . . . Her shape is very graceful and so are her movements – her Arms are good[,] her hands badish – her feet tolerable . . . . . but she is ignorant – monstrous in her behaviour flying out in all directions, calling people such names – that I was forced lately to make use of the term *Minx* . . . . .
>
> (R II, 13)

She was animated, witty, lively and spirited; and though she sometimes seemed more interested in dress-fashions than in *Paradise Lost* or Shakespeare's tragedies, Keats's interest in her became a love-relationship, and they became engaged in the autumn of 1819. He was to tell Fanny: 'I have two luxuries to brood over in my walks, your Loveliness and the hour of my death. O that I could have possession of them both in the same minute. I hate the world: it batters too much the wings of my self-will, and would I could take a sweet poison from your lips to send me out of it' (R II, 133).

A curious feature of the relationship is that after the initial phase of love-letters in the summer of 1819, Keats strove to stay away from Fanny. This feature was predictable: it reflects that conflict between the ideal and the real which had long been a preoccupation of his poetry, and it recalls the dénouement of *Endymion*, in which the ultimate identification of ideal with mundane love depended on the prior resolve of the man to part from the girl. Keats wrote to Fanny in September:

> If I were to see you to day it would destroy the half comfortable sullenness I enjoy at present into dow[n]right perplexities. I love you too much to venture to Hampstead, I feel it is not paying a visit, but venturing into a fire . . . . . Knowing well that my life must be passed in fatigue and trouble, I have been endeavouring to wean myself from you . . . . .
>
> (R II, 160)

His low finances and subsequent ill-health both barred matrimony, and in a letter to his brother and sister-in-law he said, 'A Man in love I do think cuts the sorryest figure in the world' (R II, 187). But by October he was evidently head-over-heels in love, telling Fanny:

> I have had a thousand kisses, for which with my whole soul I thank love – but if you should deny me the thousand and first – 't

*Wentworth Place, Hampstead. Keats was based here for a year and a half until May 1820, paying Charles Brown £5 per month for meals and accommodation (a bedroom and a sitting-room). During this period he produced the famous odes. The house is now known as Keats House and serves as a museum. Rooms to the left of the front door were occupied by Brown and Keats (who had a separate entrance at the side); rooms to the right were occupied by Mrs Brawne and Fanny.*

would put me to the proof how great a misery I could live through.

Again:

> I cannot exist without you. . . . . You have absorb'd me. I have a sensation at the present moment as though I was dissolving. . . . . My Creed is Love and you are its only tenet. . . . . I have endeavoured often 'to reason against the reasons of my Love.' I can do that no more – the pain would be too great – My Love is selfish – I cannot breathe without you.
>
> (R II, 222–4)

When he was dying, he wrote to Brown: 'I should have had her when I was in health, and I should have remained well. I can bear to die – I cannot bear to leave her' (R II, 351).

Keats and Fanny had often embraced, exchanging physical as well as verbal endearments, but whether they ever copulated has remained their secret. Those words, 'I should have had her when I was in health', though ambiguous, probably imply abstinence, as may some of the tones (which include the ardent and the frustrated, longing and jealous, hopeful and bitter) in his other references to the relationship. If so, his love for Fanny was appropriate to his poetic character: that of a young man constantly tantalised by goals which promise fulfilment yet recede from the quester; the plight of Endymion and of the lovers on the urn. Like the 'Joy, whose hand is ever at his lips/ Bidding adieu', Keats would recall Fanny as a figure eternally seen 'eternally vanishing'. The element of frustration in his love is harmonic with his recurrent sense of frustrated poetic ambition and, eventually, of frustrated vitality – of life receding as the lungs dissolve.

Desire tantalised is often desire intensified; and to the spirit of Tantalus, who found the grapes intangible, we may owe some of the almost tangible intensities of Keats's poetry.

## Annus mirabilis: *1819*

For all the intoxications of love for Fanny, Keats was frequently beset by depression and listlessness: though he tried to lead a secluded, industrious life as a writer, there were times when solitariness sapped his will to work and promoted a morbid brooding. He had taken to heart the death of Tom: he had seen painful lingering disease and a pointlessly curtailed life. His own health, with a recurrent sore throat, gave him nagging worries. Finances were troublesome, too. Richard Abbey had always been tightfisted and discouraging in financial and literary matters, and, when a relative contested the estate, he was prompt to use this as a

*Joseph Severn: 'Keats at Wentworth Place' (painted in Rome,* circa *1822).*
*'And there I'd sit and read all day like a picture of somebody reading', wrote*
*Keats.*

pretext for further impeding the realisation of funds. Keats, who had lent money generously to Haydon, now made fruitless efforts to reclaim it, and needed the financial help of Brown and Woodhouse; Hessey and Haslam also provided aid. Abbey was proving a severe, unloving guardian to Keats's sister Fanny, and he advised Keats to become a hatter – probably because he himself had invested money in a hatter's, and possibly as a mocking way of implying that his protégé must have been mad to abandon surgery for poetry.

Nevertheless, 1819 was Keats's *annus mirabilis* as a poet. It saw the production in January and February of 'The Eve of St. Agnes', in May of the odes 'On a Grecian Urn', 'To a Nightingale', 'On Melancholy' and 'On Indolence', and in September of 'To Autumn': works in which his poetic abilities reached their height.

'The Eve of St. Agnes', his most successful narrative poem, was influenced by his reading of Shakespeare's *Romeo and Juliet*, Mrs Radcliffe's Gothic novels, Scott's 'Lay of the Last Minstrel' (1805) and particularly Coleridge's 'Christabel' (1816); but it emerges as a distinctive and remarkably organised unity. The multiple sensuousness at the centre (the colour, the music, the banquet and the sexual embrace of Madeline and Porphyro) is elaborately and tellingly contrasted with imagery of coldness, darkness, gloom, death and decay; hot perfumed confinement opposed to the draughty stoniness of the castle, and beyond that, the bleak wintry wastes; moments of pulsing life set against the great expanse of the past and the dumb armies of the dead; a warm bedroom amid a frozen waste-land; the momentary embrace of lovers amid the endless wastes of time. Keats has discovered that a taut patterning of mutually-reinforcing contrasts can immensely increase the impact of the parts of a poem and can provide a structure which not only enriches but also extends the significance of the whole. He was to use this technique of 'dialectical description' in the great odes.

He had come to feel that a poet should be a philosopher, and accordingly in his letters had indulged in philosophical speculations, but, generally, they were inconsistent and inconclusive. Tom's death made him reflect that 'one of the grandeurs of immortality [will be that] there will be no space and consequently the only commerce between spirits will be by their intelligence of each other – when they will completely understand each other.....' (R II, 5). He had coached his sister carefully for Anglican confirmation; and he mused that the world might be 'the vale of Soul-making' in which we gain identity as preparation for immortality (102). Yet, a parson (he thought) 'must be either a Knave or an Ideot' (63). Though Keats could feel admiration for Jesus, he regretted 'that the history of the latter was written and revised by Men interested in the pious frauds of Religion' (80). And in the sonnet 'Why did I laugh tonight?', he thought of death as utter cessation rather than as a gateway to eternal life:

> Why did I laugh? I know this being's lease –
>   My fancy to its utmost blisses spreads:
> Yet could I on this very midnight cease,
>   And the world's gaudy ensigns see in shreds.
> Verse, fame, and beauty are intense indeed,
> But death intenser – death is life's high meed.

It anticipates the later sonnets of Thomas Hardy, not only in the sense, but even in the phrasing's muscular concision. The idea of 'ceasing', of lapsing into an ultimate nullity, was a recurrent temptation to Keats; here he offers it little imaginative resistance. In the great odes, life fights back valiantly.

His sensuous nature, his concern to define the individuating essence of things (the *haecceitas*, 'thisness', or what G. M. Hopkins was to call 'inscape'), his preoccupation with the kinds of immortality attainable through art, his Platonic yearnings and his down-to-earth scepticism, his death-wish and his sense of humour: all these coalesced in three of the supreme poems in the language – the 'Ode on a Grecian Urn', 'Ode to a Nightingale' and 'To Autumn'. Other important odes were 'On Melancholy', 'On Indolence' and 'To Psyche'; and this major phase included 'Lamia', 'If by dull rhymes', 'Sonnet to Sleep' and the two sonnets entitled 'On Fame'. At the same time, he was capable of producing trash. In that summer of 1819, in collaboration with Brown, he rapidly turned out the ludicrous 'tragedy', *Otho the Great*, and for a while the two had high hopes that it would be performed by Kean at Drury Lane and make their fortunes; but the management procrastinated, Kean had plans to go abroad, and these hopes fell through.

Keats had also been striving to emulate John Milton by composing a noble, stately epic: *Hyperion*. This project gave him extreme difficulty: he stopped and started, hesitated, struggled on again. Gradually he came to suspect that he was working against the grain and that the great Milton was perhaps the wrong kind of figure to emulate – Chatterton seemed more sympathetic. On 21 September he told Reynolds, 'I have given up *Hyperion* – there were too many Miltonic inversions in it – Miltonic verse cannot be written but in an artful or rather artist's humour. I wish to give myself up to other sensations. English ought to be kept up' (R II, 167). And in another letter he remarked: 'The Paradise lost though so fine in itself is a corruption of our Language..... I have but lately stood on my guard against Milton. Life to him would be death to me' (212). Turning to Dante's *Divine Comedy* for guidance, he attempted to re-work the legendary matter of *Hyperion* into *The Fall of Hyperion*, in which, poignantly, the poet himself comes to the fore as a striving yet ailing character. As in *The Divine Comedy*, the quester receives both guidance and rebuke; but now the admonisher, Moneta, is more dauntingly enigmatic than Dante's Virgil or Beatrice. Keats's self-doubts are painfully evident in the uncertain ebb and flow of the discussion in this opening, particularly when Moneta seems to define the narrator as mere dreamer rather than true poet before she relents to the extent of imparting to him her vision of the Titans. The tone of contempt, while it lasts, is sharp:

> What benefit canst thou do, or all thy tribe,
> To the great world? Thou art a dreaming thing;
> A fever of thyself. . . . .

(Canto I, lines 167–9)

Even this more fluid and autobiographic version of the material proved abortive, and with 'on he flared' in line 61 of Canto II, the poem finally guttered out.

In the course of time, Keats's conception of poetic endeavour itself was becoming more sober and self-critical. 'I have come to the resolution never to write for the sake of writing, or making a poem, but from running over with any little knowledge and experience which many years of reflection may perhaps give me – otherwise I will be dumb' (R II, 43). In June he even claimed: 'I have been very idle lately, very averse to writing; both from the overpowering idea of our dead poets and from abatement of my love of fame. I hope I am a little more of a Philosopher than I was, consequently a little less of a versifying Pet-lamb' (116). He thought of raising money by abandoning poetry and becoming a liberal journalist – 'I will write, on the liberal side of the question, for whoever will pay me. . . . . I shall apply to Hazlitt, who knows the market. . . . .' (176–7). He may have thought himself a liberal, but he still accepted the common, casual anti-Semitism of his day: 'I . . . . . am confident I shall be able to cheat as well as any literary Jew of the Market and shine up an article on anything without much knowledge of the subject, aye like an orange' (179). In the meantime, there were moments of intense pleasure – and not only in Fanny Brawne's arms. 'Talking of Pleasure, this moment I was writing with one hand, and with the other holding to my Mouth a Nectarine – good god how fine – It went down soft pulpy, slushy, oozy – all its delicious embonpoint melted down my throat like a large beatified Strawberry. I shall certainly breed.' (179) There were times of hilarity, too, as when he played a practical joke with a distastefully anti-Semitic tinge:

> Brown let his house to a Mr. Benjamin a Jew. Now the water which furnishes the house is in a tank sided with a composition of lime and the lime imp[r]egnates the water unpleasantly – Taking advantage of this circumstance I pretended that Mr. Benjamin

had written the following short note – 'Sir. By drinking your damn'd tank water I have got the gravel – what reparation can you make to me and my family? Nathan Benjamin' By a fortunate hit, I hit upon his right hethen name – his right Pronomen. Brown in consequence it appears wrote to the surprised Mr. Benjamin the following 'Sir, I cannot offer you any remuneration until your gravel shall have formed itself into a Stone when I will cut you with Pleasure. C. Brown' This of Browns Mr. Benjamin has answered insisting on an explatinon [*sic*] of this singular circumstance.

(R II, 215–16)

## The hopes of 1820

In 1820 there were distinct signs that Keats's literary reputation was burgeoning and that the high hopes of his friends were to be fulfilled by public recognition of his work. In April, *Endymion* was highly praised in Baldwin's *London Magazine*. Although the poem had palpable faults, said the reviewer, it was 'richer in promise than any other that we are acquainted with, except those of Chatterton'. 'It is the May-day of poetry..... It is the sky-lark's hymn to the day-break, involuntarily gushing forth.....' (*CH*, 147, 136). In the same month, the loyal Hunt printed 'La Belle Dame sans Merci' in *The Indicator*. Taylor and Hessey rapidly published the *Lamia* volume (containing the great odes) in July; Charles Lamb commended it warmly in the *New Times*; and subsequently several magazines (*Edinburgh, New Monthly* and Baldwin's *London*) gave generous praise, even if Gold's *London Magazine*, the *Guardian* and the *Eclectic Review* were variously mocking and scornful.

One Scottish reader, who knew Keats only from the published works, fell in love with him, and wrote passionately to say so and to offer him the hospitality of his house and library:

> ..... there is nothing selfish in my request. – It is prompted as much by the amiable qualities of your heart, which are so abundantly apparent in your productions as by the eminence which you have attained – and may yet attain by your talents. In short I love you – (as you must of necessity do me) – for yourself alone.

(R II, 325)

This letter from John Aitken provides a ludicrously extreme instance of Keats's power to attract and inspire with altruistic enthusiasm, with admiration and hope, the most diverse characters – Hunt, Haydon, Cowden Clarke, Brown, Taylor, Reynolds, Rice, Woodhouse and Severn. What attracted them was a combination of qualities – his bright-eyed enthusiasm, his vivacity and jesting, his idealism and earthy humour, the eagerness to learn and share, and his capacity for intense empathy with nature and the life around him. This mixture of qualities seemed repeatedly to bring out the best in those who knew him; for, from Hunt or Reynolds, Severn or Haydon, he drew letters which are moving testimonies of loyalty and affection and of prophetic faith in his poetic reputation to come.

## The masterpiece of the final phase

There is a Keatsian masterpiece which commentators have never appreciated as such; but, arguably, in its range, intensity, variety and pathos it transcends his acknowledged masterworks, even 'To Autumn' and 'Ode on a Grecian Urn'. That masterpiece is the account of the last year of his life, from February 1820 to February 1821, as provided mainly by the correspondence in *The Letters of John Keats*, Vol. II, pp. 251–381. It is Keatsian, because he is the central figure and the main letter-writer, but it is also collaborative, because letters by various other figures (Brown, Severn, Haydon, Shelley, Aitken, Abbey, Haslam, Woodhouse, Dr Clark, and Mrs Brawne) contribute to the story, the immediate, harrowing, vivid story, of the poet's decline and death. To read these letters is to be drawn into the very texture of that past nexus of experience; and if it is a characteristic of a masterpiece to offer a telling, memorable and searching account of life, then masterpiece is the appropriate word for this sequence. Necessarily, it is represented here only by summary and a few brief quotations; I recommend that the interested reader should study the original body of material assembled by Rollins.

Keats knew all about tuberculosis, having been a medical student and having nursed his consumptive brother Tom to the last. This made his consciousness of his own eventual situation the more acute. Early in 1820, after snow there came a sunny thaw; Keats went for a walk without wearing his great-coat and caught a cold which affected his lungs. On 3 February he had a haemorrhage and exclaimed to Brown, 'I know the colour of that blood; – it is arterial blood; – I cannot be deceived in that colour; – that drop of blood is my death-warrant; – I must die' (*KC* II, 73–4). He became a feverish invalid, confined indoors for weeks on end, though often visited and tended by Fanny Brawne (who was literally the girl next door, living in the adjacent half of Wentworth Place). He had palpitations of the heart; there were nightmares; he was often fretful, impatient and depressed. He felt that if the *Lamia* volume failed, he would abandon poetry to become an apothecary after all. Further haemorrhages came in the summer, and he moved restlessly from one home to another. He had been sharing a house with his friend Brown, but left in a jealous rage because of the older man's

*Severn: 'The* Maria Crowther'. *This water-colour shows the brig on which Keats and Severn sailed for Rome in 1820, sharing their partitioned cabin with two ladies.*

flirtatious banter with Fanny. Next, he stayed with Hunt, who tended him with affectionate care; but again there was a quarrel, and Keats moved to Kentish Town. Eventually Mrs Brawne and Fanny nursed him in their home at Wentworth Place. From Italy came a magnanimous letter from Shelley, who himself had been consumptive, urging Keats to come to stay with the Shelleys in the kind Italian climate at Pisa, adding 'I have lately read your Endymion again & ever with a new sense of the treasures of poetry it contains, though treasures poured forth with indistinct profusion'. He concluded:

> Whether you remain in England, or journey to Italy, – believe that you carry with you my anxious wishes for your health happiness & success, wherever you are or whatever you undertake. . . . .

(R II, 311)

Although Keats was never to reach Pisa, his doctor and friends urged him to avoid the English winter by setting out for Italy. Abbey, typically, denied him funds, but Keats raised money by selling the copyright of his works to Taylor and Hessey. His friend Severn nobly agreed to accompany him on the long arduous journey: a voyage which must have seemed to Severn like a descent through purgatory to the hell of the landfall. The ship, the *Maria Crowther*, set out from London into the Channel, but was soon beset by storm and tempest. Keats and Severn were cramped in a small cabin which they had to share with a Mrs Pidgeon and a young Miss Cotterell, who herself was consumptive. Severn reported:

> The trunks rolled across the Cabin – the water poured in from the skylight and we were tumbled from one side to the other of our beds. . . . . I got up and fell down on the floor from my weakness and the rolling of the ship – Keats was very calm – the ladies were much frightened – and could scarce speak – when I got up to the deck I was astounded – the waves were in Mountains – and washed the ship – the watry horizon was like a Mountainous Country – but the ship's motion was beautifully to the sea – falling from one wave to the other in a very lovely manner – the sea each time crossing the deck and one side of the ship being level with the water . . . . . but when the dusk came the sea began to rush in from the side of our Cabin from an opening in the planks – this ma[d]e us rather long faced – for it came in by pails-full – again I got out – and said to Keats – 'here's pretty music for you' – with the greatest calmness he answer[e]d me – only 'Water parted from the sea' [a quotation from a popular opera-song] . . . . . here were the pumps working – the sailes squalling the confused voices of the sailors – the things rattling about in every direction – and us poor devils pinn'd up in our

*W. Callcott: Piazza di Spagna at Rome. Keats and Severn rented an apartment on the second floor of the house on the right; here the poet died. The house is now a museum devoted to the memory of Keats and Shelley.*

beds like ghosts by day light – except Keats he was himself all the time. . . . .

(R II, 342–3)

Keats wrote to Brown, imploring him to look after Fanny Brawne:

You think she has many faults – but, for my sake, think she has not one. . . . . The thought of leaving Miss Brawne is beyond every thing horrible – the sense of darkness coming over me – I eternally see her figure eternally vanishing. . . . . Is there another Life? Shall I awake and find all this a dream? There must be we cannot be created for this sort of suffering.

(R II, 345–6)

He continued to be agonised by the thought of her – 'to see her name written would be more than I could bear'. And the illness continued its inexorable course: Keats was often feverish and sometimes bleeding from the stomach. If the cabin window were shut, the consumptive Miss Cotterell would faint for want of air; if it were open, Keats would cough and spit blood.

At last the ship reached Italy, and, after stifling quarantine at Naples, Keats and Severn travelled to Rome and took rooms at 26 Piazza di Spagna, at the corner of the steps leading up to the Church of the Trinità dei Monte, and near the sparkling fountain by Bernini. As Keats was bed-ridden, Severn worked as his nurse, cook and comforter. During the long, tormented decline from December to February, Keats was coughing blood, unable to keep food down, anguished, half suffocating. Dr James Clark, who attended him, reported that the stomach was ruined, in addition to the diseased lungs. Severn was distraught, exhausted by the strain and the sleepless nights, worried about finances:

Tolonia's – the bankers – have refused any more money – the bill is returned unaccepted – 'no effects' – and I tomorrow must – aye *must* – pay the last solitary Crowns for this cursed lodging place – yet more – should our unfortunate friend dye – all the furniture will be burnt – beds – sheets – curtains and even the walls must be scraped – and these devils will come upon me for 100£ or 150£ – the making good – but above all – this noble fellow lying on the bed – is dying in horror – no kind hope smoothing down his suffering – no philosophy – no religion to support him – yet with all the most knawing desire for it – yet without the possibility of receiving it.

(R II, 368)

Keats was coughing up clay-coloured matter, blood-streaked; his nights were restless and his body wasting: 'Yet from all these', wrote Severn, 'he might get up if he could bear over that intense feeling –

*Severn: Self-portrait. This shows him at the age of 29, around the time when he was nursing the dying Keats.*

*Severn: sketch of Keats on his deathbed. Severn has inscribed the pen-and-ink drawing: '28 Janr. 3 o'clock mng – Drawn to keep me awake – a deadly sweat was on him all this night'.*

and those unfortunate combinations and passions of mind – from which no medicine in the world can relieve him'. He begged Severn for a bottle of opium, to end his miseries, but his friend resisted the temptation and entrusted the bottle to Dr Clark. 'No one will relieve me – they all run away', grieved Severn. 'He opens his eyes in great horror and doubt – but when they fall upon me – they close gently and open and close until he falls into another sleep. . . . .' (R II, 376)

The end came on 23 February:

4 oclock afternoon – The poor fellow bade me lift him up in bed – he breathed with great difficulty – and seemed to lose the power of coughing up the phlegm – an immense sweat came over him so that my breath felt cold to him – 'don't breath[e] on me – it comes like Ice' – he clasped my hand very fast as I held him in my arms – the mucus was boiling within him – it gurgled in his throat – this increased – but yet he seem'd without pain – at 11 he died in my arms. . . . .

(R II, 378)

On 26 February, John Keats, aged twenty-five, was buried in the Protestant Cemetery at Rome, near the pyramid of Caius Cestius. Some turfs of daisies were laid on the grave. Forty years later, avid tourists stripped it of everything that was green and living.

# 2   Posthumous events

## The aftermath

Keats was deeply mourned by Fanny Brawne, who became thin and
pallid; but after twelve years she married a Sephardic Jew, Louis
Lindo (later Lindon) and spent much of her life abroad. Fanny
Keats married a Spanish liberal and author, Valentín Llanos y
Gutierrez, and went to live in Spain; during a stay in Rome she met
Severn, who after leading a precarious existence had become a
popular British Consul there. Brother George paid John Keats's
debts, discovered and claimed his legacy in Chancery, and
prospered in America. Dr Clark became physician to Queen
Victoria and was knighted.

Keats had requested the following inscription for his tombstone:
'Here lies one whose name was writ in water'. Charles Brown added
the preliminary statement, 'This Grave contains all that was
Mortal, of a YOUNG ENGLISH POET Who, on his Death Bed, in
the Bitterness of his Heart at the Malicious Power of his Enemies,
Desired these Words to be engraven on his Tomb Stone'. That
additional inscription helped to create a Romantic myth: it
melodramatised Keats as the young poet brought to an untimely
grave by the 'Malicious Power' of foes – the foes being the early
reviewers, and particularly Lockhart of *Blackwood's* and Croker of the
*Quarterly*. This myth, so appropriate to the Romantic conception of
the artist as the lonely unappreciated genius, which links Keats to
his hero Chatterton, conveniently overlooks the facts that the young
poet was winning friends among the reviewers and that, like his
brother Tom, John died of tuberculosis and not of harsh criticism.
Nevertheless, it was credited and amplified by Shelley in *Adonais*
(1821), in which the *Quarterly's* reviewer is termed a murderer.

## Shelley's Adonais

*Adonais* is one of the great English elegies; it inhabits the pastoral
and meditative traditions, and in them is superior to Spenser's
'November' and 'Astrophel' and approaches in merit Milton's
'Lycidas'.

It has some obvious faults: a monotony or predictability of literary
lamentation; a straining towards the loftily poetical; and (typical of
Shelley) a narcissistic element, as when Shelley himself enters in the
guise of

> one frail Form,
> A phantom among men; companionless

As the last cloud of an expiring storm
Whose thunder is its knell . . . . .
A pardlike Spirit beautiful and swift . . . . .

Nevertheless, the closing stanzas reach heights of eloquent intensity:

### LII

The One remains, the many change and pass;
Heaven's light for ever shines, Earth's shadows fly;
Life, like a dome of many-coloured glass,
Stains the white radiance of Eternity,
Until Death tramples it to fragments. – Die,
If thou wouldst be with that which thou dost seek!
Follow where all is fled! – Rome's azure sky,
Flowers, ruins, statues, music, words, are weak
The glory they transfuse with fitting truth to speak . . . . .

### LV

The breath whose might I have invoked in song
Descends on me; my spirit's bark is driven,
Far from the shore, far from the trembling throng
Whose sails were never to the tempest given;
The massy earth and spherèd skies are riven!
I am borne darkly, fearfully, afar;
Whilst, burning through the inmost veil of Heaven,
The soul of Adonais, like a star,
Beacons from the abode where the Eternal are.

(S, 438–9)

In stanza LII, the basic idea is Neo-Platonic, but not remote from the Christian idea; and the sense of an eternal radiant source beyond the perishable tangibles of this world is harmonic with some of the preoccupations in Keats's great odes. The image of Life as a dome of many-coloured glass which 'stains the white radiance of Eternity' has a fine ambiguity: 'stains' can mean 'renders impure, taints or pollutes' or 'enhances by adding colour to'; the many-coloured glass may deceive, by falsifying the pure light, or it may enrich, as a stained-glass window enriches daylight; and the harshness of 'Until Death tramples it to fragments' suggests the fragile beauty of that dome: so that there is a life-celebrating qualification of the overt exhortation to seek death.

As for stanza LV, this has been given immense plangency and force by the circumstances of Shelley's demise. In the verse, Shelley speaks of himself as one whose spirit's bark is driven far from the shore, submitting its sails to the tempest, seeking Adonais (Keats's spirit): and it was in the following year, in July 1822, that Shelley was drowned when his small sailing-boat was wrecked during a storm in the Bay of Spezia. The elegy for Keats's death had become an uncanny prophecy of Shelley's death. And when his body was washed up on the beach near Viareggio, a copy of Keats's *Lamia* volume was found, open, in his jacket pocket – 'doubled back', Trelawny noted, 'as if the reader, in the act of reading, had hastily thrust it away'. Shelley's corpse was burned in a funeral pyre on the beach, while Leigh Hunt, Edward Trelawny and Lord Byron attended, and the ashes were then entombed at the Protestant Cemetery where Keats lay buried.

*Blackwood's* remarked breezily: 'But what a rash man Shelley was, to put to sea in a frail boat with Jack's poetry on board! Why, man, it would sink a trireme' (XVI, 288; September 1824). And if Shelley's *Adonais* had exalted Keats as the martyred youthful genius, Byron, in *Don Juan*, offered a wryly sceptical obituary:

> John Keats, who was killed off by one critique,
> Just as he really promised something great,
> If not intelligible, without Greek
> Contrived to talk about the gods of late,
> Much as they might have been supposed to speak.
> Poor fellow! His was an untoward fate;
> 'Tis strange the mind, that very fiery particle,
> Should let itself be snuffed out by an article.
>
> (Canto XI, stanza 60)

## Keats's subsequent reputation

In his short life-time, as we have seen, Keats's poetry received a very wide range of critical responses, and there were few subsequent judgements which had not been anticipated by those early commentators. Leigh Hunt was the pioneer in intelligent appreciation entailing close attention to the details of phrasing: '*swims* is complete', he said of the well-chosen verb in the 'Chapman's Homer' sonnet; and he rightly noted that in 'The Eve of St. Agnes', the line 'And lucent syrops, tinct with cinnamon' obliges one to read 'delicately, and at the tip-end, as it were, of one's tongue' (*CH*, 42, 280). Even the notorious attacks in *Blackwood's* and the *Quarterly* made some quite valid points: Keats's rhymes ('higher' with 'Thalia', for instance) were indeed often hasty and jarring; and Croker was right to observe that Keats sometimes associates slackly, letting rhymes dictate sense. Many later complaints of the poet's unmanly self-indulgence were vigorously anticipated by Lord Byron's complaint in 1820 that Keats was a 'miserable Self-polluter of the human Mind': 'such writing is a sort of mental masturbation – f––gg––g his *Imagination*. – I don't mean that he is *indecent* but viciously soliciting his own ideas into a state which is neither poetry nor any thing else but a Bedlam vision produced by raw pork and opium' (*BTW*, 217, 225). Hazlitt complained that *Endymion* was 'soft and fleshy, without bone or muscle', and that though Keats was very talented, he lacked 'manly strength and fortitude' (*CH*, 248) – a comment which, ironically, echoes Faustus's rebuke of Mephistopheles.

1821–48.   For at least a decade after Keats's death, the little fame he had achieved seemed to be fading. In 1821 his publishers reckoned that they had lost £110 on the *Endymion* volume, and sales of his works were slow. In 1835 Taylor said, 'I should like to print a complete Edition of Keats's Poems, but the world cares nothing for him' (*CH*, 9). However, the world was slowly learning to care. In 1829 Galignani of Paris published the first collected edition of his poems; in London, the first British collected edition came in 1840; and from 1846 onwards the succession of editions was that of a classic author in steady demand. His work was slow to filter into the anthologies, but he was substantially represented in F. T. Palgrave's *The Golden Treasury* (1861), the most influential of Victorian anthologies – it was still being used in Grammar Schools in the 1950s. Thomas Hood's first volume of poems, *The Plea* (1827), contained assiduous imitations of Keats, particularly of the 'Ode on Melancholy' and 'To Autumn', and when Tennyson's early work appeared in the volumes of 1830 and 1832, reviewers widely recognised its Keatsian qualities.

Leigh Hunt had prophesied in 1828 (in *Lord Byron and Some of His Contemporaries*) that Keats would be famous 'twenty years hence'; and he was precisely correct. In 1848 R. M. Milnes's judiciously sympathetic *Life, Letters, and Literary Remains, of John Keats* firmly established Keats as a great poet, though Milnes soberly observed: 'all that he had produced was rather a promise than an accomplishment' (Vol. I, ix–x).

1848–1900.   During this period, as is shown in a subsequent section (pp. 65–8), Keats's works exerted an extensive influence on poets and artists, notably on Arnold, Tennyson, Hopkins, and the Pre-Raphaelite painter-poets associated with Dante Gabriel Rossetti. The Romantic mythologising of Keats as martyr, begun by Shelley, was maintained by George Meredith in *The Poetry of Keats* (1851) and by Elizabeth Barrett Browning's *Aurora Leigh* (1856), which compares his life to 'a tear/ Upon the world's cold cheek to make it burn/ For ever'. There were still plenty of adverse comments: the suspicion that there was an unmanly hedonism in Keats troubled Victorians concerned with moral muscularity. Cardinal Wiseman found him morally deficient, and Thomas Carlyle said: 'Keats is a miserable creature, hungering after sweets which he can't get'; 'Keats wanted a world of treacle' (*CH*, 35). Matthew Arnold initially regretted that Keats's poetry was exuberant rather than sober; but the later Arnold decided that there were, after all, 'elements of high character' in him: 'flint and iron' and 'lucidity'; and, 'in what we call natural magic, he ranks with Shakespeare'. That later view, offered by Arnold in a preface to *Ward's English Poets*, IV (1880), and subsequently in *Essays in Criticism*, Second Series (1888), did much to ensure Keats's fame by vouching for his respectability. The *Encyclopaedia Britannica* of 1857 claimed that he was the strongest influence on current poetry; while in 1882 its contributor, Algernon Swinburne, claimed fervently: 'Greater lyrical poetry the world may have seen.....; lovelier it has never seen, nor ever can it possibly see'.

1900–1980. By the end of the nineteenth century, Keats's reputation as one of the major English poets was securely established, and since then he has become a centre of the vast industry of biography, scholarship and criticism which customarily surrounds the greatest literary figures. Influential critical discussions were offered by A. C. Bradley in his *Oxford Lectures on Poetry* (1909), William Empson in *Seven Types of Ambiguity* (1930), F. R. Leavis in *Revaluation* (1936) and Cleanth Brooks in *The Well Wrought Urn* (1947). In the eighteenth century, critics valued and over-valued perspicuity and urbanity in poetry; but in the twentieth century, critics value and over-value concreteness of imagery, semantic ambiguity, paradoxes and related plays of tensions within poems: so Keats's work has amply satisfied these Modernist tastes (which largely derive from the Romantics). At the same time, his poetry speaks clearly and immediately to the 'general reader' and to both young and old; all can share his celebration of the appetites and his sense of the poignantly ephemeral richness of the world around us. One great irony is that his apparent lack of doctrine and system, the lack which so troubled him, has actually enhanced his accessibility for readers in the present sceptical phase of our culture. Harold Bloom and Lionel Trilling, assessing Keats in *The Oxford Anthology of English Literature* (1973), said: 'Clearly he is the most sympathetic of modern poets'; since Shakespeare, he is the poet 'most able to grasp the individuality and reality of selves totally distinct from his own, and of an outward world that would survive his perception of it'.

The 1970s also saw the emergence of post-structuralist or 'deconstructionist' approaches of the kind popularised by Catherine Belsey's *Critical Practice* (1980). The 'deconstructor' shared the traditional Modernist preoccupation with paradox and self-contradiction in texts; but the novelty often lay in the purportedly Marxist zeal with which the critic now sacrificed the humanity of the works on the altar of his or her ideology. The 'Ode to a Nightingale', like most other texts examined, was predictably reduced by Belsey to an illustration of the contradictions of capitalism and 'liberal humanism'. This appropriative procedure tended to impute relative wisdom to the political élite represented by the critic, and relative ignorance to the creative writers and their appreciative readers. Karl Marx, when he recognised the truth-values of literary texts (whether of Aeschylus's *Prometheus Bound* or Shakespeare's *Timon of Athens*), was shrewder than many of his putative disciples.

## Keats's influence on later writers and artists

The example of Keats's work tended to strengthen the following aspects of later poetry:
1 the sensuously descriptive;
2 presentation of states of luxurious ease or torpor;
3 the cultivation of 'Art for Art's sake';
4 idealisation of the mediaeval;
5 presentation of vacillating or oscillating attitudes on the part of the narrator; and
6 presentation of large paradoxes concerning art and reality or the ideal and the mundane.

In painting he is most directly associated with the Mediaevalism of the nineteenth century.

All six of the features listed above are prominent in the poetry of Tennyson. Early reviewers were prompt to see the influence of Keats in his first two published collections. 'The Poet's Mind' has a jaunty Aestheticism which in tone recalls some of Keats's brisker pieces; its 'dark-brow'd sophist', the destructive sceptic, may recall Apollonius in 'Lamia'. The hypnotic evocation of indolent luxury in 'The Lotos-Eaters' extends a tradition that stretches from Spenser's *Faerie Queene*, Book II, Canto vi, through Thomson's *The Castle of Indolence* to Keats's 'Sleep and Poetry' and *Endymion*. The Mediaevalist tradition, from Thomas Percy's *Reliques*, late-eighteenth-century poetry by Chatterton and others, and from the Gothic Novel, continues via Coleridge's 'Christabel' and Keats's 'Eve of St. Agnes' and 'The Pot of Basil' to Tennyson's 'Sir Launcelot and Queen Guinevere', 'The Lady of Shalott' and the later Arthurian pieces.

In turn, Coleridge, Keats and Tennyson contributed to the Pre-Raphaelite Movement. The Pre-Raphaelite painters and poets (among them Dante Gabriel Rossetti, William Morris, John Millais and Edward Burne-Jones) offered works which with clear, detailed delineation and lucid colouring sought to create an idealised mediaeval world of knights and fair maidens, castles and questers, Launcelots and Guineveres; and Keats's poems, by taking the trappings and scenery of mediaeval romance and investing them with an essentially modern, secular and erotic spirit, had provided

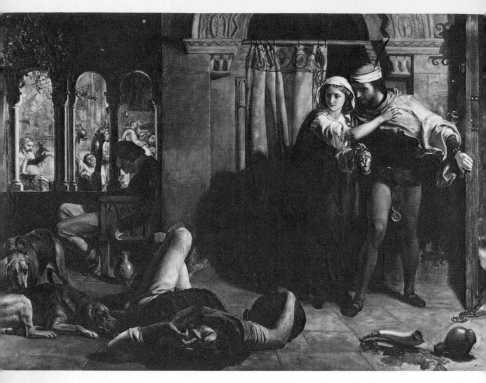

*W. Holman Hunt: 'The Eve of St. Agnes',* circa *1848.*

*Keats's relatively 'Gothic' narrative poems, 'The Eve of St. Agnes' and 'Isabella', inspired the Pre-Raphaelites, who in turn extended his fame in the nineteenth century. His work has even been termed (by Stephen Prickett) 'the most potent single influence upon the art of the Victorian era'. This painting illustrates stanza 41 of the poem:*

> *They glide, like phantoms, into the wide hall;*
> *Like phantoms, to the iron porch, they glide;*
> *Where lay the porter, in uneasy sprawl,*
> *With a huge empty flaggon by his side:*
> *The wakeful bloodhound rose, and shook his hide,*
> *But his sagacious eye an inmate owns:*
> *By one, and one, the bolts full easy slide: –*
> *The chains lie silent on the footworn stones; –*
> *The key turns, and the door upon its hinges groans.*

*Holman Hunt has carefully depicted the porter's 'uneasy sprawl', the 'huge empty flaggon', the 'wakeful bloodhound' (and a dormant one), and even the silent chains. As Timothy Hilton observes, however, 'The lovers look like actors, and the central figure surely had its origin in some academic exercise in fore-shortening' (*The Pre-Raphaelites; *London: Thames & Hudson, 1970, p. 11-*

the Pre-Raphaelites with a ready-made territory of the imagination. Repeatedly they seized on the pictorial possibilities of Keats's verse. William Bell Scott had admired him since 1832; and Holman Hunt delighted Rossetti in 1848 with his picture 'The Eve of St. Agnes'. Millais painted 'Lorenzo and Isabella' (1849) and again 'The Eve of St. Agnes' (1863); Arthur Hughes also painted an 'Eve of St. Agnes' (1856), and Holman Hunt an 'Isabella and the Pot of Basil' (1868). Rossetti made drawings from 'La Belle Dame sans Merci'; and William Morris, himself so influential as poet, painter, designer, craftsman and propagandist, spoke of his 'boundless admiration' for Keats – 'one of my masters'. (In turn, such poetic and artistic Mediaevalism helped to generate many distinctive features of Victorian architecture: neo-Gothic churches and cathedrals, castellated factories and follies, turreted mansions, and even the fashionable adornments – stained-glass windows and crenellated architraves – of villas and terraced houses.) Leigh Hunt, who was consulted by Rossetti in 1848, also contributed to the Movement, largely through his persuasive enthusiasm for the Camposanto frescoes at Pisa.

If we turn to poets outside the Pre-Raphaelite group, we find that Thomas Hood (1799–1845) was, after Leigh Hunt, the earliest precursor of the great phase of close interest in Keats's work. His 'The Sea of Death' recalls the various kinds of suspended animation in *Endymion* and *Hyperion*. More obviously, his 'Ode: Autumn' and 'Ode to Melancholy' are deliberate attempts to emulate his predecessor; but whereas Keats's 'To Autumn' was richly varied in tone and feeling, Hood's version (though proficient in versification and occasionally vigorous in expression, as in 'tear with horny beak their lustrous eyes') tends to impose a predictably melancholy tone and phraseology – the stock-response material illustrated by the following lines:

> But here the Autumn melancholy dwells,
>     And sighs her tearful spells
> Amongst the sunless shadows of the plain.
>     Alone, alone,
>     Upon a mossy stone,
> She sits and reckons up the dead and gone
> With the last leaves for a love-rosary,
> Whilst all the wither'd world looks drearily,
> Like a dim picture of the drownèd past
> In the hush'd mind's mysterious far away,
> Doubtful what ghostly thing will steal the last
> Into that distance, grey upon the grey.         (TH, 46)

Later in the century, Matthew Arnold's 'The Scholar-Gipsy' (1853) and 'Thyrsis' (1866) hold numerous echoes of 'To Autumn' and

'Ode to a Nightingale', though the comparison does emphasise the self-indulgent, weary melancholy of Arnold's poetic disposition. (The 'Cult of the Dismal' was a widespread legacy of Romanticism to the Victorian Age: 'Our determination . . . . . to be "all unhappy together", is remarkable', said Leigh Hunt in 1832.) Gerard Manley Hopkins also studied Keats's poems, and although (a loyal Jesuit) he said 'Sensuality is their fault', his own early work seems eager to surpass *Endymion* in sumptuous richness. In 'A Vision of the Mermaids', for example, we find:

> Plum-purple was the west; but spikes of light
> Spear'd open lustrous gashes, crimson-white. . . . .
>    Summer of his sister Spring
> Crushes and tears the rare enjewelling,
> And boasting 'I have fairer things than these'
> Plashes amidst the billowy apple-trees
> His lusty hands, in gusts of scented wind
> Swirling out bloom till all the air is blind
> With rosy foam and pelting blossom and mists
> Of driving vermeil-rain. . . . .

(GMH, 8, 10)

Algernon Swinburne's enthusiasm for Keats may have encouraged his tendency towards emotionalistic sensualism, and he too was influenced by Pre-Raphaelite vistas. From Keats (directly, or via Tennyson, the Pre-Raphaelites and Swinburne) a road leads to the 'Decadent' and 'Aesthetic' fashions of the late nineteenth century: to Lionel Johnson, Ernest Dowson and Arthur Symons. Keats of the drugged torpor, the blissful trance, the amoral hedonism and the quest for a superior and timeless other-world of art (the poet of 'As Hermes once', 'To Melancholy' and 'Why did I laugh tonight?') clearly anticipates Decadent writing and the realm of 'Art for Art's sake'. What is wrong with such subsequent work is its rejections and exclusions; such an art which ostentatiously turns its back on the diverse moral concerns of ordinary life in its quest for the special beauties and pleasures available to dedicated and hyper-sensitive connoisseurs will often become precious, sterile and self-defeating. Oscar Wilde, who proclaimed the Aesthete's creed in the Preface to *The Picture of Dorian Gray* ('The artist is the creator of beautiful things. . . . . All art is quite useless'), was a great admirer of the Keats who had said: 'I have lov'd the principle of beauty in all things' (R II, 263). In a sonnet, 'The Grave of Keats', Wilde mourned 'the youngest of martyrs' – 'tears like mine will keep thy memory green,/ As Isabella did her Basil-tree'.

However, though there are clear connections between Keats and some of the self-indulgent Aestheticism of the late nineteenth century, he is equally clearly connected with Preter-Aestheticism:

the outlook of those who experience the seductive appeal of Aestheticism but move beyond, submitting the claims of art to the claims of social life. As a boy, W. B. Yeats had argued with his father about Keats; and in 'Ego Dominus Tuus' the Irish poet offers this debate:

> *Ille.* What portion in the world can the artist have
> Who has awakened from the common dream
> But dissipation and despair?
> *Hic.*                          And yet
> No one denies to Keats love of the world;
> Remember his deliberate happiness.
> *Ille.* His art is happy, but who knows his mind?
> I see a schoolboy when I think of him,
> With face and nose pressed to a sweet-shop window,
> For certainly he sank into his grave
> His senses and his heart unsatisfied,
> And made – being poor, ailing and ignorant,
> Shut out from all the luxury of the world,
> The coarse-bred son of a livery stable-keeper –
> Luxuriant song.
>
> (Y, 182)

But it was not mere 'luxuriant song' that Keats evoked in Yeats. One of Yeats's supreme poems is 'Sailing to Byzantium', and it quite evidently is a close counterpart to the great odes of Keats: in particular, to 'Ode on a Grecian Urn' and 'Ode to a Nightingale'. Just as the urn had counterpoised 'cold pastoral' (the world of the urn's art, immortal yet frozen) against rich vulnerable sensual life, so Yeats's poem counterpoises the golden bird (immortal yet metallic) against the 'sensual music' of copulating humanity and mackerel-crowded seas. There emerges a similar contrast, a similar dilemma, and a kindred power similarly generated by a dialectical structure of mutually-reinforcing contrasts.

Some of the aesthetic paradoxes of 'Ode on a Grecian Urn' resonate in Wallace Stevens' poems, in 'The Man with the Blue Guitar' and 'Anecdote of the Jar', for example; and they blend with Buddhist and Christian concepts to engender the meditations of T. S. Eliot's *Four Quartets*:

> Words move, music moves
> Only in time; but that which is only living
> Can only die. Words, after speech, reach
> Into the silence. Only by the form, the pattern,
> Can words or music reach
> The stillness, as a Chinese jar still
> Moves perpetually in its stillness.
>
> ('Burnt Norton', v, lines 1–7)

*Wilfred Owen in July 1916, two years before his death on the battlefield.*
*'Owen came to Keats as Keats to Chapman's* Homer *and grew to worship him in an almost religious sense' (Jon Stallworthy:* Wilfred Owen; *London: Oxford University Press and Chatto & Windus, 1974, p. 57). Owen felt that by enlisting in the British Army during the First World War he was 'perpetuating the language in which Keats and the rest of them wrote'. His war poems combine a Keatsian linguistic richness with a distinctive determination to confront the horrors of mass-slaughter.*

70

Eliot's Chinese jar is clearly a relative of a Grecian urn which, though silent, held melodies, and which, though still, had power to move.

The career of Wilfred Owen provides the most poignant instance of Keats's influence on a twentieth-century poet. What makes it poignant is that Owen, who revered Keats's work, was himself to die at the same age, twenty-five, having gone to war partly in order to defend from Germany 'the language in which Keats and the rest of them wrote'. (He was killed in battle just a week before the Armistice of November 1918.) The young Owen had idolised Keats, twice making a pilgrimage – celebrated in a sonnet – to the house in Teignmouth where the Romantic poet had stayed; and of the biography by Dante Gabriel Rossetti he said: 'Rossetti guided my groping hand right into the wound, and I touched, for one moment the incandescent Heart.....'. The poems by Owen which are most conspicuously indebted to Keats are the fragment 'Before reading a Biography of Keats for the first time' (which recalls 'On First Looking into Chapman's Homer'), 'The Little Mermaid' (using the eight-line stanza of 'Isabella', which it echoes), and 'To My Friend (with an Identity Disc)', which invokes Keats and, in form, tone and theme, emulates 'When I have fears that I may cease to be'. Although it is the immature verse which seems most conspicuously influenced by Keats, the mature work is more subtly and effectively influenced by him. Siegfried Sassoon recalled that on reading Owen's 'Anthem for Doomed Youth',

> I now realised that his verse, with its sumptuous epithets and large-scale imagery, its noble naturalness and the depth of meaning, had impressive affinities with Keats, whom he took as his supreme exemplar.....
>
> (*Siegfried's Journey*. London: Faber, 1945, p. 59)

It should not be forgotten that though Owen's war-poetry may initially seem far removed in preoccupation from the work of Keats, stanzas XIV and XV of 'Isabella' (describing the weary hands that swelt, the whipped slaves, and the pearl-diver whose 'ears gush'd blood') provide a precedent not only for Owen's rich diction but also for his intense evocation of carnage and cannon-fodder. Even in technical details there is continuity with Keats's poems: the Keatsian principle of the half-pun ('O Attic shape! Fair attitude!') was eventually vindicated by some of Owen's most memorable lines: 'The pallor of girls' brows shall be their pall'; 'All their eyes are ice'; and 'The Poetry is in the pity'.

Owen was outlived by the ageing Thomas Hardy, whose poetic tributes to Keats include 'Rome: At the Pyramid of Cestius near the Graves of Shelley and Keats' (1887), 'At a House in Hampstead' (July 1920) and 'At Lulworth Cove a Century Back' (September

1920). The first of these offers a characteristic irony – that the Roman tribune, Caius Cestius, is remembered today not for any of his life's achievements but because; fortuitously, his commemorative pyramid guides pilgrims to the graves of two English poets. 'The Darkling Thrush' (1900), probably Hardy's most famous poem, maintains the tradition of 'Ode to a Nightingale' and Shelley's 'To a Skylark': for although Hardy gives his bird a predictably blighted landscape, its song's implication of 'some blessed Hope' echoes the traditional intimations of immortality.

Modern fiction-writers and essayists who have commented on Keats range from the Argentinian Jorge Luis Borges to the English D. H. Lawrence and the Irish Flann O'Brien. In the essay 'The Nightingale of Keats' Borges offers a resourceful Platonistic defence of the 'immortal' bird. D. H. Lawrence makes pithily irreverent comments in 'The Nightingale' (*Forum*, September 1927): 'It never was a plaintive anthem – it was Caruso at his jauntiest. But don't try to argue with a poet'. And Flann O'Brien, in *At Swim-Two-Birds* (1939) exploits the romanticism of 'Ode on a Grecian Urn' to the advantage of comic bathos:

> What neat repast shall feast us light and choice of Attic taste with wine whence we may rise to hear the lute well touched or artful voice warble immortal notes or Tuscan air? What mad pursuit? What pipes and timbrels? What wild ecstasy?
>
> Here's to your health, said Kelly.
>
> Good luck, I said.
>
> The porter was sour to the palate but viscid, potent. Kelly made a long noise as if releasing air from his interior.
>
> I looked at him from the corner of my eye and said:
>
> You can't beat a good pint.

Finally, among the work of recent poets, Tony Harrison's *A Kumquat for John Keats* (1982) offers relaxed ruminations that are fruitful in a sense, as in the following couplets which explain what a 'kumquat' is:

> I'm pretty sure that Keats, though he had heard
> 'of candied apple, quince and plum and gourd'
> instead of 'grape against the palate fine'
> would have, if he'd known it, plumped for mine,
> this Eastern citrus scarcely cherry size
> he'd bite just once and then apostrophize
> and pen one stanza how the fruit had all
> the qualities of fruit before the Fall,
> but in the next few lines be forced to write
> how Eve's apple tasted at the second bite.....

# Part Two
## *The Art of Keats*

# 3   Keats and Romanticism

## *The Romantic Movement*

The various features which give identity to the Romantic Movement can all be found in other periods. What matters is that those features have greater frequency and prominence of occurrence in the Romantic Movement than at other times. In England, the heyday of the Movement was from 1790 to 1830, though of course there is no clear-cut demarcation: some features can be traced back through the eighteenth century to the Age of Pope and beyond that to the Elizabethans, to Chaucer and ultimately to the Garden of Eden; and similarly the Movement did not suddenly cease to be, but rather flowed on, evolving and mutating, through the nineteenth century and into the twentieth.

The distinguishing features, which interlink and overlap, are these.

1 Special prestige is accorded to the greatly-talented individual who can be seen as a rebel against social tradition and convention.

2 The subjective vision becomes highly valued as a means of social therapy or transformation.

3 Instead of accepting orthodox religion, the individual seeks some absolute centre of values in intense private experience.

4 Nature, in her wilder, awe-inspiring or luxurious aspects, often provides the occasion of such intense experience.

5 The individual exists in a paradoxical situation, being pulled in opposite directions: towards solitary experience but also towards sociable experience; towards the lonely pursuit of some high ideal and yet also towards a close relationship with fellow-beings. This is related to the tension between the transcendent and the mundane. Politically the tension is between faith in some charismatic leader and faith in democratic movements.

6 The individual seeks a revolution in society or a transformation in human nature, or perhaps both at once.

7 Conversely, he may oppose revolution by appealing to the sense that society is an organism which rightly evolves slowly and steadily.

8 Anti-rational ideas become widespread. The rational, conscious mind is criticised in the name of unconscious wisdom, instinctive responsiveness, sensual hedonism, or vigorously passionate conduct.

9 Sometimes orthodox ethical judgements may be subverted by appeal to 'ontological fulness' – sheer fulness of being, as opposed to, say, constructive prudential existence.

10 Dreams and drugged or entranced states are accorded special

prestige; the outlooks of children, savages and the deranged are even regarded as privileged.

11 The status of culture-hero or tutelary spirit is assigned to men of the past who can be seen as spontaneous geniuses, breaking rules by their eruptive creativity (Shakespeare, for example), or who can be seen as lonely rebels, defying their society (the aged Milton), or as unappreciated martyrs (Chatterton); and to defiant liberators in history or legend (Prometheus), to great rebels (Milton's Satan) or brave patriots who strove to free nations from subjection (Tadeusz Kościuszko or William Tell).

12 Writers search the national past in order to establish a patriotic cultural tradition (turning perhaps to Arthurian legend and mediaeval chivalry, to ballads and folk-lore, or to the poetry of Chaucer and Spenser).

In the main, the list offers a broad contrast to the features we associate with the Augustan period. The Augustan writer (Dryden, Pope or Johnson, for example) commonly presents himself as the defender of inherited social values: he is one who seeks to guard a particular consensus against assaults from without or within, particularly against assaults from the fanatical, extreme, passionate, anarchic and eccentric elements in human nature. ('*Common quiet* is *Mankind's concern*', said Dryden.) Even intense faith in reason is something he opposes in the name of the reasonable, in the name of the common sense of civilised men. In his scepticism about the capacities of reason, in his fear of an arrogance of intellect, he may mock pedants, speculators, solitary scholars and 'enthusiasts': all whose mental labours are not governed by reference to social utility and cohesion. In this respect there are links between Augustanism and anti-rational Romanticism: for instance, 'hard' and 'soft' primitivism, commending respectively a simple life of toil and an unreflective life of Arcadian ease, have their imaginative advocates in both cultural phases.

The Romantic qualities we have listed above may readily be illustrated by reference to William Blake, who in himself was a dynamically rebellious spirit, and who so valued the subjective vision as a means to transformation of the world that his writings became increasingly apocalyptic and increasingly obscure as his symbols multiplied, subdivided and procreated. For him the creative imagination was the revolutionary power, the Godhead in man. 'All deities reside in the human breast', said Blake. 'The tygers of wrath are wiser than the horses of instruction.' 'Sooner murder an infant in its cradle than nurse unacted desires.' 'The road of excess leads to the palace of wisdom.' 'Prisons are built with stones of Law, Brothels with bricks of Religion.' He praised Milton as 'a true Poet and of the Devil's party without knowing it', and in his own poem, *Milton*, proclaimed himself the blind poet's heir and reincarnation.

Through a re-awakening of the imagination and a revolt against the 'mind-forg'd manacles' and the oppressive Establishment, he hoped to 'build Jerusalem/ In England's green and pleasant land'.

Wordsworth, too, has left on record his republican and revolutionary enthusiasms; influenced by what he had seen in revolutionary France and by Godwin's *Political Justice*, as a young man he had hoped for a splendid transformation of European society: 'Bliss was it in that dawn to be alive'. Subsequently disillusioned, as so many were, by the descent of the French Revolution into a waste of futile carnage followed by the dictatorship of Napoleon, Wordsworth concentrated on the *inner* revolution: an amelioration of human nature through communion with the greater Nature beyond. Intermittently, his anti-rationalism and preoccupation with childhood may remind us of Blake (as will his determination to experiment with 'ballads' using simple and even banal diction): 'Books! 'tis a dull and endless strife . . . . . / Let Nature be your teacher'; 'Our meddling intellect/ Misshapes the beauteous forms of things;/ – We murder to dissect' ('The Tables Turned'). Milton was a culture-hero to Wordsworth as well as to Blake, *The Prelude* being born of Wordsworth's attempt to write an epic worthy of the author of *Paradise Lost*. The 1800 Preface to the *Lyrical Ballads* is often treated as a Romantics' manifesto, but already it shows Wordsworth reacting against some forms of Romanticism. On behalf of a sober, meditative outlook, he is combating the sensational, violent and vulgar Romanticism of 'frantic novels, sickly and stupid German Tragedies, and deluges of idle and extravagant stories in verse'. When he states the maxim 'All good poetry is the spontaneous overflow of powerful feelings', he does so not as one coining and commending that maxim but rather as one quoting a dangerous prevalent idea which needs to be qualified, checked and virtually contradicted. 'For all good poetry is the spontaneous overflow of powerful feelings; but though this be true, Poems to which any value can be attached, were never produced on any variety of subjects but by a man who being possessed of more than usual organic sensibility had also thought long and deeply.' Again: 'Poetry is the spontaneous overflow of powerful feelings: it takes its origin from emotion recollected in tranquillity'. In each case, the effect of the second part of the statement, which stresses peaceful recollection, is almost to reverse the effect of the first, which stresses spontaneous overflow. It is in keeping with this stepping-back from the threshold of the violently or anarchically romantic that Wordsworth should gradually have become conservative in politics (so that when Keats called at his home, he was out helping the Tory candidate's election campaign) and orthodox in religion, retreating from nature-mysticism towards Anglicanism. In his 'To a Skylark' (1825), the bird proves to be respectably Victorian in aspiration, pious and domesticated: 'True to the kindred points of Heaven and Home!'

In the career of Wordsworth's collaborator, Coleridge, there is a similar trajectory. In 1794 he had written of the French Revolution:

..... slumb'ring freedom roused by high disdain
With giant fury burst her triple chain!.....
Red from the tyrant's wound I shook the lance,
And strode in joy the reeking plains of France!
('To a Young Lady, with a Poem on the French Revolution')

The young radical republican who hoped to found in America a new communal society, a 'Pantisocracy', became the old organicist conservative who urged the unity of Church and State. Nevertheless, in his most celebrated poems (including 'The Rime of the Ancyent Marinere', 'Kubla Khan' and 'Christabel') Coleridge splendidly displays various Romantic characteristics: a potent evocation of dream-states and nightmares, of phantasmagoria rich and oppressive, appealing to the sense of the occult and the mystical. (Like Keats, Crabbe, Shelley and De Quincey, he took laudanum – tincture of opium.) In the figure of the Ancient Mariner, he drew on potent archetypes, creating a new version of the figure that haunts the Romantic imagination – the cursed wanderer, like Cain or Ahasuerus or, later, the Flying Dutchman. (Coleridge published a prose 'Canto' entitled 'The Wanderings of Cain'.) In 'Kubla Khan' he celebrates the fantastic, exotic and ecstatic; the poet is imagined as a seer possessed, to be regarded with 'holy dread' –

For he on honey-dew hath fed,
And drunk the milk of Paradise.

The honey-dew and milk are at once the song and music of an imagined Abyssinian maid, the manna of the Biblical prophets in the wilderness, and probably, in the everyday world, the drug laudanum that had first induced in Coleridge the vision of the poem.

If Blake, Wordsworth and Coleridge (born between 1757 and 1772) belong to the 'first generation' of the great Romantic poets, Byron, Shelley and Keats (born between 1788 and 1795) belong to the second generation. In his own life, Lord Byron exemplified many of the Romantic characteristics that we have listed, being self-consciously a rebel against convention who shocked and fascinated society by his cynicism, extravagance and defiantly promiscuous sexuality. He died in his thirty-sixth year at Missolonghi, whither he had travelled to help the Greeks in their fight for liberation from the Turkish Empire. In his *Childe Harold* he had dramatised the hero as eternal quester, solitary and misunderstood: the exile and outcast, oppressed by society but consoled by Nature. In the far superior poem *Don Juan*, Byron assails fellow-Romantics, including Wordsworth, Coleridge, Southey and Keats, and by rapid modulations from the lofty to the ludicrous, the pensive to the satiric, seeks to break away from various clichés of Romanticism. Obviously, some crucial Romantic features remain: the narrator is a person who prides himself on his scornfully independent stance, mocking virtually all the societies that he surveys; he has yearnings for hedonistic innocence; and he expresses the traditional Romantic hostility to tyrants and conquerors while praising patriots and liberators (George Washington, Tadeusz Kościuszko and William Wilberforce, for example). And though *Don Juan* is a comic poem, it still, in its scale and scope, offers some justification for Byron's terming it 'an epic'.

Shelley, too, was a major Romantic by life-style as well as by verse: expelled from Oxford for his share in *The Necessity of Atheism*, he tried unsuccessfully to raise the Irish to revolt, deserted his young wife in order to elope with William Godwin's daughter, and was drowned at the age of 29. Like the Byron of *Childe Harold*, he liked to dramatise himself in his poems as the lonely, idealistic but misunderstood martyr; and he hoped that his works, notably *Queen Mab* and *Prometheus Unbound*, might further a vast revolution in which tyrants would be toppled and the world transformed by freedom and joy. Adopting the views of Godwin's *Political Justice*, but with an ecstatic enthusiasm that was all his own, he believed that 'the chains fall off of themselves, when the magic of opinion is dissolved' – men had only to will their freedom, and they would attain it. Like Blake, Shelley believed that the poetic imagination was the chief means to liberation. (He defined the poet so generously as to be able to rank Jesus and Socrates as poets.) His *Defence of Poetry* claims:

> The great instrument of moral good is the imagination; and poetry administers to the effect by acting upon the cause. . . . . Poetry is indeed something divine. It is at once the centre and circumference of all knowledge. . . . . It is at the same time the root and blossom of all other systems of thought. . . . . Poets are the unacknowledged legislators of the world.
>
> (*DP*, 33, 53, 59)

Like Blake, he saw Satan as the hero of *Paradise Lost*: 'Nothing can exceed the energy and magnificence of the character of Satan. . . . . Milton's Devil as a moral being is . . . . . far superior to his God' (*DP*, 46–7).

It will have been seen that Keats fulfils many of the criteria in our list. The sense of rebellion against social tradition and convention is shown not only in his choice of cultural heroes (Milton, Wordsworth, Byron and the jailed Hunt) but also in his own lonely determination to fulfil himself as a poet instead of following the professional path to the career of apothecary or surgeon. He was unable to accept Christian orthodoxy, though he speculated at times about a blissful Heaven and about this earth as 'The vale of Soul-making'; while the assumption of the specially privileged nature of intense private experience is made repeatedly in his letters and poems. As 'Nature in her wilder, awe-inspiring or luxurious aspects' is important to the Romantics, we see Keats celebrating such aspects in his enthusiastic responses to the Lake District and to Fingal's Cave in Scotland (the wild and awe-inspiring) and in his enjoyment of the floral, rich and mellow countryside (the luxurious). The familiar Romantic dichotomy in which the writer is pulled in conflicting directions, drawn now towards lonely pursuit of some ideal and now towards the gratifications of warmly sociable existence, is exemplified in Keats's personal life by his ambivalent attitude to Fanny Brawne: now deliberately exiling himself from her in order to concentrate on his poetic vocation, and now staying close to her and treating her as his life-centre. In his literary work, that Romantic dichotomy is the central preoccupation, from *Endymion*, with the choice between far-off Cynthia and the immediate Indian Maid, to the 'Ode on a Grecian Urn' with its contrast between the enduring but cold perfection of art and the 'breathing human passion' that is ephemeral and may disappoint.

The sixth entry in the list was this: 'the individual seeks a revolution in society or a transformation in human nature, or perhaps both at once'. We have seen that Keats was of the republican left wing in politics, and, though not revolutionary in outlook like Blake or Shelley, he certainly looked with keen interest and sympathy on radical figures (like Henry 'Orator' Hunt and Richard Carlile) who were prepared to defy the law; furthermore, like Blake, Shelley and the younger Wordsworth and Coleridge, he opposed monarchy and militarism. The anti-rational element which is so important in Romanticism is implicit in his sensuous hedonism and, to a large extent, in his speculations about 'Negative Capability'; and, again like Blake, Shelley, Wordsworth and Coleridge, he stressed the importance of the imagination as a source of greater wisdom than 'consequitive reasoning'. We saw that there is a strong similarity, though not identity, between the Blake who said 'What is now proved was once only imagin'd' and the Keats who says 'What the imagination seizes as Beauty must be truth – whether it existed before or not'. The importance of ontological fulness as opposed to orthodox virtue is suggested in the letters by statements like 'What shocks the virtuous philosop[h]er, delights the camelion Poet', and in the poems by (for example) the potency with which the embrace of the lovers in 'The Eve of St. Agnes' defies the claims of prudence or Christian chastity. Dreams and drugged or entranced states are frequently accorded special prestige in his works, from 'Sleep and Poetry' onwards, though some of the best poems, particularly 'Ode to a Nightingale', dramatise not only the appeal of such states as a source of visionary knowledge but also the value of wakeful resistance to them. The anti-rational primitivism (the commendation of the culturally primitive) which leads other Romantics to ascribe privileged status to the supposed outlooks of savages is treated with a qualified, partly-sceptical sympathy by Keats in *The Fall of Hyperion*:

> Fanatics have their dreams, wherewith they weave
> A paradise for a sect; the savage too
> From forth the loftiest fashion of his sleep
> Guesses at heaven.....

Finally, we see that Keats amply fulfils the eleventh and twelfth critieria in our list, as he shares the Romantic enthusiasm for Shakespeare (this was the time of vivid new appraisals by his acquaintances Coleridge and Hazlitt); like Blake, Wordsworth and Shelley, he was deeply impressed by Milton; he praised Chatterton, admired Chaucer and Spenser, and lauded the patriot-warriors Kościuszko and Tell, William Wallace and King Alfred.

In the quest for intense private experience which could be accorded the status of an ultimate centre of values, the Romantic can be seen as one who seeks a compensatory, consolatory alternative to the sustenance which, once, orthodox religion might have provided. There were various reasons why religious orthodoxy no longer seemed to provide such sustenance. One was the political recognition that the Church was in various ways allied to an oppressive Establishment; another was the recognition of the claims of philosophical scepticism (advanced by Hume, Voltaire, Paine, Godwin and their disciples). The introspective egotism of the Romantics can be seen as, in part, a half-secularised transmutation of the Calvinistic concern with the salvation of the individual soul and its distrust of formal intermediaries between man and the divine. There is indeed a quality of inverted Puritanism about Romanticism: the new endeavour to liberate unruly emotions and appetites is often as zealous as was the former endeavour to subject them to ascetic discipline. The community of 'Saints' is superseded by a poetic élite; the Pilgrim's Progress to Heaven is superseded by the wanderer's search for a lost Eden on earth; and not the Bible but the book of Nature (and the obscurer passages of human nature) becomes the oracular text. The more the historic reality was seen to be dominated by urbanisation and the dark satanic mills, the more the rural world was idealised. The Romantic mystification of the poet's rôle by the poets themselves and their sympathisers can be seen as a consolatory endeavour: a compensation for the fact that in an age which increasingly valued practical economic activity, the artist might increasingly appear to lack social justification. The Augustan poets were often close to the centres of power; the Romantics often lacked such access to authority. Their compensatory activity was, as a cultural phenomenon, vastly successful: it changed (sometimes for worse, sometimes for better) people's ways of seeing the world and the self. In its protean manifestations, Romanticism eventually contributed to every part of the political spectrum: to Fascism (the charismatic leader, the nationalist resurgence); to 'Marxist' totalitarianism (the Promethean ideal, the myth of historical teleology, the dictatorial élite); to conservatism (organicist patriotism); to right-wing liberalism (competitive individualism); to democratic liberalism and socialism (the concern to extend individual liberty while reducing social injustice); and to libertarian anarchism (faith in human nature and hostility to all state institutions created by that nature). Romanticism pervades the twentieth century, and is often most influential when least recognised.

## The precursors; Thomas Chatterton

It is easy to think of Blake, Wordsworth and Coleridge as 'the first generation' of English Romantic poets; but of course they had many precursors.

In the poetry and prose of the eighteenth century, from James Thomson's pity for both the hooked worm and the fish in *The Seasons*, to Pope's 'poor Indian' in *An Essay on Man*, to Goldsmith's 'The Deserted Village', Sterne's *Sentimental Journey* and Mackenzie's *The Man of Feeling*, there flourished the 'Cult of Sensibility' and the related cult of the Sentimental. These encouraged emotional sensitivity, particularly a sympathetic, pitying or charitable responsiveness to the poor, humble, needy and afflicted; to people, animals, birds. Another important factor was that (even before the appearance of the *Lyrical Ballads*) the Gothic Novel, particularly the very successful *Mysteries of Udolpho* (1794) by Mrs Radcliffe, had popularised various Romantic attitudes: feelings of awe before the 'sublime' in Nature and in art; relish for the mysterious, numinous and uncanny; and the belief that the enthusiastic appreciation of music and poetry is the sign of an admirable character. Amongst the poems of the first half of the century, *The Seasons* is particularly notable. Even though Thomson's Augustanism is apparent in his latinate orotundity and his relatively public and pompous tone, this long meditative work anticipates Wordsworth's *Prelude* by its celebrations of the power and pleasures of rural nature. Occasionally it even offers hints of Keats's odes: of 'To Autumn', when Thomson describes 'The downy orchard, and the melting

*Henry Wallis: 'The Death of Chatterton' (1856).*

    *Wallis visited Chatterton's attic when making this painting, and the poet George Meredith is said to have acted as the model. In this sharply-detailed, vivid and lurid 'secular* pietà*' the young suicide is beautified as a Romantic martyr.*

    *The painting expresses memorably the preoccupations of early Pre-Raphaelite art: theatrical poses, strongly linear designs, narrative clues, glowing light and colour, and minute fidelity to texture. The Victorians' love of such story-telling works partly explains yet proleptically challenges the Modernists' excessive hostility to traditional narrative structures.*

82

pulp/ Of mellow fruit', and 'Ode on a Grecian Urn', when he writes:

> on the marble tomb
> The well-dissembled mourner stooping stands,
> For ever silent, and for ever sad.
>
> ('Summer', lines 1220–2)

Other poetic precursors were Thomas Gray, whose 'The Bard' had presented the figure of poet-prophet, seer, sage and martyr; Crabbe of *The Village* (1783), who sought a new sombre realism in the presentation of rural life; and Robert Burns, who introduced a fresh pungency of Scots idiom and folk-lore. (Keats imitated Burnsian jauntiness in 'Ah! ken ye what I met the day'.) But perhaps the oddest of the precursors, and arguably the most important to Keats, was Thomas Chatterton.

Chatterton, born in 1752, was the posthumous child of a poor Bristol school-master. He possessed extremely precocious talents as a poet, publishing his first poems before he was twelve and proceeding to write prolifically. Through studying the muniments of the Church of St. Mary Redcliffe he became fascinated by the mediaeval, and wrote numerous documents in pseudo-mediaeval diction, ascribing these works to 'Thomas Rowley', an imaginary monk. He supplied these to James Dodsley and Horace Walpole; they attracted considerable interest, and a controversy about their authenticity followed. Unable to pay his way as a poet in London, Chatterton poisoned himself with arsenic in 1770, dying at the age of seventeen. The 'Rowley' poems were published in 1777, 1778 and 1782, and brought him tardy recognition as a writer of eccentric yet lyrical originality.

Subsequently he became legendary, being seen as the poet-martyr, the tragically short-lived rebel. To Wordsworth (in 'Resolution and Independence') he was

> Chatterton, the marvellous Boy,
> The sleepless Soul that perished in his pride;

while Coleridge described him as

> Bristowa's bard, the wondrous boy!
> An amaranth, which earth scarce seem'd to own,
> Blooming 'mid poverty's drear wintry waste,
> Till disappointment came, and pelting wrong
> Beat it to earth.....
>
> ('On Observing a Blossom on the First of February, 1796')

and evisaged him singing in Heaven 'Amid the blaze of Seraphim' ('Monody on the Death of Chatterton', 1794). Keats may be echoing Coleridge's amaranthine lines when, in his early sonnet 'Oh Chatterton', he says:

83

>                                      Thou didst die
> A half-blown flower, which could blasts amate.
> But this is past. Thou art among the stars
>    Of highest heaven; to the rolling spheres
> Thou sweetly singest – naught thy hymning mars,
>    Above the ingrate world and human fears.

To Shelley, he was one of 'The inheritors of unfulfilled renown' whose spirit re-appeared as a mourner for Keats:

>                                      Chatterton
> Rose pale, – his solemn agony had not
> Yet faded from him.....
>
>                    (*Adonais*, stanza XLV, lines 3–5)

In 1835 appeared Alfred de Vigny's highly successful play *Chatterton*, which treats him as the idealist martyred by a materialistic society.

Today, Chatterton's works appear to have little intrinsic value. When he writes in normal English, the results generally seem thin or derivative: in 'Kew Gardens', for example, there are facile or banal echoes of Rochester:

> Woman, of every happiness the best,
> Is all my heaven, – religion is a jest.

As for the extensive works of 'Rowley', these now seem a ludicrous hokum, a demented virtuosity, the 'Mediaeval' spellings derived from Chaucer, Spenser or fancy being ludicrously imposed on matter that seems variously sentimental or melodramatic:

> Before yonne roddie sonne has droove hys wayne
> Throwe halfe hys joornie, dyghte yn gites of goulde,
> Mee, happeless mee, hee wylle a wretche beholde,
> Mieselfe, and al that's myne, bounde ynne myschaunces
>                                                    chayne.
>                              (*Ælla*, lines 119–22)

Chatterton's pseudo-Mediaeval writings appealed to an age which enjoyed the *frisson* of an encounter with the 'Gothic' past and was not greatly concerned about the genuineness of the occasion: this was the age of the 'folly', the faked ruin. It relished antiquarian trappings and a veil of cobwebs. From 1747 Horace Walpole arranged for his mansion, Strawberry Hill, to be extended and furnished in Gothic style, and in 1796 William Beckford commissioned James Wyatt to design his country house, Fonthill, as a ruined convent. Walpole pretended that his novel, *The Castle of Otranto* (1764), had been written in the Middle Ages and printed in Italy in 1529. Percy's *Reliques of Ancient English Poetry* (1765) was an influential collection of ballads; James Macpherson produced 'translations' of imaginary works by the ancient Gaelic poet, Ossian; and Coleridge gave antique spellings and phrasings to his 'The Rime of the Ancyent Marinère' (1798).

Chatterton's 'Rowley' poetry, which now seems foolishly fraudulent – neither truly Mediaeval nor forthrightly of the eighteenth century – was enticingly exotic and mysterious to Keats and others of his period; furthermore, Keats enjoyed poetry which proclaimed, by oddities of phrase and diction, that it was distinctively poetry and not versified prose. There is little doubt, however, that like the verse of Spenser and Milton, Chattertonian verse constituted a temptation that Keats needed to outgrow (a temptation towards the escapist and the quirky – as in that archaic 'amate', meaning 'destroy', in his sonnet to Chatterton that was quoted above); and it is troubling that when Keats rightly turned away from the example of Milton, he then turned back mentally towards Chatterton. He would have found Chatterton's hedonistic scepticism congenial; and Keats's callow dismissal of the Augustan poets as riders not on Pegasus but on a rocking-horse (in 'Sleep and Poetry', lines 184–7), may derive from Rowley's complaint against contemporaneous poets:

> Instedde of mountynge onn a wyngèd horse,
> You onn a rouncy dryve yn dolefull course.
> ('Letter to the Dygne Mastre Canynge', lines 79–80)

Keats's worthiest debt to 'Rowley' is to the Third Minstrel's song of Autumn, in *Ælla* (lines 296–307):

> Whanne Autumpne blake and sonne-brente doe appere,
> With hys goulde honde guyltenge the falleynge lefe,
> Bryngeynge oppe Wynterr to folfylle the yere,
> Beerynge uponne hys backe the ripèd shefe;
> Whan al the hyls wythe woddie sede ys whyte;
> Whanne levynne-fyres and lemes do mete from far the syghte;
>
> Whann the fayre apple, rudde as even skie,
> Do bende the tree unto the fructyle grounde;
> When joicie peres, and berries of black die,
> Doe daunce yn ayre, and call the eyne arounde;
> Thann, bee the even foule, or even fayre,
> Meethynckes mie hartys joie ys steyncèd wyth somme care.

Keats obviously recalled this song when he was writing his ode 'To Autumn'. Chatterton's fair ruddy apples which 'bende the tree unto the fructyle grounde' are recalled in Keats's lines

> To bend with apples the moss'd cottage-trees,
> And fill all fruit with ripeness to the core;

and Chatterton's personification of Autumn as a labourer, 'Beerynge uponne hys backe the ripèd shefe', may have suggested Keats's personification of Autumn as harvester and as gleaner bearing a basket on his head. It is not surprising that Keats once remarked: 'I always somehow associate Chatterton with autumn' (R II, 167).

Keats's early *Endymion* had been dedicated 'to the memory of Thomas Chatterton'. One of the greatest ironies of his career is that he was encouraged in his poetic ambitions by the frustrated ambitions of young Chatterton, whom he helped to make into a figure of Romantic myth; and that he himself, by his own brevity of life, became a twin-figure of the poet as young martyr.

## Opium and the Romantic imagination

Opium is an addictive drug derived from the poppy. Laudanum is a solution of opium in alcohol. Generally in the form of laudanum, opium was widely taken in the Romantic period as a pain-killer, soporific and tranquilliser. Children were liberally dosed with it; adults of all classes (including Jane Austen's mother) took it as a night-cap. Indeed, its use seems to have been almost as common as that of aspirin in the twentieth century. The drug's dangers were slow to be recognised; of the famous Romantic writers, De Quincey, Crabbe and Coleridge became addicted. Byron, Lamb, Moore, Shelley, Southey and Scott are known to have taken it. In 1830 Britain imported 22,000 lb (10,000 kilogrammes) of solid opium, and not until 1868 was the first parliamentary legislation passed to control its availability.

The Romantics valued the imagination and sought inspiration from the sub-rational or irrational: from dreams, reveries and ecstatic states, from strange or surrealistic visions. Laudanum induced vivid dreams and seemed to open wide the doors of the private imagination. Coleridge, who claimed (in *Literary Remains*, Lecture XIII) that 'there is in genius itself an unconscious activity; nay, that is the genius in the man of genius', left a detailed record of his opium trances. For example:

> a dusky light – a purple *flash*
> crystalline splendor – light blue –
>    *Green* lightnings. –
> in that eternal and & delirious misery –
>    wrathfires –
>          inward desolations –
>    an horror of great darkness
>      great things that on the ocean
>       counterfeit infinity –.

(STC, 273)

This example (dated 1796) clearly anticipates, and may partly have prompted, the nightmarish sea-scapes of his 'The Rime of the Ancyent Marinere'; and opium apparently laced the 'honey-dew' which nourished the poet of 'Kubla Khan', for Coleridge stated that this poem resulted from the administering of 'an anodyne' – 'two grains of Opium'.

It is certain that Keats had laudanum with him on his final journey to Rome, for there he implored Severn to supply a fatal dose. (Pious Severn's refusal can be justified on Keatsian as well as Christian grounds.) He may have taken laudanum intermittently from his student days. As a medical student and qualified apothecary he would be familiar with the drug, and may well have taken it as a pain-killer during his long bouts with a sore throat and in the early stages of tuberculosis: laudanum was often recommended as a protection against consumption. Furthermore, Charles Brown says that in the winter of 1819–20 Keats 'was secretly taking, at times, a few drops of laudanum to keep up his spirits' (*KC*, II, 73).

When Keats asked Fanny Brawne for a consolatory love-letter, he said: 'make it rich as a draught of poppies to intoxicate me' (R II, 123). From the beginning to the end of his poetic career, Keats's works are sprinkled with references to the opium-poppy: repeatedly, dreams and sleep are associated with the flower. Endymion's dream of Cynthia comes when he has fallen asleep on a bank of 'sacred ditamy, and poppies red':

> Moreover, through the dancing poppies stole
> A breeze, most softly lulling to my soul;
> And shaping visions all about my sight
> Of colours, wings, and bursts of spangly light.....
>
> (*Endymion* Book I, lines 555, 566–9)

In *The Fall of Hyperion*, the poet is overcome by a 'domineering potion' –

> No Asian poppy, nor elixir fine.....
> Could so have rapt unwilling life away.
>
> (Book I, lines 47, 51)

The late sonnet, 'To Sleep', says: 'thy poppy throws/ Around my bed its lulling charities'; and in the great ode 'To Autumn', Autumn himself sleeps 'Drows'd with the fume of poppies'.

This associative cluster (poppy – sleep – pleasant dreams) is, of course, an ancient and traditional poeticism. Ovid's *Metamorphoses*, Book XI, line 605, had linked the poppy with Morpheus, god of dreams. (The drug morphine derives its power from opium and its name from the god.) Shakespeare's Iago had said of Othello:

not poppy, nor mandragora,
Nor all the drowsy syrups of the world,
Shall ever medicine thee to that sweet sleep
Which thou owedst yesterday.

(Act III, scene iii, lines 335–8)

Andrew Marvell's Thyrsis and Dorinda plan to 'pick poppies and them steep/ In wine' and 'smoothly pass away in sleep'. In Keats's writing, however, the association of poppies with dreams is more recurrent and significant than in other poets', and there were related features in his experience. Alethea Hayter, in *Opium and the Romantic Imagination* (London: Faber and Faber, 1971, pp. 315–20), conjectures that the taking of laudanum by Keats might explain the alternation of excitement and despondency which Haydon noted in him in spring 1819; it may have given him the waking vision (on the morning of 19 March) of three vase-figures passing by; and some time in April it may have caused the following strange dream:

> The dream was one of the most delightful enjoyments I ever had in my life – I floated about the whirling atmosphere . . . . . with a beautiful figure to whose lips mine were joined a[s] it seem'd for an age – and in the midst of all this cold and darkness I was warm – even flowery tree tops sprung up and we rested on them sometimes with the lightness of a cloud till the wind blew us away again . . . . . o that I could dream it every night.
>
> (R II, 91)

Alethea Hayter comments: 'This dream has several of the classic constituents of an opium vision: the feeling of blissful buoyancy, the extension of time . . . . . , contrasts of temperature, the bliss of the outcast'. (One result was his visionary sonnet, 'As Hermes once'.) Of course, the dream had its literary sources: Dante's *Inferno*, Canto V, lines 73–87, in which Paolo and Francesca 'seem so light upon the wind'; Shakespeare's *Measure for Measure*, Act III, scene i ('To be imprison'd in the viewless winds/ And blown with restless violence round about/ The pendent world'); and Keats's own 'The Eve of St. Agnes', with its warm waking-dream embrace amid the coldness. Similarly, the great temple of Moneta in *The Fall of Hyperion* may have been suggested by the Young Memnon statue in the British Museum, the natural columns of Fingal's Cave, the long nave of Winchester Cathedral, and infernal palaces in the pages of Milton and Beckford; nevertheless, with its vast gloom, drifting incense, numbing cold, massive columns and colossal statues, it resembles the dream-buildings later described in De Quincey's *Confessions of an English Opium-Eater* and which in turn resemble Poe's eponymous City in the Sea and Francis Thompson's Palace of the Occident in *Sister Songs*.

When W. J. Courthope complained in 1872 that Keats's work had been vitiated by 'intellectual opium-eating' (*CH*, 33), he may have been close to the truth. Keats always dreamt with ease; to generate his best poetry he needed not laudanum but the play of critical intelligence and the feel of recalcitrant reality.

As the Romantic Movement extended into the twentieth century, high claims for drug-experience continued to be made from time to time (notably by Aldous Huxley in *The Doors of Perception*); and the recourse to drugs by various writers and musicians became as well known as the often lethal social consequences of addiction. One partial analogy for the difference between drug-vision and the undrugged perception of life is the difference between solitary masturbation and a mutual embrace. Keats's best work did not neglect such differences.

## *The influence of Shakespeare:* Otho the Great

Shakespeare has not always enjoyed the unquestioned pre-eminence as poet-dramatist that he has enjoyed in this century and the last. In 1679 Dryden could refer to *Troilus and Cressida* as 'that heap of Rubbish, under which many excellent thoughts lay wholly bury'd', and could proceed to re-write the play on predictable Neoclassical principles. Similarly, in Dryden's hands *Antony and Cleopatra* became the tritely sentimental *All for Love; or, The World Well Lost*. It is virtually certain that, in the eighteenth century, anyone who saw a production of *King Lear* saw not Shakespeare's bleak play but Nahum Tate's transformation of it (1681, prevailing until 1823), in which, when the wicked have perished, Lear and Gloucester live on to applaud the happy marriage of Edgar to Cordelia. Even Dr Johnson, the greatest of eighteenth-century critics, having weighed the merits of the two versions, finally (after honest misgivings) gave his vote to Tate's, explaining:

> since all reasonable beings naturally love justice, I cannot easily be persuaded, that the observation of justice makes a play worse. . . . .
> In the present case the publick has decided.
> (*Johnson on Shakespeare*. New Haven: Yale, 1968, Vol. II, p. 704)

The Romantic period saw a great revival of interest in Shakespeare, and his prestige rose to immense new heights amid the acclaim of Coleridge, Lamb and Hazlitt, while on stage Edmund Kean gave passionate life to the rôles. What Dryden and the other Neoclassical critics had seen as disorder now seemed a natural abundance and diversity. Shakespeare and Milton exerted a profound influence on the English Romantic poets; but it was, in some respects, unfortunate. The prestige of Tragedy and Epic as forms, maintained by the related prestige of Shakespeare and Milton, encouraged the belief that to be a great writer one had to produce big works – full-length plays or very long poems. Consequently, Romantic poet after Romantic poet struggled to produce his tragedy or his epic, and the result was often a lamentable waste of time and energy.

The great Romantic poets produced numerous plays, and almost all of them are bad. Blake attempted a play about King Edward III and got as far as the prologues to *King Edward IV* and *King John*. Wordsworth wrote *The Borderers: A Tragedy*. Coleridge wrote *Zapolya, Remorse: A Tragedy, The Fall of Robespierre: An Historical Drama; The Piccolomini,* and *The Death of Wallenstein.* Byron wrote *Manfred: A Dramatic Poem, Marino Faliero: An Historical Tragedy, Sardanapalus: A Tragedy, Cain: A Mystery, Heaven and Earth: A Mystery, Werner: A Tragedy,* and *The Deformed Transformed: A Drama.* Shelley wrote *The Cenci: A Tragedy, Hellas: A Lyrical Drama,* and part of *Charles the First.* And Keats, of course, wrote *Otho the Great.* Keats's play had one performance: as a literary curiosity, in 1950, just 130 years after it was written. Shelley's *The Cenci* is occasionally revived. But virtually all these plays have died the death: they are unperformed and forgotten; and the reason is that they are generally poor plays.

An obvious problem arises: why is it that such great poets, whose shorter works include masterpieces, were so unfortunate when they turned to drama? There are several explanations.

The first is linguistic. Shakespeare so overshadowed the realm of drama that when they wrote plays these Romantics were repeatedly drawn towards his kinds of versification, his kinds of diction and blank verse. They borrowed from him and imitated him consciously or unconsciously. The result, all too often, is a never-never-land speech: a literary confection that takes something from the Elizabethan and Jacobean periods and something from the preoccupations of the Romantic era, but seldom emerges as an untrammelled and fully-effective vocal medium. Another reason is that the Romantic sensibility, which gives priority to intense private experience, is good for personal poetry – e.g. for short odes or lyrics or meditative pieces – but not good for drama, which requires an ability to create a credible diversity of characters in social interaction. It is almost as though the English Romantics were too self-centred to create characters who stand free as plausible and memorable beings. A third explanation is that the prestige attributed by the Romantics to intense emotion led to plays which contain a lot of bombast and melodramatic histrionics: 'ohs' and 'ahs' and exclamation marks abound. These writers persistently responded to Shakespearian authority and example by looking to the past for their subjects and their idioms. (Fear of prosecution for 'seditious' writing was an important inhibitor.) The way ahead was quite different. That way ahead was to be found by Büchner in *Woyzeck*, by Ibsen and Strindberg, and by Shaw – men who turned to the contemporary world and used the phrasings of the middle class and working class, and who employed a charged idiomatic prose rather than the blank verse which had been the appropriately dominant dramatic medium in the Elizabethan age.

Queen Elizabeth once said in anger: 'I am Richard II: know ye not that?' She knew, Essex's rebels knew, and Shakespeare knew, that when Shakespeare dealt with past history he was tackling contemporary problems: the political and religious arguments were cogently topical. When the English Romantics tried to emulate Shakespeare, they mimicked his tones and tried to copy his subjects, but the works were not rooted in social realities; at best, they seem energetic pastiche; at worst, ludicrous fustian. Keats's *Otho the Great* is a mixture of both.

Keats felt that his reputation needed the prestige that a tragedy would bring: 'My name with the literary fashionables is vulgar – I am a weaver to them – a Tragedy would lift me out of this mess'; and he hoped to make money quickly by it, so as to repay a debt to Charles Brown: 'Mine I am sure is a tolerable tragedy – it would have been a bank to me' (R II, 186). His enthusiasm had been aroused by the dynamic, passionate acting of Edmund Kean, and he wrote *Otho the Great* with Kean in mind, hoping that it would produced by Drury Lane. The tragedy was provisionally accepted there, and for a while it did seem that Kean might take the leading rôle, that of Ludolph; but deferments followed, it was sent to Covent Garden and rejected, and it was never performed until long after Keats's death.

The play was written in a rushed and rather absurd collaboration. Brown says:

> I engaged to furnish him with the fable, characters, and dramatic conduct of a tragedy, and he was to embody it into poetry. The progress of this work was curious; for, while I sat opposite to him, he caught my description of each scene, entered into the characters to be brought forward, the events, and every thing connected with it. Thus he went on, scene after scene, never knowing nor enquiring into the scene which was to follow, until four acts were completed. It was then he required to know, at once, all the events which were to occupy the fifth act.
>
> (*KC* II, 66)

It will be seen that this 'method' is likely to ensure a result which is bitty, confused and confusing.

The central plot of *Otho* concerns amatory deception. Ludolph, who had rebelled against his father but then fought valiantly for him in disguise, is reconciled to him and marries Auranthe. (The virtuous Erminia, who truly loves Ludolph, has been foully

'*Edmund Kean*': *a portrait (attributed to G. Clint) which well conveys the energetic intensity which made Kean famous and evoked Keats's admiration.*

slandered.) On learning, too late, that Auranthe has adulterously deceived him, Ludolph becomes deranged. She dies inexplicably; he, on hearing of this, also expires. The location is Germany, the time vague but long ago, and the verse varies between energetic pastiche of Shakespeare (with echoes of *Macbeth, Antony and Cleopatra, Hamlet, Coriolanus* and *Richard II*) and bathetic nineteenth-century colloquialisms (for example, 'Perchance I might . . . . . chuck it them/ To play with' and 'Was't to this end I louted. . . . .?'). Here is a sample of the descent from the Shakespearian to the ridiculous:

> *Albert*:    To-night, upon the skirts of the blind wood
> That blackens northward of these horrid towers,
> I wait for you with horses. Choose your fate.
> Farewell!
> *Auranthe*: Albert, you jest; I'm sure you must.
> (Act IV, scene i, lines 147–50)

It is sobering to recall that this wretched play was written by Keats in the same year as his great odes. Attention to *Otho* not only helps to define, by contrast, the strengths of the odes, but also saves us from taking them for granted. The more imperilled such achievements are, the more exciting they appear.

## *The influence of Milton*: Hyperion

The reasons for Milton's profound influence on the Romantics are numerous. In the first place, his character made a political appeal to them. They were generally (in their early years at any rate) republican and anti-monarchic in spirit; and Milton had been spokesman for the Parliamentarians who had defeated the Royalists and executed Charles I. He could be seen as a valiantly patriotic subversive. Then he could also be seen as a nobly tragic figure, for in his late years, with the Restoration, he felt himself encompassed by enemies; and he was blind, so he could think of himself as a Samson, 'eyeless in Gaza, at the mill with slaves'. Yet, though blind, he had completed his great epic, *Paradise Lost*, and could therefore be regarded as an indomitably heroic figure.

The epic enjoyed, with tragedy, the highest prestige as a literary form. Of all the British attempts at the epic, Milton's achievement seemed most assured and imposing: he had dared to 'justify the ways of God to men', dared with astonishing imaginative and intellectual presumption to describe and explain Heaven, Earth and Hell, the fall of Satan and the fall of man; so the sheer scale was impressive.

In 1757 Edmund Burke, in his *A Philosophical Enquiry into the Origin of Our Ideas of the Sublime and the Beautiful*, had made an important and influential distinction between sublime effects and beautiful effects in art and life. Our sense of the beautiful, he said, was dependent on our sense of pleasure, and was evoked by objects which were small rather than big, were smooth, delicate or fragile, clear, bright and diversified in colour. An attractive woman would sufficiently fulfil these conditions. Our sense of the sublime, on the other hand, was dependent on feelings of fear or pain: it was evoked by objects which were vast, rugged, angular, massive, obscure and gloomy. Such objects seem to threaten us. Examples included Leviathan, in the Book of Job, and Stonehenge. *Paradise Lost* was a rich repository of instances of the sublime: Burke cited the description of Death in Book II; and the account of Hell yielded obvious examples. Romantic poets and artists were repeatedly prompted and inspired by the poem, from Blake, in 'The Marriage of Heaven and Hell', to John Martin, with his painting 'Pandemonium'.

Romantics had sympathy with bold, lonely rebels; and so forcefully had Milton dramatised the power, resilience and eloquence of Satan that it was easy for Romantics to invert the avowed theology of the poem and see Satan as the hero. Blake, of course, claimed that Milton was 'a true Poet and of the Devil's party without knowing it'. Shelley said:

> Milton's poem contains within itself a philosophical refutation of that system of which, by a strange and natural antithesis, it has been a chief popular support. Nothing can exceed the energy and magnificence of the character of Satan as expressed in *Paradise Lost*..... Milton's Devil as a moral being is as far superior to his God, as one who perseveres in some purpose which he has conceived to be excellent in spite of adversity and torture, is to one who in the cold security of undoubted triumph inflicts the most horrible revenge upon his enemy.....
>
> (*DP*, 46–7)

When Frankenstein's monster wanders in the Alps, he finds a portmanteau which, of course, contains the reading required of a *Romantic* monster: Goethe's *Sorrows of Werther* (*Die Leiden des jungen Werthers*), Plutarch's *Lives* (containing 'the histories of the first founders of the ancient republics') and Milton's *Paradise Lost*. He reflects of the last:

> It moved every feeling of wonder and awe that the picture of an omnipotent God warring with his creatures was capable of exciting..... Like Adam, I was apparently united by no link to any other being in existence..... Many times I considered Satan as the fitter emblem of my condition, for often, like him, when I viewed the bliss of my protectors, the bitter gall of envy rose within me.

(Mary Shelley: *Frankenstein*: in *Three Gothic Novels*, Penguin, 1968, p. 396)

Milton's Satan inspired numerous Romantic figures who display defiant scorn and who persevere in a quest that seems doomed or wicked. He influenced the 'Byronic hero' and Byron's own more saturnine moods and postures, as well as the ambivalent heroic villains of Gothic and post-Gothic fiction, from Walpole's Manfred to Emily Brontë's Heathcliff and Melville's Ahab. Repeatedly, writers in the Romantic tradition are tempted by the idea that the ontological criterion may be superior to the moral criterion: that is, that sheer charismatic fulness of being, however violent and destructive, may be superior to decent, constructive and conventional conduct.

Bertrand Russell had this in mind when (in *A History of Western Philosophy*, Chapter 18) he likened Romanticism to Frankenstein's monster. The monster is initially benevolent, but when the world does not welcome him affectionately, he becomes vengeful and destructive. Russell argues that Romanticism, for all its idealism, basically celebrates egotism; and he suggests that the reason for the Romantic preoccupation with incestuous passion (of which there are examples in Byron's personal life, Byron's play *Manfred*, Shelley's *The Cenci*, Wagner's Siegmund and Sieglinde, and even Keats's *Otho*) is that the Romantic, being egoistic, wishes to love a person who resembles himself as closely as possible: a blood-relation is thus well qualified. And because of the predilection for irrationalism and the egoistic will, the culmination of Romanticism, says Russell, comes with Hitler and Auschwitz. (It is true that there are Romantic elements in Nazism: for example, the cult of the charismatic leader, the mass-irrationalism, and even the Wagnerian influence. But Romanticism is so complex that it leads in every political direction. As we have noted, it has nourished conservatism, liberalism, socialism, communism and libertarian anarchism.)

The example of Milton sometimes caused the English Romantics to waste huge amounts of time and energy. Because the epic had high prestige, and because Milton had written a powerful English epic, the Romantic poets attempted to emulate him. The results, generally, were costly. Blake wrote longer and longer poems (one of them *Milton*) which became increasingly obscure. Southey attempted an epic. Wordsworth wrote two poems of epic length: *The Prelude* and the incomplete *Excursion*. Both these pay explicit tribute to Milton, and *The Prelude* is a personal epic which purportedly arises from the narrator's failure to write a public epic 'on some theme/ By Milton left unsung'. Its first two books have numerous admirable passages, but of this and *The Excursion* the reader may remark, as F. R. Leavis remarked of *Paradise Lost*, that 'a good deal . . . . . strikes one as being almost as mechanical as bricklaying' (L, 56). There was an inherent conflict between Romanticism, with its emphasis on the primacy of individual (and individualistic) experience, and the epic, with its use of a publicly accepted system of theology and mythology. The Romantics may have had epic ambitions, but they lacked the traditional, public, theological material to fulfil them. Blake retreated into private mythology. Wordsworth, with characteristic egotism, attempted to make an epic of an autobiography by describing in immense detail the development of his own beliefs. Perhaps the best solution of the problem was Byron's in *Don Juan*: instead of trying to *resolve* the tension between tradition and the solitary ego, he exploited it with gusto for ironic and comic effect. Though he repeatedly promises an epic as he writes, he does so tongue-in-cheek; and a parody-epic, lurching and veering giddily from the whimsical and the poignant to the farcical and ludicrous, is the engaging result: the most intelligent long poem of the period.

John Keats, however, did not have the particular poetic resources which wealth for travel and a subversively patrician temperament gave to Lord Byron, and his endeavours to write an epic were to cause him much painful effort and frustration. His early admiration of Milton is attested in numerous poems (including 'Written on the Day That Mr. Leigh Hunt Left Prison', 'Ode to Apollo', 'To George Felton Mathew', 'O! how I love', 'To Charles Cowden Clarke' and 'Seeing a Lock of Milton's Hair'); and it was with *Hyperion* that he made his great attempt at emulation. The debt to *Paradise Lost*, in plot and verse, is all too apparent. Book I of *Paradise Lost* had told how the rebel angels, stunned after their defeat, gradually recover: Satan rouses Beelzebub; they take stock of their plight, and summon an assembly of the fallen. In Book II the rebels debate their situation, and Satan sets out for earth. In *Hyperion*, Book I, Saturn and his fellow-Titans are stunned after their defeat by Jupiter; Thea rouses Hyperion, and Hyperion addresses the defeated masses. In Book II the Titans debate their situation, the speakers being introduced (like their Miltonic counterparts) with lofty descriptions. Keats's distinctive contribution is the strong evocation of massive brooding stasis, as in the imagery of 'branch-charmèd oaks' (Book I, lines 72–9) and 'Druid stones, upon a forlorn moor' (Book II, lines 33–40). Generally, though, the many echoes of Milton's narrative, the Miltonic characterisations, the Miltonic epic similes and weighty phraseology, serve only to reverberate the central hollowness of the Keatsian endeavour. To Milton, the legends were realities. The Bible was the word of God; the pagan deities (Moloch, Beelzebub and the rest) were real devils and not fictions; and he knew so thoroughly and intimately the classical mythology that when he dreamt of his dead wife, Alcestis came to mind. For him the passions

*Michelangelo: Two 'Captives' (circa 1530–33). Left: 'The Young Giant';
right: 'Atlas'.*

    *Michelangelo never completed these sculptures, which were intended to grace
the tomb of Pope Julius II but long stood in the Boboli gardens at Florence.
Half-emergent from the marble block, these figures offer symbolic equivalents
to the Titans of Keats's incomplete* Hyperion, *who are only half-emergent
from the stupor of their downfall and whose story is only partly-emergent from
Keats's imagination.*

    *Keats's friend Haydon, when comparing Raphael with Michelangelo (in
the* Examiner, 9 May 1819), *remarked:* 'Raphael *was at the mercy of
Pleasure, from his sensibility to Beauty.* Michael Angelo *disdained it, from
his intense awe of Immortality!'*

and polemics of theology were politics, and those of politics were theology: *Paradise Lost*, an epic of a rebellion which both succeeded and failed, drew energy from the period of the Civil War, Commonwealth and Restoration in which the Puritan rebellion also succeeded and failed. The Bible had little authority for Keats, and his knowledge of the classics, though eagerly diverse, was sometimes eclectically superficial. Most important: for Keats, remote from the practicalities of politics and temperamentally detached from the masses, there were few emotions proper to epic that he could naturally tap. He sensed what was wrong when, at the opening of the abortive Book II of *Hyperion*, he wrote:

> Thus, in alternate uproar and sad peace,
> Amazèd were those Titans utterly.
> O leave them, Muse! O leave them to their woes;
> For thou art weak to sing such tumults dire:
> A solitary sorrow best befits
> Thy lips, and antheming a lonely grief.

There followed the second version. In *The Fall of Hyperion*, as we have seen, Keats attempted to make the problem into the poem, the impediment into the impetus, the contradiction into the sustaining paradox. The very conflict between the egoistic outlook of the Romantic and the social concerns of epic are the matter of debate between the narrator and Moneta. As she says:

> 'What benefit canst thou do, or all thy tribe,
> To the great world? Thou art a dreaming thing;
> A fever of thyself – think of the earth;
> What bliss even in hope is there for thee?
> What haven?. . . . .
>          Art thou not of the dreamer tribe?
> The poet and the dreamer are distinct,
> Diverse, sheer opposite, antipodes.
> The one pours out a balm upon the world,
> The other vexes it.'

> (Book I, lines 167–71, 198–202)

Furthermore, this apparent rebuke to dreamers is offered by a visionary figure who herself is part of the narrator's 'dream': a paradox portending the impasse which the moribund *Fall of Hyperion*, so memorably bleak and sepulchral, was soon to reach. In August 1819 Keats had written: 'Shakespeare and the paradise Lost every day become greater wonders to me – I look upon fine Phrases like a Lover'; 'the Paradise Lost becomes a greater wonder – The more I know what my diligence may in time probably effect; the more does my heart distend with Pride and Obstinacy' – like that of the Miltonic Satan (R II, 139, 146). But in September he wrote:

'Miltonic verse cannot be written but in an artful or rather artist's humour. I wish to give myself up to other sensations' (R II, 167). *The Fall of Hyperion* was abandoned; and the dark, massive shadow of Milton lifted from pale Keats.

# 4   Keats's views

> I must once for all tell you I have not one Idea of the truth of any
> of my speculations.....
>
> (R I, 243)

In his short life, Keats never formed a settled doctrine. He
speculated in various directions; his moods veered and changed;
and he was influenced in different ways by the books he read and
the people he met. Though retaining liberal sympathies and a
faith in the value of poetry, he emerged from his school-days largely
innocent of doctrine, system and theology. This gave him a sense of
inferiority to men with doctrine and philosophies to expound
(Milton, Wordsworth and Coleridge, for example); but it also gave
him a fresh openness to experience, and, gradually, the sense that if
he lacked certitude he gained freedom. I give samples of his opinions
below. They should not be treated as settled convictions; but they do
help to illuminate his work and, therefore, our lives. Their main
truths reside in their lively texture rather than in their
paraphrasable claims.

## Keats on Art

From a letter of 22 November 1817 (R I, 184–6 – the reference to
'Adam's dream' is to *Paradise Lost*, Book VIII, lines 452–90):

> Men of Genius are great as certain ethereal Chemicals operating
> on the Mass of neutral intellect..... they have not any
> individuality, any determined Character.....
> I am certain of nothing but of the holiness of the Heart's
> affections and the truth of Imagination – What the imagination
> seizes as Beauty must be truth – whether it existed before or not –
> for I have the same Idea of all our Passions as of Love they are all
> in their sublime, creative of essential Beauty..... The
> Imagination may be compared to Adam's dream – he awoke and
> found it truth. I am the more zealous in this affair, because I have
> never yet been able to perceive how any thing can be known for
> truth by consequitive reasoning – and yet it must be – Can it be
> that even the greatest Philosopher ever arrived at his goal without
> putting aside numerous objections – However it may be, O for a
> Life of Sensations rather than of Thoughts! It is 'a Vision in the
> form of Youth' a Shadow of reality to come – and this
> consideration has further conv[i]nced me for it has come as
> auxiliary to another favorite Speculation of mine, that we shall
> enjoy ourselves here after by having what we called happiness on

Earth repeated in a finer tone and so repeated..... I scarcely remember counting upon any Happiness – I look not for it if it be not in the present hour – nothing startles me beyond the moment. The setting sun will always set me to rights – or if a Sparrow come before my Window I take part in its existince and pick about the Gravel..... I sometimes feel not the influence of a Passion or Affection during a whole week.....

From a letter of 21 December 1817 (R I, 192–4 – the picture discussed is Benjamin West's 'Death on the Pale Horse'):

..... the excellence of every Art is its intensity, capable of making all disagreeables evaporate, from their being in close relationship with Beauty & Truth – Examine King Lear & you will find this examplified throughout; but in this picture we have unpleasantness without any momentous depth of speculation excited, in which to bury its repulsiveness..... it struck me, what quality went to form a Man of Achievement especially in Literature & which Shakespeare posessed so enormously – I mean *Negative Capability*, that is when man is capable of being in uncertainties, Mysteries, doubts, without any irritable reaching after fact & reason – Coleridge, for instance, would let go by a fine isolated verisimilitude caught from the Penetralium of mystery, from being incapable of remaining content with half knowledge. This pursued through Volumes would perhaps take us no further than this, that with a great poet the sense of Beauty overcomes every other consideration, or rather obliterates all consideration.

From a letter of 3 February 1818 (R I, 224–5 – Keats is thinking of Wordsworth's poems):

We hate poetry that has a palpable design upon us..... Poetry should be great & unobtrusive, a thing which enters into one's soul, and does not startle it or amaze it with itself but with its subject. – How beautiful are the retired flowers! how would they lose their beauty were they to throng into the highway crying out, 'admire me I am a violet! dote upon me I am a primrose![']
Modern poets differ from the Elizabethans in this..... I don't mean to deny Wordsworth's grandeur & Hunt's merit, but I mean to say we need not be teazed with grandeur & merit – when we can have them uncontaminated & unobtrusive. Let us have the old Poets, & Robin Hood.....

From a letter of 27 February 1818 (R I, 238–9):

In Poetry I have a few Axioms, and you will see how far I am from their Centre. 1st I think Poetry should surprise by a fine excess and not by Singularity – it should strike the Reader as a wording of his own highest thoughts, and appear almost a Remembrance – 2$^{nd}$ Its touches of Beauty should never be half way therby making the reader breathless instead of content . . . . . but it is easier to think what Poetry should be than to write it – and this leads me on to another axiom. That if Poetry comes not as naturally as the Leaves to a tree it had better not come at all.

From a letter of 13 March 1818 (R I, 242):

I am sometimes so very sceptical as to think Poetry itself a mere Jack a lanthern to amuse whoever may chance to be struck with its brilliance – As Tradesmen say every thing is worth what it will fetch, so probably every mental pursuit takes its reality and worth from the ardour of the pursuer – being in itself a nothing. . . . .

From a letter of 27 October 1818 (R I, 386–7):

As to the poetical Character itself, (I mean that sort of which, if I am any thing, I am a Member; that sort distinguished from the wordsworthian or egotistical sublime; which is a thing per se and stands alone) it is not itself – it has no self – it is every thing and nothing – It has no character – it enjoys light and shade; it lives in gusto, be it foul or fair, high or low, rich or poor, mean or elevated – It has as much delight in conceiving an Iago as an Imogen. What shocks the virtuous philosop[h]er, delights the camelion Poet. It does no harm from its relish of the dark side of things any more than from its taste for the bright one; because they both end in speculation. A Poet is the most unpoetical of any thing in existence; because he has no Identity – he is continually in for – and filling some other Body – The Sun, the Moon, the Sea and Men and Women who are creatures of impulse are poetical and have about them an unchangeable attribute – the poet has none . . . . . not one word I ever utter can be taken for granted. . . . .

From 'Where's the Poet? Show him! show him!', written around October 1818:

Where's the Poet? . . . . .
'Tis the man who with a man
   Is an equal, be he king,
Or poorest of the beggar-clan. . . . .

## Keats on Religion

From 'Written in Disgust of Vulgar Superstition', 22 December 1816:

The church bells toll a melancholy round.....
Still, still they toll, and I should feel a damp,
   A chill as from a tomb, did I not know
That they are dying like an outburnt lamp.....

From a letter of 16 December 1818 (R II, 5):

That will be one of the grandeurs of immortality – there will be no
space and consequently the only commerce between spirits will
be by their intelligence of each other – when they will completely
understand each other – while we in this world merely
comp[r]ehend each other in different degrees .....

From a letter of 14 February 1819 (R II, 63):

A Parson is a Lamb in a drawing room and a lion in a Vestry –
The notions of Society will not permit a Parson to give way to his
temper in any shape – so he festers in himself..... His mind is
against every Man and every Mans mind is against him – He is
an Hippocrite to the Believer and a Coward to the
unbeliever.....

From a letter of 19 March 1819 (R II, 80–1):

I go among the Feilds and catch a glimpse of a stoat or a
fieldmouse peeping out of the withered grass – the creature hath a
purpose and its eyes are bright with it – I go amongst the
buildings of a city and I see a Man hurrying along – to what? The
Creature has a purpose and his eyes are bright with it. But then
as Wordsworth says, 'we have all one human heart'..... I have
no doubt that thousands of people never heard of have had hearts
comp[l]etely disinterested: I can remember but two – Socrates
and Jesus..... It is to be lamented that the history of the latter
was written and revised by Men interested in the pious frauds of
Religion. Yet through all this I see his splendour..... May there
not be superior beings amused with any graceful, though
instinctive attitude my mind m[a]y fall into, as I am entertained
with the alertness of a Stoat or the anxiety of a Deer? Though a
quarrel in the streets is a thing to be hated, the energies displayed
in it are fine; the commonest Man shows a grace in his quarrel –
By a superior being our reasoning[s] may take the same tone –
though erroneous they may be fine – This is the very thing in
which consists poetry; and if so it is not so fine a thing as
philosophy – For the same reason that an eagle is not so fine a
thing as a truth.....

From a letter of 21 April 1819 (R II, 102):

Call the world if you Please 'The vale of Soulmaking'

103

..... There may be intelligences or sparks of the divinity in millions – but they are not Souls till they acquire identities, till each one is personally itself..... I will call the *world* a School instituted for the purpose of teaching little children to read – I will call the *human heart* the *horn Book* used in that School – and I will call the *Child able to read, the Soul* made from that school and its hornbook. Do you not see how necessary a World of Pains and troubles is to school an Intelligence and make it a soul?

From a letter to Fanny Brawne, June(?) 1820 (R II, 293):

I long to believe in immortality..... If I am destined to be happy with you here – how short is the longest life.....

From a letter to Brown, 30 September 1820 (R II, 346):

Is there another Life? Shall I awake and find all this a dream? There must be we cannot be created for this sort of suffering.....

From a letter from Severn to William Haslam, 15 January 1821 (R II, 368 – the 'noble fellow' is Keats):

..... this noble fellow lying on the bed – is dying in horror ..... no philosophy – no religion to support him ..... he says in words that tear my very heartstrings – 'miserable wretch I am – this last cheap comfort – which every rogue and fool have – is deny'd me in my last moments – why is this – O! I have serv'd every one with my utmost good – yet why is this – I cannot understand this'.....


## Keats on Politics

'Lines Written on 29 May, the Anniversary of Charles's Restoration, on Hearing the Bells Ringing':

Infatuate Britons, will you still proclaim
His memory, your direst, foulest shame?
    Nor patriots revere?
Ah! when I hear each traitorous lying bell,
'Tis gallant Sidney's, Russell's, Vane's sad knell,
    That pains my wounded ear.

*Endymion*, Book III, lines 1–12:

There are who lord it o'er their fellow-men
With most prevailing tinsel: who unpen
Their baaing vanities, to browse away
The comfortable green and juicy hay

*H. M. Paget: 'Peterloo, 1819'.*

*On 16 August 1819, between sixty thousand and one hundred thousand people gathered in St. Peter's Field, Manchester, to hear Henry 'Orator' Hunt advocate democratic rights; and the crowds were attacked by Hussars and the 'Yeomen's Cavalry', who killed eleven people and wounded over four hundred. In the three decades following the French Revolution of 1789, the apprehensive British Government had become systematically repressive; the 'Peterloo' massacre was widely seen as proof of its ruthlessness.*

*In* Endymion, *Keats had expressed his republican hostility to martial authority, and a sense of defeated republican aspirations may have contributed to the tone of* Hyperion. *Not personal inclination alone, but also the repressive factors in Keats's England, tended to generate the seemingly 'non-political' characteristics of much of his poetry.*

From human pastures; or, O torturing façt!
Who, through an idiot blink, will see unpack'd
Fire-branded foxes to sear up and singe
Our gold and ripe-ear'd hopes. With not one tinge
Of sanctuary splendour, not a sight
Able to face an owl's, they still are dight
By the blear-eyed nations in empurpled vests,
And crowns, and turbans.

From a letter of 18 September 1819 (R II, 193–4 – 'Carlisle' is Richard Carlile [1790–1843], the freethinking bookseller, jailed for publishing Tom Paine's *Age of Reason*):

All civil[is]ed countries become gradually more enlighten'd and there should be a continual change for the better . . . . . Then in every kingdom therre was a long struggle of kings to destroy all popular privileges. The english were the only people in europe who made a grand kick at this. They were slaves to Henry 8th but were freemen under william 3rd at the time the french were the abject slaves under Lewis 14th The example of England, and the liberal writers of france and england sowed the seed of opposition to this Tyranny – and it was swelling in the ground till it burst out in the french revolution – That has had an unlucky termination. It put a stop to the rapid progress of free sentiments in England; and gave our Court hopes of turning back to the despotism of the 16 century. They have made a handle of this event in every way to undermine our freedom . . . . . This makes the business about Carlisle the Bookseller of great moment in my mind. He has been selling deistical pamphlets, republished Tom Payne and many other works held in superstitious horror . . . . . the Trials would light a flame they could not extinguish. Do you not think this of great import?

# 5  Critical discussions

### 'On First Looking into Chapman's Homer'

> Much have I travell'd in the realms of gold,
>     And many goodly states and kingdoms seen;
>     Round many western islands have I been
> Which bards in fealty to Apollo hold.
> 5 Oft of one wide expanse had I been told
>     That deep-brow'd Homer ruled as his demesne;
>     Yet did I never breathe its pure serene
> Till I heard Chapman speak out loud and bold:
> Then felt I like some watcher of the skies
> 10    When a new planet swims into his ken;
>     Or like stout Cortez when with eagle eyes
> He star'd at the Pacific – and all his men
> Look'd at each other with a wild surmise –
>     Silent, upon a peak in Darien.

This sonnet was written in October 1816 (the occasion is described on pp. 13–14). It was first published in Hunt's *Examiner* on 1 December 1816. The draft and the *Examiner* text give the seventh line as 'Yet could I never judge what Men could mean'.

The form is that of the Petrarchan sonnet, in this case rhyming ABBA ABBA CDCDCD. Keats had to strain language to maintain the taxing rhyme-scheme: 'Round . . . . . islands have I been' is what hostile reviewers would have termed a Cockneyism ('I've been round the islands!') in which the verb 'to be' is substituted for the verb of travel which the sense properly requires; and some strain is also indicated by the use of the bookishly literary rhyme-words 'demesne' (meaning 'dominion'), 'serene' (meaning 'air', from the Latin *serenum*, 'clear sky') and 'his ken' (meaning 'his awareness'). 'Realms of gold', clarified by the reference in line 4 to Apollo, the poets' god, means 'realms of the poetic imagination': Sir Philip Sidney's *Defence of Poesie* (1595) had said '[Nature's] world is brazen, the poets only deliver a golden'. Line 12, 'He star'd at the Pacific – and all his men', is irregular, having one syllable too many; it would read more smoothly if the last phrase were 'and his men'.

For some readers, the poem is blemished by a factual error which reminds us of the occasional superficiality of Keats's memory and of the rapid (and sometimes careless) way in which he composed his poems. The conquistador who discovered the Pacific when climbing the isthmus of Darien was not 'stout Cortez' but Balboa. Keats has been recalling J. M. Robertson's *History of America*, and has confused Robertson's account of Balboa's discovery of the 'South Sea' with his account of Cortés's soldiers' amazement on first seeing Mexico City. Robertson writes that when Balboa, on the summit, beheld the South Sea (the Pacific) he knelt and thanked God, while his followers 'rushed forward to join in his wonder, exultation, and gratitude'. Keats may also be recalling William Gilbert's commentary on his poem, 'The Hurricane', quoted by Wordsworth in *The Excursion*: this says that the man who 'contemplates, from a sudden promontory, the distant, vast Pacific – and feels himself a freeman in this vast theatre' experiences 'exaltation . . . . . not less than imperial'. Keats's error has not marred the poem for most readers, because most readers trust Keats's word. Those who know the error know a less satisfactory poem; however, they may mentally substitute 'Balboa' for 'stout Cortez', weakening the alliterative patterns using 'st' but strengthening the patterns using 'l'. This pedantry may gratify Balboa's shade and amuse Keats's.

The secrets of the poem's power are interesting. We have a metaphoric exploration (journeys in 'realms of gold', 'states and kingdoms', 'islands') to describe the narrator's experience of reading various poets. Then, to account for the effect of reading Chapman's translation of Homer, we are referred to actual historic discoveries – the discovery of a new planet by some astronomer, and, more concretely and specifically, to the historic discovery of the Pacific by a conquistador and his followers. Thus there is a fine inter-relationship of abstract and concrete, metaphoric and historic, literary exploration and topographical exploration, cultural discovery and territorial discovery. The paradox is that after the reading of poetry has been metaphorically likened to travel around a world, a historic example of travel and discovery is used to convey the shock of a literary discovery. The glowing, shimmery vagueness of the opening makes more startlingly realistic and precise the final close-up on the conquistador and his amazed followers; and that realistic vista of the group is, after all, but a simile to convey the amazement of the solitary speaker. Ironically, Chapman's 'speak[ing] out loud and bold' is likened to an event in which all were 'Silent'.

As Leigh Hunt noted, 'the word *swims* is complete' – it suggests with precision the way in which a planet may seem to move, undulating, into the vision of a man adjusting a telescope. Other felicities are, as so often with Keats, the rich use of assonance and alliteration. In the last five lines, if we take line 10 as our starting-point, we hear the 'n' of 'When' echoed in 'new', 'ken', 'when', 'men', 'Silent', 'upon', 'Darien'; the 'p' of 'planet' echoed in 'Pacific' and 'peak'; the 'l' of 'planet' in 'like', 'Look'd' and 'Silent'; and the 's' of 'swims' in 'stout', 'star'd', 'Pacific', 'surmise' and 'Silent'. 'Wild' and 'Silent' re-echo the 'i' of 'like' in line 11. The effect of such patterning is to slow the reading, making it more deliberate and self-aware, giving sensuous pleasures to the oral and aural powers. This may either intensify the meaning of the poem by rendering it more memorable or veil it by operating as a seduction which lulls the conceptualising intelligence. Two or three readings bring the conceptual and the sensuous into a fully effective harmony. The result is a poem which, with considerable originality, inter-relates and illuminates widely-ranging experiences. This is not to overrate it. Its popularity with Arthur Ransome's children in *Swallows and Amazons* emphasises its obvious quality of boyish, self-dramatising Romanticism: the narrator (who sounds young, dreamy and starry-eyed) associates himself flatteringly with a bold conquistador, a tough man of action.

One of the main claims made in this *Preface to Keats* is that at the heart of Keats's creative imagination was a preoccupation with threshold-states. It is, therefore, fitting that in his first famous sonnet, when he himself stood on the threshold of remarkable work, the most memorable image should be that of explorers on the threshold of the astonishing unknown.

## Endymion

Keats completed this lengthy poem in 1817, as a trial of strength. Book I tells how Endymion, the shepherd, was smitten with melancholy, and eventually revealed to his sister, Peona, the cause: he had had a dream-vision (while slumbering amid poppies) that the moon-goddess had descended from the skies and embraced him passionately; now, he pines for her. This book had opened with the subsequently-famous exordium, 'A thing of beauty is a joy for ever'; Book II opens with the Huntian doctrine that lovers are far more important than conquerors – Juliet and Imogen are better than Alexander and Ulysses. The latter book tells how Endymion wanders in the underworld, meeting Venus and Adonis, before experiencing a further embrace with Cynthia the moon-goddess ('long time they lay/ Fondling and kissing every doubt away'): she promises that eventually she will translate him to the heavens to live with her. He hears the lament of the ever-parted lovers, Alpheus, the river-god, and the nymph Arethusa. Book III opens with another Hunt-like political exordium, the denunciation of monarchs, tyrants and exploiters, men of battle and conquest. Endymion now meets Glaucus, who tells at length the tale of his unfortunate love for Scylla, who was changed by Circe into a monster. The advent of Endymion means that Glaucus can be rejuvenated and united with the restored Scylla, while all lovers drowned in storms are resurrected (the amatory resurrection adumbrated in 'I stood tip-toe'). Venus promises that Endymion will attain happiness when he has eventually 'Escap'd from dull mortality's harsh net'. In Book

IV, Endymion meets an Indian maid and falls in love with her; he still loves Cynthia but decides that earthly pleasures with the Indian are better than a pining for the transcendental:

> 'There never liv'd a mortal man, who bent
> His appetite beyond his natural sphere,
> But starv'd and died. My sweetest Indian, here,
> Here will I kneel, for thou redeemèd hast
> My life from too thin breathing: gone and past
> Are cloudy phantasms.'

(lines 646–51)

The Indian maid, however, says that she is forbidden to make love with Endymion. He declares that he will become 'a hermit young', while she can live with his sister Peona, and he will love her as another sister. The dusky Indian is then transformed into fair Cynthia, and explains:

>          'Drear, drear
> Has our delaying been; but foolish fear
> Withheld me first; and then decrees of fate;
> And then 'twas fit that from this mortal state
> Thou shouldst, my love, by some unlook'd for change
> Be spiritualiz'd.....'

(lines 988–93)

– and she and Endymion vanish away.

It will be seen that the tale is open to various allegorical interpretations, and the most obvious one is that which relates to much of Keats's subsequent work. Endymion's attraction to both the moon-goddess and the dusky maid expresses the dilemma of men generally and the Romantic poet in particular, divided between aspiration after some high ideal and satisfaction with the pleasures of this world. In the speech about 'cloudy phantasms' quoted previously, the poet seems to be saying, 'Beware of frustrating ideals; opt for the pleasures of the real'. But the subsequent ascetic emphasis on chastity as a key to salvation gives a contrastingly neo-Platonic quality to the discussion. The eventual meaning appears to be that a time of disciplined self-restraint actually permits the eventual reconciliation of the ideal and the real, the spiritual and the sensual, virtue and pleasure, the other world and this one. The transformation of Indian maid into Cynthia is Keats's way of imaginatively resolving that extreme tension in his nature between ambitious yearnings (for wisdom, stature, fame; some kind of immortality) and sensuous hedonism (whether gratified by nature's beauties, claret, masturbatory reveries or a girl like Fanny Brawne). We may see the poem as a personal, consolatory allegory which tells Keats that if he perseveres as a poet, he may succeed in attaining historic immortality by expressing within poetic disciplines his love for the rich luxuries and beauties of this world.

The tale of *Endymion* is not only slow to unfold; it is also indecisive over a crucial matter. As is shown by the last passage quoted previously, Cynthia gives a confusing number of reasons for the delay in the consummation of her love for Endymion: one being 'foolish fear', another 'decrees of fate', and another, which makes better moral sense, that it was first necessary for Endymion to be 'spiritualiz'd'. The first reason is not really compatible with the other two; and whereas the phrase 'foolish fear' implies that a rapid consummation was right (implying, therefore, approval of the sensuously hedonistic), the postulated need for the spiritualisation of Endymion implies a relatively austere moral, compatible with the Christian and neo-Platonic doctrine of pre-marital chastity. This suggestion of self-contradiction at the crucial point indicates that Keats's imagination could not fully overcome the tension which the paradoxical merging of Indian and Cynthia was intended to resolve. The finest resolution of the same tension would eventually be provided in the adroit, economical and lucidly lyrical 'Ode to a Nightingale'.

The faults of *Endymion*, then, are: a crucial uncertainty; the tediously slow exposition (the episodes of Glaucus and Alpheus are themselves excessively long); the surfeit of descriptive scene-setting, and the monotony induced by too predictable a preoccupation with the rather escapist realm of romanticised classicism – a mixture of Ovid's *Metamorphoses*, Baldwin's *Pantheon*, Lempriere's *Classical Dictionary*, Spenser, Marlowe, Claude and Poussin. (In such a context, the radical republicanism of Book III, lines 1–22, though incongruous, is a refreshing shock.)

The strengths are the familiar ones: in particular, a richness of sensuous description, of which the poem offers a multitude of examples. Here are two:

> A shout from the whole multitude arose,
> That lingered in the air like dying rolls
> Of abrupt thunder, when Ionian shoals
> Of dolphins bob their noses through the brine.
> (Book I, lines 308–11)

> [The butterfly] began to dip,
> As if, athirst with so much toil, 'twould sip
> The crystal spout-head: so it did, with touch
> Most delicate, as though afraid to smutch
> Even with mealy gold the waters clear.
> (Book II, lines 87–91)

The sensuousness of observation is enriched by a sensuousness of diction created by the dense interweaving of oral patterns. Thus, in the first example, we have these alliterative sounds: 'multitude', 'thunder', 'dolphins'; 'thunder', 'through'; 'abrupt', 'bob', 'brine'; 'whole', 'multitude', 'rolls', 'shoals', 'dolphins'; and these assonances: 'whole', 'arose', 'rolls', 'Ionian', 'shoals', 'noses'; 'dolphins', 'bob'; 'like dying', 'Ionian', 'brine'. In the second example we find these alliterative sounds: 'touch', 'smutch'; 'much', 'most', 'smutch', 'mealy'; 'delicate', 'mealy', 'clear'; 'toil', 'crystal', 'gold'; and these assonances: 'touch', 'smutch'; 'so', 'most', 'though', 'gold'; 'even', 'mealy', 'clear'. These are only selections: more examples from each quotation could be given. The fact that 'mealy', like the vigorously idiomatic 'smutch', appears in three of these groups helps to explain its effectiveness and, indeed, the secret of such poetry. (Keats had been taught the association of 'mealy' with butterflies' wings by Shakespeare's *Troilus and Cressida*, Act III, scene iii, lines 78–9.) We are given mouth-filling sounds; the sensuous aspects of diction are given prominence (though not so much as to swamp the sense); thus there is aural harmony with the visually attractive description, and this not because particular sounds necessarily evoke any particular pictures – sounds in themselves very seldom do – but because in both cases, though in very different ways, the poem offers gratification to the sensuous appetites.

Romantic literature is full of lonely characters pursuing elusive goals, so centrally *Endymion* is conventional. Furthermore, there is an obvious debt to Shelley's *Alastor*, which Keats had read a short time previously. In *Alastor* a noble figure, clearly representing the Poet, embraces in a dream a beautiful female form; he awakes, yearning and dissatisfied, and wanders through the world, across sea and mountain, seeking that ideal beauty; eventually he dies. Not only does this poem have that initial sexual dream-embrace which recurs in *Endymion*, not only is there a quest through a succession of visionary landscapes; but also in Shelley's narrative there is 'an Arab maiden' who loves and tends the Poet, and who perhaps suggested Keats's 'Indian maid'; and though the moon-goddess does not embrace Shelley's hero, 'the great moon' figures prominently in several of the descriptions. Of course, there are many differences: Shelley's hero dies, while Keats's is translated; but in both tales one senses that the central figure is a glamorised representative of the author (who is not immune to self-pity); and both poems have considerable descriptive virtuosity. Characteristically, Shelley's descriptions are *faster* than Keats's: they solicit a more rapid, impetuous reading, and often what they describe is a headlong motion; and Shelley is very interested in colourful, mobile optical effects. Here is a good example:

As one that in a silver vision floats
Obedient to the sweep of odorous winds
Upon resplendent clouds, so rapidly
Along the dark and ruffled waters fled
The straining boat. – A whirlwind swept it on,
With fierce gusts and precipitating force,
Through the white ridges of the chafèd sea.
The waves arose.....
   Evening came on,
The beams of sunset hung their rainbow hues
High 'mid the shifting domes of sheeted spray
That canopied his path o'er the waste deep.....

       (S, 22, lines 316–23, 333–6)

Although there are clear differences in descriptive emphasis, there is no doubt that *Alastor* exerted a dialectical influence on *Endymion*: it offered the challenge to which *Endymion* was the response. As A. C. Bradley once remarked (*Oxford Lectures on Poetry*, London: Macmillan, 1909, p. 241), 'It seems almost beyond doubt that the story of Cynthia and Endymion would not have taken this shape but for *Alastor*'.

Keats added an extremely apologetic preface to the work: he declared that

the reader ..... must soon perceive great inexperience, immaturity, and every error denoting a feverish attempt, rather than a deed accomplished. The two first books, and indeed the two last, I feel sensible are not of such completion as to warrant their passing the press.....

[T]here is not a fiercer hell than the failure in a great object.....

The imagination of a boy is healthy, and the mature imagination of a man is healthy; but there is a space of life between, in which the soul is in a ferment, the character undecided, the way of life uncertain, the ambition thick-sighted: thence proceeds mawkishness.....

Clearly, this preface was not likely to encourage the wavering purchaser; and there is accuracy in its recognition of a quality of adolescent immaturity about *Endymion*. Adolescence has other aspects; but we may regard as 'adolescent' qualities a sensuous excitability, an emotional vagrancy, vague ambitions and yearnings, a tendency to confuse ideals with auto-erotic reveries, and a lack of that discipline and control provided by sufficient experience of the real world with its multiple demands and responsibilities. Throughout Keats's poetic career, there were to be weaknesses related to these 'adolescent' characteristics; but, as is shown by that preface (and indeed by the allegory of *Endymion* itself), he was aware of these deficiencies and concerned to control them.

## The odes

ON THE TERM 'ODE'. The word 'ode' comes from the Greek ψδή (*ōidē*), meaning 'song'. Originally an ode was a poem to be sung. Gradually the term came to mean 'a poem of exalted, lyrical or enthusiastic tone, generally addressed to some living or inanimate object'. It varies in length between 30 and 200 lines. There is a tradition of relatively sober, 'personal' odes extending from Horace (Andrew Marvell's 'Horatian Ode' is an example), and there is a tradition of relatively excited, 'choral' odes extending from Pindar (Gray's 'The Progress of Poesy' and 'The Bard' provide examples). Stanzas may be regular, as in Shelley's 'Ode to the West Wind', or irregular (in which case they may be termed 'strophes'), as in Wordsworth's 'Intimations of Immortality'. Thus, like some other literary-generic terms, the term 'ode' has become so capacious as to be little informative.

Of Keats's odes, 'To Psyche' is in the tradition of irregularity established by Cowley and Dryden (who had apparently not seen that Pindar was regular, and thought they were imitating him): the strophes vary in length, the rhyme-scheme is elaborate and varies from strophe to strophe, and though most lines have five feet, some have three. The ode 'Lines on seeing a Lock of Milton's Hair' is extremely irregular. In the sonnet 'If by dull rhymes our English must be chain'd', Keats had complained that the traditional rhyme-schemes of the sonnet imposed severe limitations; the stanzas of his odes may partly result from his desire to give greater flexibility to the sonnet. 'On Melancholy', 'On Indolence', 'To a Nightingale' and 'On a Grecian Urn' use a ten-line stanza whose rhyme-scheme combines the quatrain of a Shakespearian sonnet (ABAB) with the sestet of a Petrarchan sonnet (normally CDECDE, which Keats sometimes varies as CDEDCE or CDECED). 'Ode to a Nightingale' substitutes a trimeter for a pentameter in the eighth line of each stanza. 'To Autumn' has an eleven-line stanza, the Shakespearian quatrain (ABAB) being followed by a septet (rhyming CDEDCCE, CDECDDE and CDECDDE respectively).

G. S. Fraser writes: 'These ten- and eleven-line stanzas are just long enough to express a complex modulation of thought and feeling but not so long as to run the risk of becoming, like a sonnet in a sonnet-sequence, isolated poems in themselves'; and he rightly points out that these odes owe less in spirit to previous odes than to Shakespeare's sonnets, 'in their erotic evocation of spring and autumn weather, [and] in their combination of formal beauty and opulence of rhetoric with extreme intimacy of tone' (GSF, 13, 14).

If, as we read, we become very conscious of the form of a poem, this often indicates that something is going wrong with the poem: we may have sensed jarring rhymes or an awkward juggling with phrases. One measure of the success of the odes written by Keats in 1819 is the extent to which we are unaware of their formal patterning until we choose to count the rhymes and make formal analysis. Though not unblemished, these odes are among the finest in the language: the formal restraints generally intensify the experience (or generate the experience of intensification), while the formal flexibility permits fluency.

'ODE TO PSYCHE' and 'ODE ON INDOLENCE'. In the subsequent sections, I give close attention to the most complex and problematic of the odes. In this section, I give a briefer commentary on the 'Ode to Psyche' and 'Ode on Indolence', which are more straightforwardly descriptive and less searching in thought.

In classical legend, Cupid, the winged love-god, had fallen in love with the nymph Psyche and had often made love to her by night in blissful Arcadian bowers; eventually, after Cupid's intercession with Jupiter, Psyche became a winged goddess. In the 'Ode to Psyche', Keats changes the legend so that she is already 'winged' at the time of the sylvan embraces. (The Latin word *cupido* means 'desire' or 'love'. Cupid has wings because love can come and go rapidly, can surmount obstacles, and can make one feel exalted. The Greek word *psyche*, φῡχή, means both 'soul' and 'butterfly', and sometimes 'moth'. Psyche has wings because the soul is thought to transcend the body, just as the butterfly arises from the caterpillar's 'corpse', the chrysalis. The legend of Cupid's love for Psyche is, among other things, a way of saying not only that a lover may seek to engross the very soul of his beloved, but also that the exaltation of love may encourage belief in the transcendent power of the soul.) In the ode, the poet first describes his vision of the two lovers embracing 'on the bedded grass'; he then praises the beauty of Psyche, regrets that she was admitted too late to the Pantheon to be the object of rituals of worship, and says that to make amends he will himself be her priest and will create in his imagination a natural sylvan and floral temple for her glory and pleasure.

The poem has the customary Keatsian abundance of literary sources. Lemprière's *Bibliotheca Classica* had provided the idea of Psyche's tardy godhead ('this personification ..... is posterior to the Augustan age'). The version of the legend given in William Adlington's translation (1566) of *The Golden Ass* of Apuleius may have suggested the idyllic sylvan and floral setting. Mrs Tighe's *Psyche* (1811) provided a precedent for the poem's reference to Psyche as a dove. Spenser's description of 'The Garden of Adonis' in *The Faerie Queene* (Book III, Canto vi) and Milton's 'On the Morning of Christ's Nativity' probably provided further descriptive hints. What emerges is a celebratory vision of idealised love, enthusiastic and affirmative, unclouded by Keats's familiar doubts, misgivings and sense of mortality. The poet is almost too much at ease in this dream of 'soft delight'; but there are still some ripples of linguistic energy, as in the concluding lines:

> A rosy sanctuary will I dress
> With the wreath'd trellis of a working brain,
>   With buds, and bells, and stars without a name,
> With all the gardener Fancy e'er could feign,
>   Who breeding flowers, will never breed the same:
> And there shall be for thee all soft delight
>   That shadowy thought can win,
> A bright torch, and a casement ope at night,
>   To let the warm Love in!

It is the 'wreath'd trellis of a working brain' that most commands interest: a bold fusion of the imagined garden with the brain doing the imagining. The 'wreath'd trellis' is, firstly, the wooden trellis-work of the imaginary bower, interwoven by the entwining rose-growth, and created by the poet's mind; secondly, and subordinately, it is a metaphor for the working of that mind, for as the rose seeks to intertwine the trellis, so the fancy seeks to enrich in images of life and beauty the framework of intersecting ideas (as in this ode itself); and thirdly, fleetingly, it evokes the very physical texture and appearance of the brain's surface which (as the former medical student knew) is a delicately elaborate organic trellis-work of lines and whorling wrinkles.

As for the concluding images: their felicity lies largely in the transition from the imaginary pastoral bower of bliss to more familiar, tangibly domestic, places of bliss in the present: that 'casement', implying a hinged window and therefore a house arising from the fanciful Arcadia, invites Love to travel from dreamlands of ancient legend to now – perhaps to Wentworth Place, Hampstead, where Keats and Fanny were neighbours in 1819. A torch at an open window would be an appropriate signal for the god who was so often depicted in poem and painting as a torch-bearer; it could be a beacon guiding a human lover to the sexual destination; and we all know that on a warm dark summer's night, when a lamp is burning in the room, various winged creatures fly in through the open casement, drawn to the hot brightness from the garden's blackness. The phrase 'the warm Love' evokes simultaneously three things: one, a tangible Cupid; two, the incarnate ideal of human love; and three, a particular human being who is the ideal's incarnation.

'Ode on Indolence' proves that virtually any attitude can be lent sanction by judicious quotation from the Bible. Its epigraph is 'They toil not, neither do they spin': a quotation from the Gospel of St. Matthew, Chapter vi, verse 28, in which Jesus had been commending the example of the idle and beautiful lilies of the field. The narrator of the ode determines to follow, in his way, the Biblical precept. He says that he has had a waking-dream vision of three mysterious white-robed figures; he identified them as 'Love', 'Ambition' and 'my demon Poesy'. Initially, he longed to follow them, but now he is resolved to dismiss all three:

> They faded, and, forsooth! I wanted wings:
> O folly! What is Love? and where is it?
> And for that poor Ambition – it springs
> From a man's little heart's short fever-fit;
> For Poesy! – no, – she has not a joy, –
> At least for me, – so sweet as drowsy noons,
> And evenings steep'd in honied indolence;
> O, for an age so shelter'd from annoy,
> That I may never know how change the moons,
> Or hear the voice of busy common-sense!

And thus Keats makes poetry out of the rejection of poetry, and works hard on a formally-taxing ode which celebrates mere 'honied indolence'. The poet dismisses this sequence of visions in order to turn to less troublesome ones:

> Farewell! I yet have visions for the night,
> And for the day faint visions there is store.....

An ascetic reader may wish to repudiate sternly the poem's unmanly commendation of the Deadly Sin of Sloth. A sympathetic reader may notice that the poem's strength, such as it has, is related to the possible virtue of truth – a measure of truth to common experience of states of feeling. Although the three robed figures are distinctively Keatsian – three characters in search of a Grecian Urn – the drowsy waking-dream state is persuasively evoked, and we are reminded of the intermittent appeal of 'evenings steep'd in honied indolence'. The descriptive passages have some characteristic felicities: 'flowers, and stirring shades, and baffled beams'; 'The open casement press'd a new-leaved vine,/ Let in the budding warmth'. Equally, there is some derivative-sounding poetical diction: 'throstle's lay' and 'in her lids hung the sweet tears of May'. A significant weakness is the element of callow posturing, as in:

> For I would not be dieted with praise,
> A pet-lamb in a sentimental farce!

When Keats aspires to the magisterial, he sometimes attains the petulant.

### I

No, no, go not to Lethe, neither twist
   Wolf's-bane, tight-rooted, for its poisonous wine;
Nor suffer thy pale forehead to be kiss'd
   By nightshade, ruby grape of Proserpine;
5  Make not your rosary of yew-berries,
    Nor let the beetle, nor the death-moth be
     Your mournful Psyche, nor the downy owl
A partner in your sorrow's mysteries;
    For shade to shade will come too drowsily,
10    And drown the wakeful anguish of the soul.

### II

But when the melancholy fit shall fall
   Sudden from heaven like a weeping cloud,
That fosters the droop-headed flowers all,
   And hides the green hill in an April shroud;
15  Then glut thy sorrow on a morning rose,
    Or on the rainbow of the salt sand-wave,
     Or on the wealth of globèd peonies;
Or if thy mistress some rich anger shows,
    Imprison her soft hand, and let her rave,
20    And feed deep, deep upon her peerless eyes.

### III

She dwells with Beauty – Beauty that must die;
   And Joy, whose hand is ever at his lips
Bidding adieu; and aching Pleasure nigh,
   Turning to poison while the bee-mouth sips:
25  Ay, in the very temple of Delight
    Veil'd Melancholy has her sovran shrine,
     Though seen of none save him whose strenuous tongue
Can burst Joy's grape against his palate fine;
    His soul shall taste the sadness of her might,
    And be among her cloudy trophies hung.

This poem, written probably in May 1819, is one of the great odes of Keats, and it has a sumptuous sensuousness; but the logical structure is not always clear, and the commentator may find himself nudging, prodding and pulling at the sense here and there in order to increase the validity of the poem's reasoning. I shall try to resist the temptation to smooth the sense and will preserve some of its awkwardness.

    *Paraphrase. Stanza 1:* Do not go to Lethe, the river in the underworld that gives oblivion to the dead when they drink of it, and do not commit suicide by taking the poisons wolfsbane or deadly nightshade, nor turn to things associated with graveyards and death; for then in the underworld your shade (your ghost) will remain too drowsy in its meeting with other shades, instead of preserving a wakeful anguish. (Keats's heterodox idea appears to be that if you poison the body you drug the soul, so that in the after-life the soul of a suicide will be stupefied.)

*Stanza 2:* Instead, do this. When a fit of melancholy falls as suddenly as an April shower that fosters the flowers and enshrouds the hill, glut your sorrow by contemplating the beauty of a morning rose, or the rainbow caused by sunlight shining through sea-spray, or the wealth of peonies in bloom. Or, if your mistress is angry, grip her hand, let her rave on, and enjoy the beauty of her incomparable eyes.

*Stanza 3:* She is one with Beauty (which must die), with Joy (which is always transient), and with aching pleasure (a nectar which turns to poison as you sip it). Indeed, the very temple of pleasure contains Melancholy's shrine, though this will be recognised only by the most strenuous pleasure-seeker; his soul will be vanquished by Melancholy and hung among her other cloudy trophies.

Thus it ends. The central paradox emerges if we summarise the poem in one sentence. When you are melancholy, do not commit suicide; instead, seek palliatives – the beauties and pleasures of life; although, the more intensely you seek such palliatives, the more you will be conquered by Melancholy, who lurks at the heart of them! The logic of the poem is rather fuzzy: if melancholy is by definition a state in which one does not experience joy, then the recommendation of beauties and pleasures as though they were a concomitant of melancholy ('glut thy sorrow on a morning rose') seems to verge on self-contradiction. Of course, we can make sense of the reasoning by thinking of these pleasures as mitigating intervals within a prevailing mood of sadness; but this reading is resisted by the poem's initial dramatisation of contrast.

In the first stanza, the logical relationship between 'go not to Lethe' and the subsequent advice not to commit suicide by poisoning, is not very clear, since the phrasing ('go not to Lethe, neither twist . . . . .') suggests that Lethe's oblivion is an alternative to suicide; yet the soul of the suicide would in the underworld have access to the river Lethe. If 'going to Lethe' means merely 'seeking oblivion in *this* world', its classical image is conflictingly confused with the later classical imagery of the otherworld ('shade to shade will come too drowsily'). In lines 6–7, the reference to Psyche ('Nor let the beetle, nor the death-moth be/ Your mournful Psyche') constitutes an etymological pun, since Psyche is the Greek word for both 'soul' and 'butterfly'. The sense is: 'Don't let your soul, which should be represented by a butterfly, be represented by base or ugly insects associated with graveyards and mortality – the beetle and the death's-head moth.'

The lines 'Ay, in the very temple of Delight/ Veil'd Melancholy has her sovran shrine', coming after the reference to the mistress (and to 'aching' pleasure and a sipping bee-mouth), acquire the central meaning that even the intensities of sexual pleasure entail sorrow; though a central meaning is not the sole meaning, and the abstractness of the phrasing also permits the more general gloss, that melancholy is to be found at the heart of every pleasure. The justifications for the claim are:

1 the traditional maxim, *post coitum homo tristis* – that after coitus one feels sad;
2 the physiological and psychological fact that feelings of pleasure are generally proportionate to prior feelings of displeasure – the pleasure of drinking a glass of water is proportionate to the previous displeasure of thirst; and
3 the logical fact that pleasure and displeasure, joy and sadness, are mutually defining concepts, so one is logically dependent on the other.

The attempt at paraphrase draws attention to those parts of the ode which are either too vague or too good to be paraphrased readily. An example of the vagueness is the conclusion:

> His soul shall taste the sadness of her might,
> And be among her cloudy trophies hung.

Here the idea of a soul which is capable of tasting and which yet can be hung up like a suit of armour or some other trophy of war strains the visualising imagination; but it resembles the mixed metaphors of Shakespeare, and Keats may have in mind Shakespeare's sonnet 31, lines 9–10:

> Thou art the grave where buried love doth live,
> Hung with the trophies of my lovers gone.....

Keats marked these lines in his copy of Shakespeare's poems, making the marginal note 'conceit'.

Another Shakespearian passage marked by Keats was *Troilus and Cressida*, Act III, scene ii, lines 19–24:

> What will it be
> When that the wat'ry palate tastes indeed
> Love's thrice-repurèd nectar? Death, I fear me;
> Sounding destruction; or some joy too fine,
> Too subtile-potent, tun'd too sharp in sweetness
> For the capacity of my ruder powers.....

This passage appears to lie behind the imagery of Keats's lines

23–8, with their linkage of nectar, intense pleasure, a 'palate fine' and death.

Phrasing so good that it defies paraphrase occurs at lines 22–3: 'And Joy, whose hand is ever at his lips/Bidding adieu'. The boldness of the living rendition of the abstract again evokes Shakespeare, particularly the Shakespeare of that *Troilus and Cressida* period ('Time hath, my lord, a wallet at his back/Wherein he puts alms for oblivion'). The paradox of the simultaneously eternal yet transient ('ever at his lips, bidding adieu') anticipates the paradoxes of the Grecian Urn, and here generates an oddly vivid picture of a smiling figure, ever receding yet never vanishing, blowing kisses as he dwindles. (Keats, dying, was to say of Fanny Brawne, 'I eternally see her figure eternally vanishing' [R II, 345].)

There are numerous examples of Keats's power of sensuous diction. One of the best is:

> Then glut thy sorrow on a morning rose,
> > Or on the rainbow of the salt sand-wave,
> > > Or on the wealth of globèd peonies.....

Particularly forceful here is the rich word 'glut', which Keats substituted for his original weaker choice, 'feed'. 'Glut', apart from its oral fulness, has the useful ambiguity of suggesting both 'feed to the full' and 'overcome by abundance', linking the idea of indulging one's melancholy with the idea of overcoming it. The double alliteration of 'gl' in 'glut' is echoed in 'globèd', which in turn gives a sense of three-dimensional hollow bulginess to the idea of round blooms. Another memorable allusion whose evocative precision is enriched by the interlacing of assonance and alliteration is:

> him whose strenuous tongue
> Can burst Joy's grape against his palate fine.

This ode shows that Keats has an important position as an intermediary between the 'Cult of Sensibility' of the eighteenth century and the Aestheticism of the nineteenth century. The former cult, illustrated by parts of Sterne's *Tristram Shandy* and *A Sentimental Journey*, and particularly by Mackenzie's *The Man of Feeling*, encouraged the reader to relish melancholy and sorrow, to value those occasions which elicit a pitying tear accompanied, perhaps, by a wistful smile. 'Sensibility' may encourage charity to those deserving it; or it may encourage a rather narcissistic indulgence in emotion, an aesthetic connoisseurship of the world of suffering rather than an altruistic concern for that world. We see the temptation of aesthetic connoisseurship in lines 18–20 of this ode:

> Or if thy mistress some rich anger shows,
> > Imprison her soft hand, and let her rave,
> > > And feed deep, deep upon her peerless eyes.

This is all very well for the lover but may justly exacerbate the fury of the angry mistress. The lines anticipate the self-indulgent feelings which became stock matter of the minor poetry of the late nineteenth century, in which love and beauty are so often associated with sorrow and mourning, and woman is so often seen as a beautiful extern for mournful contemplation rather than as an active being in a social world.

Thus, although the 'Ode on Melancholy' is one of Keats's best poems, it has a clear relationship to much decadent, stock-response poetry. However, a father is not necessarily to blame for the sins of wayward sons; and a comparison of samples of Aesthetic melancholy verse (for example, Yeats's 'The Sad Shepherd', 'The Cloak, the Boat and the Shoes', 'The Falling of the Leaves' and 'Ephemera', or Arthur Symons's 'Wanderer's Song') with Keats's ode emphasises the predictable downward drift of feeling in the former and the energetically resilient movements of feeling and imagination in the latter.

Let us look at Yeats's 'Ephemera', published in 1899:

> 'Your eyes that once were never weary of mine
> Are bowed in sorrow under pendulous lids,
> Because our love is waning.'
>                    And then she:
> 'Although our love is waning, let us stand
> By the lone border of the lake once more,
> Together in that hour of gentleness
> When the poor tired child, Passion, falls asleep.
> How far away the stars seem, and how far
> Is our first kiss, and ah, how old my heart!'
> Pensive they paced along the faded leaves,
> While slowly he whose hand held hers replied:
> 'Passion has often worn our wandering hearts.'
>
> The woods were round them, and the yellow leaves
> Fell like faint meteors in the gloom, and once
> A rabbit old and lame limped down the path;
> Autumn was over him: and now they stood
> On the lone border of the lake once more:
> Turning, he saw that she had thrust dead leaves
> Gathered in silence, dewy as her eyes,
> In bosom and hair.
>              'Ah, do not mourn,' he said,
> 'That we are tired, for other loves await us;
> Hate on and love through unrepining hours.
> Before us lies eternity; our souls
> Are love, and a continual farewell.'

Some of the ingredients resemble those of Keats's ode: melancholy, transience, love, beauty, a woman whose hand is held by her lover. But even that last reference points a difference: the lover in Yeats's poem is 'he whose hand held hers', whereas in Keats's ode the lover is told to 'Imprison her soft hand' – *imprison* being a much stronger verb that implies attempted resistance, a will to escape. In 'Ephemera', everything tones in, predictably and unsurprisingly: sorrow, waning love, lone border of a lake, sleeping passion; eyelids are pendulous; the leaves are (of course) fading, yellow and dead, and if they fall like meteors, these must be 'faint' meteors; the time of year is inevitably autumn; and the rabbit has to be an old and lame one which cannot run but can only limp down the path. The poem has an easy and predictable unity of feeling; one is invited to enter a soft drift of melancholy emotion; intelligence can rest. Compared with that, Keats is taxing and astringently intelligent: his poem warns us against a drowsy fate and offers us contrasts: against wolfsbane, nightshade and the death-moth he sets April showers, roses and peonies; against poison, he sets the bursting of Joy's grape upon the fine palate. Yeats seeks to entrance, Keats to engage.

'ODE TO A NIGHTINGALE'

### I

My heart aches, and a drowsy numbness pains
　　My sense, as though of hemlock I had drunk,
Or emptied some dull opiate to the drains
　　One minute past, and Lethe-wards had sunk:
5　'Tis not through envy of thy happy lot,
　　But being too happy in thine happiness –
　　　That thou, light-wingèd Dryad of the trees,
　　　　In some melodious plot
　　Of beechen green, and shadows numberless,
10　　　Singest of summer in full-throated ease.

### II

O, for a draught of vintage! that hath been
　　Cool'd a long age in the deep-delvèd earth,
Tasting of Flora and the country green,
　　Dance, and Provençal song, and sunburnt mirth!
15　O for a beaker full of the warm South,
　　Full of the true, the blushful Hippocrene,
　　　With beaded bubbles winking at the brim,
　　　　And purple-stainèd mouth;
　　That I might drink, and leave the world unseen,
20　　　And with thee fade away into the forest dim:

*Keats's early draft of 'Ode to a Nightingale'.*

This illustration shows the first page of the draft. There are numerous petty differences between this text and that published in 1820: for example, 'the Nightingale' became 'a Nightingale', 'the true and blushful' became 'the true, the blushful', 'cluster'd bubbles' became 'beaded bubbles', and the punctuation was regularised. Particularly interesting are the alterations of first to second thoughts: 'painful numbness falls' changes to 'drowsy numbness pains', 'minute hence' to 'minute past', 'Cooling an age' to 'Cool'd a long age', and 'pale and thin and old' to 'pale and spectre-thin and dies'.

### III

Fade far away, dissolve, and quite forget
    What thou among the leaves hast never known,
The weariness, the fever, and the fret
    Here, where men sit and hear each other groan;
25  Where palsy shakes a few, sad, last gray hairs,
      Where youth grows pale, and spectre-thin, and dies;
        Where but to think is to be full of sorrow
        And leaden-eyed despairs,
      Where Beauty cannot keep her lustrous eyes,
30       Or new Love pine at them beyond to-morrow.

### IV

Away! away! for I will fly to thee,
    Not charioted by Bacchus and his pards,
But on the viewless wings of Poesy,
    Though the dull brain perplexes and retards:
35  Already with thee! tender is the night,
      And haply the Queen-Moon is on her throne,
        Cluster'd around by all her starry Fays;
        But here there is no light,
      Save what from heaven is with the breezes blown
40       Through verdurous glooms and winding mossy ways.

### V

I cannot see what flowers are at my feet,
    Nor what soft incense hangs upon the boughs,
But, in embalmèd darkness, guess each sweet
    Wherewith the seasonable month endows
45  The grass, the thicket, and the fruit-tree wild;
      White hawthorn, and the pastoral eglantine;
        Fast fading violets cover'd up in leaves;
        And mid-May's eldest child,
      The coming musk-rose, full of dewy wine,
50       The murmurous haunt of flies on summer eves.

### VI

Darkling I listen; and, for many a time
    I have been half in love with easeful Death,
Call'd him soft names in many a musèd rhyme,
    To take into the air my quiet breath;
55  Now more than ever seems it rich to die,
      To cease upon the midnight with no pain,
        While thou art pouring forth thy soul abroad

In such an ecstasy!
Still wouldst thou sing, and I have ears in vain –
60      To thy high requiem become a sod.

## VII
Thou wast not born for death, immortal Bird!
No hungry generations tread thee down;
The voice I hear this passing night was heard
In ancient days by emperor and clown:
65 Perhaps the self-same song that found a path
Through the sad heart of Ruth, when, sick for home,
She stood in tears amid the alien corn;
The same that oft-times hath
Charm'd magic casements, opening on the foam
70      Of perilous seas, in faery lands forlorn.

## VIII
Forlorn! the very word is like a bell
To toll me back from thee to my sole self!
Adieu! the fancy cannot cheat so well
As she is fam'd to do, deceiving elf.
75 Adieu! adieu! thy plaintive anthem fades
Past the near meadows, over the still stream,
Up the hill-side; and now 'tis buried deep
In the next valley-glades:
Was it a vision, or a waking dream?
80      Fled is that music: – Do I wake or sleep?

The nightingale is a bird with a long literary pedigree, from Ovid's
*Metamorphoses* to T. S. Eliot's *The Waste Land* and beyond. Because
Romantics valued spontaneous lyrical utterance, this bird and her
song (like the skylark and hers) were especially prominent in
Romantic poetry; and Keats was probably familiar with Cowden
Clarke's 'The Nightingale', with Charlotte Smith's 'To a
Nightingale' and 'On the Departure of the Nightingale' in her
*Elegiac Sonnets* (1784), and Coleridge's 'To the Nightingale' (1796)
and 'The Nightingale: A Conversation Poem' (1798). On 11 April
1819 he had walked on Hampstead Heath with Coleridge, who
discoursed on 'Nightingales, Poetry – on Poetical sensation –
Metaphysics – Different genera and species of Dreams' (R II,
88–9). Keats's poem stands out from the others by virtue of its
adroit oscillations in response and its vivid patterning of contrasts.
    Stanza VII was apparently influenced, probably subconsciously,
by Wordsworth's 'The Solitary Reaper' (1807), which describes a
girl singing as she works in a remote corn-field. This (and Cowden
Clarke's claim that the bird's song is 'full of ruth') may have

suggested to Keats 'the sad heart of Ruth . . . . . amid the alien corn';
and his

> magic casements, opening on the foam
> Of perilous seas, in faery lands forlorn

may stem from a recollection of Wordsworth's second stanza:

> No Nightingale did ever chaunt
> More welcome notes to weary bands
> Of travellers in some shady haunt,
> Among Arabian sands:
> A voice so thrilling ne'er was heard
> In spring-time from the Cuckoo-bird,
> Breaking the silence of the seas
> Among the farthest Hebrides.

(WP, 230)

Keats's nightingale was engendered by a real bird as well as many
literary ones. Charles Brown recalled:

> In the spring of 1819 a nightingale had built her nest near my
> house. Keats felt a continual and tranquil joy in her song; and
> one morning he took a chair from the breakfast-table to the
> grass-plot under a plum-tree, where he sat for two or three hours.
> When he came into the house, I perceived he had some scraps of
> paper in his hand, and these he was quietly thrusting behind the
> books. On inquiry, I found those scraps, four or five in number,
> contained his poetic feeling on the song of our nightingale. . . . .

(KC II, 65)

The poem's pattern of oscillations, its recurrent pressure towards
paradox, is established in the very first stanza. 'My heart aches, and
a drowsy numbness pains/ My sense': the speaker is numbed and
drawn down towards a deathly oblivion – but not through grief, we
learn with surprise, but through an excess of happiness occasioned
by the bird's carefree song of summer. The early stress on
drowsiness, numbness and dulness heightens by contrast the later
emphasis on the bird's freedom, mobility, joy, fluency and bright
surroundings.

The poet then calls for wine, 'a beaker full of the warm South',
that he may drink and fade away into the forest with the nightingale;
thus he would escape 'the weariness, the fever, and the fret' of
human life with its sorrows. But he changes his mind: he will fly to
the bird not through intoxication but through the agency of the
poetic imagination; and for a moment he thinks he is succeeding:

> Already with thee! tender is the night,

> And haply the Queen-Moon is on her throne,
>   Cluster'd around by all her starry Fays.....

But at once common sense obtrudes. The poet isn't up there amid moon and stars – he's down here in the gloom:

> But here there is no light,
> Save what from heaven is with the breezes blown
>   Through verdurous glooms and winding mossy ways.

However, although he cannot *see* the flowers at his feet or the blossoms above, he can use his nose to discriminate between the rich perfumes in the darkness: hawthorn, eglantine, violets, and vinous musk-rose.

Death has often seemed attractive to him; and now it would be particularly rich to die while the bird is singing so ecstatically – but then, if he were dead, he wouldn't be able to hear it. In any case, the bird was not born for death: it is immortal, for this same song was heard in the past by high and low; the Biblical Ruth, in exile, may have been consoled by it; and the song may have sounded in 'faery lands forlorn' – 'forlorn' meaning 'long lost, untrodden by men'. But, of course, that word 'forlorn' has a sadder meaning – 'forsaken, alone and desolate' – which reminds the poet of his own situation, not in distant fairy lands but here and now; he has not, after all, been seduced by fanciful notions. And the bird itself is flying away, so that its song fades:

> Was it a vision, or a waking dream?
> Fled is that music: – Do I wake or sleep?

In other words: 'In my entranced state, was I having a visionary insight or merely a daydream? Now that the music has gone, am I awakened to reality or merely returned to that slumber of the spirit which is everyday existence?'

It is a sign of the strength of the poem that the final questions are hard to answer: the evidence for the alternative answers has been so evenly presented. The transcendental and the mundane, the lofty and the earthy, have been richly contrasted yet also intermingled.

The poem works admirably as a whole; but, within that whole, notable areas of richness are lines 11–18, with their evocation not merely of wine but of the sunny south and the land of festive pastoral (which emphasise by contrast the weariness and ill-health stressed in the next stanza); and lines 38–50, with their description of the odorous plenitude of night. The phrasing

> no light,
> Save what from heaven is with the breezes blown
>   Through verdurous glooms and winding mossy ways

is question-begging (how can light be blown?) but answers the question deftly by summoning up recollections of the kind of gleam and shimmer created by breezes blowing through leaves and over mossy grass on moonlit nights. Stanza V is full of pleasures for oral sensualists, the best occurring at the end:

> And mid-May's eldest child,
> The coming musk-rose, full of dewy wine,
> The murmurous haunt of flies on summer eves.

The sensuousness is accentuated by the alliteration of 'm', which approaches onomatopoeia ('mid-May', 'coming', 'musk', 'murmurous', 'summer'), by the 'f' repetition ('full', 'flies'), the assonance ('child', 'wine', 'flies'; 'murmurous', 'summer') and by the resultant interplay of related sounds ('m', 'f', 'v'). (In these lines Keats is both beckoning Tennyson and partly echoing *A Midsummer Night's Dream*, Act II, scene i, lines 249–52, in which Oberon describes a floral bank over-canopied 'with luscious woodbine,/ With sweet musk-roses, and with eglantine'.)

Such sensuous pleasures have their place in a complex dialectical structure. It's a sign of the strength of this ode that just as the reader begins to think 'Oh, this is too airy-fairy, this is too fanciful, this is too conventionally romantic' – at exactly those places the poet himself briskly shifts stance, challenging his own temptations. At lines 35–7, for example, we have what promises to be the rather prissily poetical and literary, signalled by the slightly archaic diction (*'haply* the Queen-Moon is on her throne', 'Cluster'd around by *all her starry Fays'*): yet blunt common sense promptly enters with 'But here there is no light', just as the ideal of death amid ecstasy is deflated at lines 59–60 by simple fact – 'Still wouldst thou sing, and I have ears in vain –/ To thy high requiem become a sod.' (The juxtaposition with the loftily abstract and latinate 'high requiem' makes the Germanic word 'sod' seem the more curt and earthy.)

The claim (in line 61) that the nightingale is immortal drew the hostile comment from Robert Bridges that this idea is 'fanciful or superficial, – man being as immortal as the bird in every sense but that of sameness': but it is the very idea of 'sameness' that provides the poetic vindication of the claim. Men sing a diversity of songs; their utterances down the ages make a cacophony, a babel; they have a multitude of languages. But the nightingale, as known by its song, is beautiful, eloquent and unchanging; the song endures and knows neither historical nor geographical frontiers. This point is well made by the contrasts in stanza VII: the nightingale is heard 'by emperor and clown'; it may have been heard by the historic Ruth and in enchanted lands. 'Alien corn' is a tersely precise phrase; and 'the *foam* of perilous seas' gives brief reality to those 'faery lands' from which the poet will rapidly be recalled to the present.

There are a few weaknesses. For example, the list of men's woes, at lines 23–30, is rather facile and predictable. Nevertheless, a passage on earthly wretchedness has a valuable part to play in the whole argumentative structure; and the line 'Where youth grows pale, and spectre-thin, and dies' will have plangent resonance for readers who remember that Keats's brother Tom had wasted away with tuberculosis and died a few months previously at the age of nineteen. (The incorporation of such extra-textual information in one's response to the poem is entirely proper: the frequency of deaths by consumption in those days would have made the line more factual and less sentimental than it would seem to a modern reader ignorant of such mortality. Ignorance that deprives one of both understanding and pleasure is not worth preserving.)

Another fault is that in the last stanza the word 'elf' jars:

> Adieu! the fancy cannot cheat so well
> As she is fam'd to do, deceiving elf.

One reason for the jarring effect is that an elf (a creature often mischievous or malignant) seems an inappropriate personification of a 'fancy' which has been intermittently equated with the consolatory or aspiring imagination; and another reason is that to use the oddly fanciful term 'elf' seems unsuitable at a time of recollection from the fanciful to the mundane. My explanation of this elf is that Keats needed a rhyme-word for 'self' at the end of line 72, and 'elf' came by reflex. The *Concordance to the Poems of John Keats* (1981), verified by my computer-analyses, lists seven other occasions on which Keats uses the word 'elf' in a poem. In six cases, 'elf' comes at the end of a line and as a rhyme-word; and in all six cases, it rhymes with the syllable 'self'. Of course, this blemish is tiny, and computers are seldom humane to elves. The poem as a whole remains one of the finest dramatised meditations on man, mortality, nature and beauty.

If we want to know what a nightingale looks like, Keats's ode will be no use to us: for the naturalist's data, we should read John Clare's 'The Nightingale's Nest'. What Keats provides is a dramatisation of the bird's cultural significance to a self-aware poet of the Romantic Movement; and as Romanticism (commending attitudes varying from altruistic idealism to selfish hedonism) continues today, so does the relevance of his ode.

'ODE ON A GRECIAN URN'

I

Thou still unravish'd bride of quietness,
    Thou foster-child of silence and slow time,

130

Sylvan historian, who canst thus express
    A flowery tale more sweetly than our rhyme:
5  What leaf-fring'd legend haunts about thy shape
        Of deities or mortals, or of both,
            In Tempe or the dales of Arcady?
    What men or gods are these? What maidens loth?
    What mad pursuit? What struggle to escape?
10          What pipes and timbrels? What wild ecstasy?


## II

Heard melodies are sweet, but those unheard
    Are sweeter; therefore, ye soft pipes, play on;
Not to the sensual ear, but, more endear'd,
    Pipe to the spirit ditties of no tone:
15 Fair youth, beneath the trees, thou canst not leave
        Thy song, nor ever can those trees be bare;
            Bold lover, never, never canst thou kiss,
    Though winning near the goal – yet, do not grieve;
        She cannot fade, though thou hast not thy bliss,
20      For ever wilt thou love, and she be fair!


## III

Ah, happy, happy boughs! that cannot shed
    Your leaves, nor ever bid the spring adieu;
And, happy melodist, unwearièd,
    For ever piping songs for ever new;
25 More happy love! more happy, happy love!
        For ever warm and still to be enjoy'd,
            For ever panting, and for ever young;
    All breathing human passion far above,
        That leaves a heart high-sorrowful and cloy'd,
30      A burning forehead, and a parching tongue.


## IV

Who are these coming to the sacrifice?
    To what green altar, O mysterious priest,
Lead'st thou that heifer lowing at the skies,
    And all her silken flanks with garlands drest?
35 What little town by river or sea shore,
        Or mountain-built with peaceful citadel,
            Is emptied of this folk, this pious morn?
    And, little town, thy streets for evermore
        Will silent be; and not a soul to tell
40      Why thou art desolate, can e'er return.

O Attic shape! Fair attitude! with brede
  Of marble men and maidens overwrought,
With forest branches and the trodden weed;
  Thou, silent form, dost tease us out of thought
45  As doth eternity: Cold Pastoral!
  When old age shall this generation waste,
    Thou shalt remain, in midst of other woe
  Than ours, a friend to man, to whom thou say'st,
  'Beauty is truth, truth beauty,' – that is all
50    Ye know on earth, and all ye need to know.

This is the best of Keats's odes and the greatest of his poems. Here, the main tensions of his creative nature find their most succinct, epigrammatic and elegant expression. This ode has generated a huge and ever-growing body of critical analysis and interpretation; and this body, in all its diversity, validates the poem by confirming the central claim about the urn – that it can 'tease us out of thought'.

The poem's strength lies in the pattern of interwoven paradoxes. The first stanza is quick to breed them. The urn is initially associated with the static and the silent ('quietness', 'silence', 'slow time'), yet by lines 9–10 it has apparently become the scene of wild motion and noise:

What mad pursuit? What struggle to escape?
  What pipes and timbrels? What wild ecstasy?

The paradox is compounded by the fact that initially the urn is associated with the virginal ('still unravish'd bride'), yet the ending of the stanza associates it with the amatory, ecstatic and orgiastic. The very first line has a useful ambiguity: 'still unravish'd' can be read as 'still, unravished' (that is, static and unravished) or as 'still unravished' (that is, unravished as yet). Though a bride, the urn remains intact; she is wedded to quietness, and is unbroken. She is a 'foster-child of silence and slow time' because the artist who made the urn, the 'father', died long ago, and the urn has been adopted by silence and slow time. (The epigrammatic strength of this poem is shown by the way in which it taxes or defies paraphrase. If, for example, you substitute 'history' for 'slow time' you at once lose the important sense that the urn inhabits its own dimension, its own alternative realm whose values are proper to it and different from ours.) Another paradox follows: though the urn is associated with silence, it is a 'historian' – for it tells a story and records a cultural era; and it is a 'sylvan' historian, because its legend is 'leaf-fring'd' – there are overhanging boughs fringing its picture-story, and it offers us a glimpse of the history of a pastoral region. Though silent, it tells a story more ably than a poet can – or so, to compound the paradox, our poet tells us:

> Sylvan historian, who canst thus express
> A flowery tale more sweetly than our rhyme.....

The urn has a distinctive character: it (or she) is mysterious and teasing. The poet speculates about the meaning of the 'leaf-fring'd legend', the pictures on its surface. Is the location Tempe or Arcady? Are these figures men or gods? What does the wild action mean?

The paradox of silent utterance, set by the urn in stanza I, is maintained in stanza II. 'Heard melodies are sweet, but those unheard/ Are sweeter': the pipes in the picture play exquisite music –

> therefore, ye soft pipes, play on;
> Not to the sensual ear, but, more endear'd,
> Pipe to the spirit ditties of no tone.....

The idea is Platonic: that there is an ideal world of eternal abstract forms, of which the familiar world offers only base, material, perishable imitations. As the noblest side of man has access to the ideal world, so here it is 'the spirit' and not 'the sensual ear' which hears the music. 'Ear' generates a half-pun, 'endear'd'. The paradox that the stillness of the urn holds a superior life is maintained in the subsequent lines: the youth's song is endless, the trees will never lose their leaves; and though the lover will never reach the girl to kiss her, his love and her beauty will last for ever.

In stanza III the poet enthuses over the happiness of the urn's world, where spring is permanent, where the piper's melodies are 'ever new', and where love is

> For ever warm and still to be enjoy'd,
> For ever panting, and for ever young;
> All breathing human passion far above.....

The words 'warm' and 'panting' have the effect of imparting the mobile life of flesh and blood to the beings of the urn, while yet this 'panting' world is contrasted with the inferior 'breathing' world of ordinary life in which passion

> leaves a heart high-sorrowful and cloy'd,
> A burning forehead, and a parching tongue.

Then, as though the urn were slowly revolving before the poet's gaze, he questions the new scene revealed: a scene of ritual sacrifice, at which a garlanded heifer is to be sacrificed at an altar. The phrases 'lowing at the skies' and 'silken flanks' again perform the trick of investing with audible, tangible life the urn's world. A town has been emptied of its people to supply the procession; and in mock-pathos the poet commiserates with it:

little town, thy streets for evermore
Will silent be; and not a soul to tell
Why thou art desolate, can e'er return.

If 'little town' sounds sentimental, the sentimentality is feigned and tongue-in-cheek: for the poet knows, as we do (after our brief reprise in which we shake off the imaginative seductions of the phrasing), that the town always has been empty and that the emptiness is no more real than the town.

In the last stanza the poet makes a final survey of the urn; observes that it can 'tease us out of thought', yet is a 'Cold Pastoral'; and says that in the future, amid life's woes, the urn will remain

a friend to man, to whom thou say'st,
'Beauty is truth, truth beauty,' – that is all
Ye know on earth, and all ye need to know.

This conclusion is, of course, the major crux in Keats's work; and critic after critic has grappled with its difficulties of syntax and sense. Miriam Allott summarises the range of options:

> Opinions about the meaning of the beauty-truth equivalent and its relevance to the rest of the poem can be roughly divided as follows: (1) philosophically defensible but of doubtful relevance (Murry); (2) a 'pseudo-statement', but emotionally relevant (I. A. Richards); (3) expressing the paradoxes in the poem and therefore dramatically appropriate (C. Brooks); (4) meaningless and therefore a blemish (T. S. Eliot); (5) an over-simplification, but attempting a positive synthesis of the oppositions expressed in the poem (F. W. Bateson); (6) emotionally and intellectually relevant when properly understood, but 'the effort to see the thing as Keats did is too great to be undertaken with pleasure' (W. Empson).

(A, 538)

We can begin to resolve the problem by supplying the punctuation that the imaginative sense requires. The punctuation should be:

to whom thou say'st,
'"Beauty is truth, truth beauty," – that is all
Ye know on earth, and all ye need to know.'

What this punctuation shows clearly is that the whole of the last two lines is an utterance by the urn. The poet introduces the urn's statement, and 'ye' is an appropriate form of address when a superior being (like this urn) is talking down to inferiors (like mere mortals) – as when Marlowe's Tamburlaine cries 'Holla, ye pampered jades of Asia'. Why, then, is the maxim 'Beauty is truth, truth beauty,' enclosed in further quotation-marks? The answer is that the urn is making a quotation. The urn has endured a long time

134

and has acquired a considerable store of wisdom. (Some real urns did in fact bear moral maxims as inscriptions.) Furthermore, the urn has a distinctive character – it likes to tease us out of thought: it (or she) is a mocking, teasing, paradoxical creature. From its store of wisdom it produces a maxim from Lord Shaftesbury's *Characteristicks* (1711): 'Beauty is truth'; and it elaborates the maxim so as to make it even more difficult. It's as though the urn, teasing, says: 'Here's a paradox for you: "Beauty is truth": and to make the riddle even harder, I'll add its mirror-image: "truth beauty". Sort *that* out if you can. And to make matters even more tantalising, I will tell you "that is all / Ye know on earth" – as though you have already grasped this fact – and that that is "all ye need to know" – as though this riddle provided all things needful.'

And ever since the urn set that riddle, hundreds of commentators have obediently striven to solve it. Such commentators may cite Keats's letters, particularly the passage in which Keats says: 'I am certain of nothing but the holiness of the Heart's affections and the truth of the Imagination. What the imagination seizes as Beauty must be truth.....' (R I, 184), and 'The excellence of every Art is its intensity, capable of making all disagreeables evaporate, from their being in close relationship with Beauty & Truth' (R I, 192). They may cite Shakespeare's 'The Phoenix and the Turtle', with its lines:

> Truth and beauty buried be.
> To this urn let those repair
> That are either true or fair.

And we, trying to make our sense of the last two lines of the ode, may produce glosses like the following. Aesthetic perfection and conceptual truth are ultimately identical; our only real knowledge consists of this intuition, which is implicit in the feeling of aesthetic wonder; and since this is our only real knowledge it is our only necessary knowledge. (The lines have thus become a Platonic hyperbole.) Or again: artefacts suggest that the temporal and the mortal can be translated into the timeless and immortal: the sense of beauty contains this truth, and this truth is at the heart of what we call the sense of beauty.

Thus we may proceed, filling our margins with more and more attempts to solve the riddle of 'Beauty is truth, truth beauty'. *And the urn laughs at our attempts.* The key to the ending is provided by the earlier words:

> Thou, silent form, dost tease us out of thought
> As doth eternity.....

The point about 'eternity' is that it is a word in common use which is immediately understood (when the parson talks of eternity, I know at once what he means) and yet whose meaning utterly defies the imagination when we strive to grasp and visualise it there. We can imagine a year, a thousand years, a million; but if we attempt to imagine eternity, the imagination struggles, flinches and gives up the attempt. That's why the term teases us out of thought.

And the maxim 'Beauty is truth, truth beauty' is like that word 'eternity'. It seems simple and straightforward at first; it sounds as though it has an obvious, immediate sense (and we have all seen pictures and statues that were both beautiful and accurate, just as we have heard truths that were beautifully expressed); yet as soon as we attempt to elucidate its meaning, then, as with the attempt to grasp 'eternity', we find that we are floundering; the explications become more and more entangled, more and more remote from the initial laconic brevity. In short, the ending of the ode is a statement in character by the riddling, paradox-loving urn; and one which appropriately concludes this teasing poem. To enjoy this ode the reader needs a sense of humour. In its play of feeling and intelligence, its dazzling ability to tease and confound, to oscillate between the earnest and the witty, it evokes some of the strengths of the best Metaphysical poetry of the seventeenth century, notably Marvell's 'To His Coy Mistress' and 'Dialogue Between the Soul and the Body'.

The urn is a consolatory 'friend to man'; but also a mocking, tantalising one. The phrase 'Cold Pastoral!' seems less a reproach than an oxymoronic apostrophe. I think that it is a weakness of this fine poem that in stanza III, with the exclamatory repetition of 'happy' ('Ah, happy, happy boughs!..... happy melodist, ..... happy love! more happy, happy love!'), the poet seems to be trying to hypnotise himself into imaginative belief in the urn-world; he protests too much; the note is forced.

Another blemish is the opening of the final stanza:

O Attic shape! Fair attitude! with brede.....

'The last stanza', said Robert Bridges, 'enters stumbling on a pun' – the supposed pun being the part-echo of 'Attic' (meaning 'of Attica, Grecian') in 'attitude' (meaning 'stance or presence'). William Empson says that the line is 'very bad.....; the half pun suggesting a false Greek derivation and jammed against an arty bit of Old English ['brede'] seems to me affected and ugly'. I think Empson is right: the phrasing makes us search for an etymological pun, and we find that there is none; the flow of the poem is interrupted by this obtrusion. 'Attitude' is a weak and inappropriate word; a person can adopt a particular physical attitude, but we strain the sense if we apply the word to an immobile urn. 'Brede' is an archaic poeticism (archaic in Keats's day) meaning 'braid, frieze or woven patterning'. Just possibly Keats intends a homophone with 'breed', so that we may think not only of a pattern of interwoven men and maidens but also of a living generation (breed) of 'marble men and maidens': another oxymoron. However, 'overwrought' fits 'brede' so well as to greatly diminish the homophonic association. 'Overwrought' possibly has a subsidiary sense, referring to the maidens who are overwrought (that is, they are overcome emotionally and physically by the men who struggle with them), as well as the obvious main sense, referring to the artistic working of the design on the surface of the urn.

Although the ode conveys an aestheticised Platonism, whereby works of art are the portals of an eternal other-realm which is superior to mundane actuality, the strength of the poem resides not in any such paraphrasable (and questionable) doctrine, but rather in its complex imaginative dramatisation of tensions, in its interplay of 'cold' and 'warm' life, mobile and immobile, mortal and immortal. The meaning lies in the total experience, which memorably and intelligently evokes an array of questions and notions about the relationship between art and reality. Personally, I do not believe that beauty is truth, for beauty can often deceive; nor do I believe that truth is beauty, for some truths (e.g. about Auschwitz) are ugly. To Platonists, the urn may seem truthful; to empiricists, she may seem a liar. Nevertheless, provided that we preserve a sceptical recognition of her ways, the encounter with the urn's living paradoxes will enhance our eventual understanding of art and life, of various truths and various beauties.

The importance of Keats's choice of a Grecian urn as the artefact for poetic contemplation is made clear if we attempt to substitute, say, a canvas painted by Giorgione. Pigment and canvas are relatively perishable (they darken, crack and rot) whereas an urn may survive without apparent change for thousands of years. A canvas is flat; the urn is round and three-dimensional, and its picture encircles it, so that the design has an endlessness unattainable by the painting. An urn is mineral, cold, hard to the knuckles; the depicted life therefore inhabits a particularly alien environment. The urn is hollow and may be a repository for ashes of the dead. A Grecian urn is a product of, and records, a bygone civilisation long idealised by artists; it has outlasted the culture that produced it. And ancient Greece, as the urn reminds us, is the land both of pastoral and of Plato.

'TO AUTUMN'

I

Season of mists and mellow fruitfulness,
  Close bosom-friend of the maturing sun;
Conspiring with him how to load and bless

With fruit the vines that round the thatch-eaves run;
5   To bend with apples the moss'd cottage-trees,
    And fill all fruit with ripeness to the core;
      To swell the gourd, and plump the hazel shells
    With a sweet kernel; to set budding more,
  And still more, later flowers for the bees,
10 Until they think warm days will never cease,
    For summer has o'er-brimm'd their clammy cells.

### II

  Who hath not seen thee oft amid thy store?
    Sometimes whoever seeks abroad may find
  Thee sitting careless on a granary floor,
15   Thy hair soft-lifted by the winnowing wind;
  Or on a half-reap'd furrow sound asleep,
    Drows'd with the fume of poppies, while thy hook
      Spares the next swath and all its twinèd flowers:
  And sometimes like a gleaner thou dost keep
20   Steady thy laden head across a brook;
    Or by a cyder-press, with patient look,
      Thou watchest the last oozings hours by hours.

### III

  Where are the songs of spring? Ay, where are they?
    Think not of them, thou hast thy music too, –
25 While barrèd clouds bloom the soft-dying day,
    And touch the stubble-plains with rosy hue;
  Then in a wailful choir the small gnats mourn
    Among the river sallows, borne aloft
      Or sinking as the light wind lives or dies;
30 And full-grown lambs loud bleat from hilly bourn;
    Hedge-crickets sing; and now with treble soft
    The red-breast whistles from a garden-croft;
      And gathering swallows twitter in the skies.

If 'Ode on a Grecian Urn' is the most brilliant of the odes, 'To Autumn' is the most assured and free from blemishes. The others had been written in spring 1819; this one, appropriately, was composed in September. On the 21st of that month, Keats, at Winchester, wrote to Reynolds:

> How beautiful the season is now – How fine the air. A temperate sharpness about it. Really, without joking, chaste weather – Dian skies – I never lik'd stubble fields so much as now – Aye better than the chilly green of the spring. Somehow a stubble plain looks warm – this struck me so much in my sunday's walk that I composed upon it.
>
> (R II, 167)

The poem was prompted by art, of course, as well as by nature. We have noted previously the debts to Chatterton's *Ælla*; other probable literary sources were 'Summer' and 'Autumn' in James Thomson's *The Seasons* (1730) and Coleridge's 'Frost at Midnight' (1798). Virgil's *Aeneid*, Book VI, lines 309–12 (referring to autumn leaves and migrating birds) may have provided hints. The lines

> Then in a wailful choir the small gnats mourn
> Among the river sallows, borne aloft
> Or sinking as the light wind lives or dies.....

may have been suggested by *An Introduction to Entomology*, Vol. II (1817), by William Kirby and William Spence: they say on p. 4:

> tribes of *Tipulidæ* (usually, but improperly, called gnats) assemble in sheltered situations ....., and form themselves into choirs, that alternately rise and fall with rapid evolutions.

To cite literary sources, particularly such scholarly ones, seems almost sacrilegious, since 'To Autumn' appears so fresh and spontaneous in its response to nature. Keats had always been good at sensuous poetry, but his ventures into paradoxical odes in the spring of 1819 had given him a familiarity with dialectical structures which led to the diversity, discrimination and finely-modulated contrasts of this poem.

The opening emphasises 'mellow fruitfulness': autumn is seen as a time of plenitude, the fruition of the warmth of the summer: vines, orchards and gardens produce in abundance. The whole stanza has a mouth-filling, mouth-watering sumptuousness created by apt observation, a precision in the use of tellingly descriptive words, and a dense patterning of alliteration and assonance. The tactile as well as the visual effects are strong: consider, for example, the line 'To bend with apples the moss'd cottage-trees'. If we substitute 'load' for 'bend' we at once lose the sense of an active mass of fruit, and 'moss'd' lends an unexpected yet accurate textural contrast while aurally having an apparent inevitability created by the assonance with 'cottage'. The use of an adjective, 'plump', as a verb, in 'to plump the hazel shells/With a sweet kernel', is appropriately vigorous; and again, the word meshes with several alliterative patterns using 'm' and 'p' or 'b'. Another strongly tactile word is 'clammy' in 'For summer has o'er-brimm'd their clammy cells', conveying the dark dankness of the hive.

Stanza I had stressed edible plenitude; stanza II stresses activity, by visualising the spirit of Autumn as incarnate, now sitting in the granary, now dozing at harvest-time, now carrying a basket of gleanings on his head across a brook, or now watching the cyder-press. (Although the poem leaves Autumn's gender indeterminate, the season is traditionally masculine, not only in

Latin, French and German vocabularies but also in such English sources as Thomson's *Seasons* and Chatterton's *Ælla*; and it is masculine in Keats's 'Apollo to the Graces'.) The precision of evocative observation is remarkable: realistic details give force to the personification. Sitting on the granary floor, his hair is 'soft-lifted by the winnowing wind'; drowsing in the cornfield, his sickle 'spares the next swath and all its twinèd flowers'. In the next two lines,

> And sometimes like a gleaner thou dost keep
> Steady thy laden head across a brook[,]

F. R. Leavis rightly noted the peculiarly appropriate verse-movement: 'In the step from the rime-word "keep", across (so to speak) the pause enforced by the line-division, to "Steady" the balancing movement of the gleaner is enacted' (L, 216). The inversion of the first metrical foot of the second line, shifting the heavy stress from the second to the first syllable, creates an irregularity or syncopation at 'Steady' which gives way to regularity with 'thy laden head across a brook', so that we experience, as we read, a temporary loss of balance and a restoration of it: this helps us to imagine a weighted person overcoming an obstacle. Leavis did not note that we here encounter a subtle recurrent associative cluster, but in the early poem 'I stood tip-toe', lines 72–5 (quoted on p. 24), we similarly find the association of (1) the idea of main-taining balance against a stream, (2) the trochaic inversion of the first iambic foot, and (3) the assonantial recurrence of the sounds 'ē', 'e' and 'ā'. At the end of the stanza, with Autumn patient at the cyder-press, the line 'Thou watchest the last oozings hours by hours' is typically expressive: 'oozings' is the most forceful word, and its force derives partly from Keats's boldly unorthodox use of the verb 'oozing' as a noun, and partly from the recurrent 's' and 'z' sounds in the line ('watchest', 'last', 'oozings', 'hours' and 'hours').

The third stanza opens, by contrast, briskly and challengingly: 'Where are the songs of spring? Ay, where are they?' The tone is almost contemptuous, certainly mocking. Spring is celebrated for song, but autumn has its own distinctive music too, and this stanza finely discriminates between the various sounds that may be heard: the 'wailful choir' of gnats; the bleating of lambs; the cricket's song; the whistling of a robin, and the twittering of gathering swallows. The phrasing is lucid and charged with linguistic delicacies inviting nimble tongue-work, as when those gnats mourn 'Among the river sallows, borne aloft/ Or sinking as the light wind lives or dies'. The final reference to the 'gathering swallows', preparing to migrate to southern warmth, reminds us of the approach of winter, and appropriately closes the poem.

This ode celebrates not only the abundance of transient autumn but also the diverse responsiveness of the human senses. As John

Barnard has said:

> Autumn's particular beauty is dependent upon its transience, and the stanzas can be seen as moving through the season, beginning with pre-harvest ripeness, moving to the repletion of harvest itself, and concluding with the emptiness following the harvest, but preceding winter. It also progresses from the tactile senses, to the visual, culminating in the auditory senses, and focuses first on the vegetable world, then on the human activity in gathering the harvest, and concludes in the world of animals, birds, and insects. It has also been read as a movement from morning to evening. The interconnectedness of maturity, death, and regeneration is implicit throughout.
>
> (*John Keats: The Complete Poems*. Harmondsworth: Penguin, 1973, p. 675)

After Andrew Marvell's 'The Garden', Keats's 'To Autumn' is probably the best nature-poem in the language: richly resourceful yet alert and unsentimental. Anyone who doubts this should compare it with Hood's imitation, 'Ode: Autumn', part of which was quoted on p. 67.

However, nature-poetry always includes something additional to (and other than) nature as she might appear if we were actually living and working in that rural setting. One reason for the enduring success of 'To Autumn' may be its combination of realism and consolatory fantasy. The fantasy lies in the cumulative suggestion that nature produces her bounty either spontaneously or by the agency not of sweaty labourers but of the Nature-Spirit, Autumn himself; there is a consolatory veiling of rural toil and squalor. In *The Village* (1783), George Crabbe had gone to the other extreme: while claiming to be soberly truthful, he offered a realism which repeatedly modulated into pessimistic fantasy. In his grim landscapes, the weeds triumph mockingly over wretched humanity. Lines 53–72 of *The Village* provide a famous example:

> I paint the Cot,
> As Truth will paint it, and as Bards will not:
> Nor you, ye Poor, of letter'd scorn complain,
> To you the smoothest song is smooth in vain;
> O'ercome by labour, and bow'd down by time,
> Feel you the barren flattery of a rhyme?
> Can poets soothe you, when you pine for bread,
> By winding myrtles round your ruin'd shed?
> Can their light tales your weighty griefs o'erpower,
> Or glad with airy mirth the toilsome hour?
>   Lo! where the heath, with withering brake grown o'er,
> Lends the light turf that warms the neighbouring poor;
> From thence a length of burning sand appears,

141

Where the thin harvest waves its wither'd ears;
Rank weeds, that every art and care defy,
Reign o'er the land, and rob the blighted rye:
There thistles stretch their prickly arms afar,
And to the ragged infant threaten war;
There poppies nodding, mock the hope of toil;
There the blue bugloss paints the sterile soil. . . . .

The contrast provided by these pessimistic lines makes us more aware of the relatively optimistic selectivity of Keats's. To Keats, poppies bring pleasant dreams; to Crabbe, they are mocking weeds. Furthermore, the metronomic rhythm of Crabbe's couplets makes contrastingly evident the much subtler and more flexible verse-movement of Keats's ode, just as Crabbe's more declamatory voice serves to define its relatively variable and intimate tones. We learn from both writers that good nature-poetry is not only a searchingly selective evocation of the rural but also a detailed dramatisation of a state of mind in a particular cultural phase.

John Constable's famous painting, 'The Hay-Wain', was completed in 1821, the year after the publication of Keats's 'To Autumn'; and there are some clear analogies between these enduringly appealing works. In both cases there is an appeal based on our recognition of truth: the appeal of apparent realism. In both cases there is the attraction of consolatory refuge – refuge from the familiar urban, industrialised world. Another appeal is that of craftsmanship: we note how well Constable has captured the scene in paint, and how well Keats has captured the season in words. Each work implies a double moral exhortation: such natural phenomena are good to observe; such artefacts are worth making and good to contemplate. In each work there is an aesthetic distancing and filtering of actuality: the two men on the hay-wain provide 'human interest', lending variety to the rural panorama; no doubt they are doing a job, but, as with the reaper, gleaner and cyder-watcher in the poem, the labour seems to have a close resemblance to leisure and holiday-pursuit; pain and worry are absent, as are drizzle, maggots and disease. While alerting us to nature as it really appears, removing veils of familiarity from our perception, both artists have 'improved' nature by selectivity and harmonisation. In the painting, the trees, the house-wall, the dog facing right and the hay-wain facing left across the ford (and even the leftward-extended arm of one of the labourers) lead the eye in an artful anti-clockwise spiral; rectangles contrast with curves, walls with wheels; the water reflects and contrasts with the open sky above; colours harmonise interestingly. We collaborate with the conventions, and are aware not only of nature and the painting as worthy of contemplation, but also of our very activity of contemplative collaboration. The ode, too, orders, selects, inter-relates, and invites our conscious

*John Constable: 'The Hay-Wain' (1821).*

As Keats's 'To Autumn' adapts James Thomson's 'Summer' and 'Autumn'
*by a more attentive concern for the sensuous immediacy of the English
countryside, so Constable's 'Hay-Wain' adapts Rubens' 'Château de Steen'.
Constable's 'realism' is artfully structured: this vista is more expansive than
the actual vista he observed; the house on the left of the painting is more
steeply-roofed, for the sake of the composition, than Willy Lott's cottage
which was its counterpart. Similarly, the fine harmonies of Keats's ode depend
partly on a selective re-ordering of the features of an English autumn. The
more urbanised and industrialised a society becomes, the more it may value
artefacts that present agrarian life as apparently detached from the economy of
which it is an essential part.*

> *The Millfield Lane looked like a Constable,*
> *And all the grassy hillocks spoke of Keats.*
> *(John Betjeman:* Summoned by Bells)

co-operation. The selections, omissions and structural artifices are truth-seeking in proportion to our recognition of the range of effects being selectively achieved and the diverse human needs that such effects supply. Both 'The Hay-Wain' and 'To Autumn' offer awakening and repose; both offer an ideal vision of an English green-world of plenitude and peace in which man is one with the tranquil cycles of the fields and the skies. George Crabbe, Thomas Hardy and Ted Hughes offer strongly contrasting visions. In the democracy of the arts, the major truths lie in the plurality of changing views and of conspicuous selectivity; and, to the observer who recognises this, the arts will always possess a mode of objectivity denied to the labours of the scientist.

## Aspects of sensuous verse

Keats may at first seem the most sensuous of English poets; but other poets are quite as sensuous, in their various ways. What creates the impression of Keats's supremacy in this respect is partly that the other poets are often doing additional things at the same time, whereas in him the sensuous tends to be isolated: they may put the experience in a critical framework, whereas he tends to relish it relatively uncritically.

Sensuous verse has a content which may make a strong appeal to the senses and employs techniques which simultaneously exploit the sensuous aspects of language (among them, rhythm, alliteration, assonance and onomatopoeia, generating clusters of mouthfilling sounds). A complicating factor is that in the past there has been a strong tradition of Christian asceticism, warning people against the seductions of the senses; so that consequently much sensuous writing embodies a 'placing' or criticism of the attractions cited. This is illustrated by examples, 1, 2 and 3 below.

Since Keats's day, various poets have attempted to give extreme aural richness to poetic diction. Examples 4 and 5 suggest that such verbal sensuousness offers dangers as well as pleasures, and may be self-defeating: sound may obscure meaning, and a lack of contrast can devalue the insistent diction. These two passages may help us to appreciate the implicit tact, the generally happy relationships of meaning and technique, in Keats's poetry.

1    I am giddy: expectation whirls me round.
    Th'imaginary relish is so sweet
    That it enchants my sense. What will it be
    When that the watery palate tastes indeed
    Love's thrice repurèd nectar? – death, I fear me,
    Swooning distraction, or some joy too fine,
    Too subtle-potent, tuned too sharp in sweetness,
    For the capacity of my ruder powers.

2    Thy baths shall be the juice of July-flowers,
Spirit of roses, and of violets,
The milk of unicorns, and panthers' breath
Gathered in bags and mixed with Cretan wines.
Our drink shall be preparèd gold and amber,
Which we will take until my roof whirl round
With the vertigo; and my dwarf shall dance.....

3    My foot-boy shall eat pheasants, calvered salmons,
Knots, godwits, lampreys. I myself will have
The beards of barbels served instead of salads;
Oiled mushrooms; and the swelling unctuous paps
Of a fat pregnant sow, newly cut off,
Dressed with an exquisite and poignant sauce;
For which, I'll say unto my cook, 'There's gold;
Go forth, and be a knight!'

4    Wherefore did Nature pour her bounties forth
With such a full and unwithdrawing hand,
Covering the earth with odours, fruits, and flocks,
Thronging the seas with spawn innumerable,
But all to please, and sate the curious taste?
And set to work millions of spinning worms,
That in their green shops weave the smooth-hair'd silk
To deck her sons; and that no corner might
Be vacant of her plenty, in her own loins
She hutcht th'all-worship ore, and precious gems.....

5    I caught this morning morning's minion, king-
       dom of daylight's dauphin, dapple-dawn-drawn Falcon, in
                               his riding
    Of the rolling level underneath him steady air, and striding
High there, how he rung upon the rein of a wimpling wing
In his ecstasy! then off, off forth on a swing.....

6    Beasts who sleep good and thin,
Hist, in hogsback woods! The haystacked
Hollow farms in a throng
Of waters cluck and cling,
And barnroofs cockcrow war!
O kingdom of neighbours, finned
Felled and quilled, flash to my patch
Work ark.....

In passage 1, Troilus (in Shakespeare's *Troilus and Cressida*, Act III, scene ii, lines 18–25) is thinking in appetitive terms of his future sexual embrace with Cressida: he imagines that the pleasure may be so great as to overwhelm his senses. Shakespeare frequently links the appetitive with warfare and anarchy within the individual and within the state. His great comic character, Falstaff, is a walking image of appetite, big and fat, and he is also a subversive force who would destroy justice if he came to power. In *Troilus and Cressida*, Ulysses warns the Greeks that if they disobey the traditional hierarchical principle with its moral laws, chaos follows:

> Then everything includes itself in power,
> Power into will, will into appetite;
> And appetite, an universal wolf,
> So doubly seconded with will and power,
> Must make perforce an universal prey,
> And last eat up himself.

(Act I, scene iii, lines 119–24)

'Appetite', connoting egotism, greed for power, sexual lust, and greed for food, is the term that links the 'war' theme and the 'love' theme: the senses overcome the moral judgement. Paris has abducted the beautiful Helen, and the long brutal war results; Hector's acquisitive appetite for 'sumptuous armour' leads him into the path of Achilles, who murders him; and Troilus's appetite for Cressida (gratified outside marriage) results in disillusionment, for she betrays him. The terms in which Troilus, in the quoted speech, describes his desires, imply criticism of those desires and of him.

Keats loved *Troilus and Cressida* and marked this speech by Troilus; and, as we noted, he may be partly recalling it in the 'Ode on Melancholy'. Whereas Shakespeare presents the appetitive critically, however, Keats tends to indulge it; a tendency of which we are forewarned by the letter in which the young poet hedonistically identifies himself with the character (whose name he mis-spells 'Triolus'):

> I throw my whole being into Triolus and repeating those lines, 'I wander, like a lost soul upon the stygian Banks staying for waftage,' I melt into the air with a voluptuousness so delicate that I am content to be alone.

(R I, 404)

Keats saw Troilus, rightly, as a Romantic fore-runner; but he was less willing to see that Shakespeare, in that characterisation, was offering a proleptic warning against Romanticism and its tendency to encourage the egoistic and anarchic appetites.

This principle of double dramatisation of the appetitive – a dramatisation both persuasive and critical – is maintained in examples 2, 3 and 4. In 2, Ben Jonson's Volpone, the charismatic but vicious trickster, is attempting to seduce the chaste Celia (*Volpone*, Act III, scene ii, lines 220–6). The sensuous description – again vertiginous – is deliberately carried to a point of fantastic excess verging on absurdity or derangement ('panthers' breath/ Gathered in bags'), and the reference to the dwarf reminds us that Volpone's servants, a dwarf, a eunuch and a hermaphrodite, are living warnings of the moral perversity and sterility behind his rhetoric. For all his talk of 'July-flowers' and 'violets', when Celia resists him the tempting rhetoric becomes a cry of 'Yield, or I'll force thee!'

In passage 3, Sir Epicure Mammon in Jonson's *The Alchemist* (Act II, scene ii, lines 80–7) is dreaming of the luxuries he will enjoy when he makes his fortune. The sensuous is tinged with the excessive, perverse and destructive – those 'swelling unctuous paps/ Of a fat pregnant sow' sound rich but slightly disgusting, and when he adds 'newly cut off' we perceive the destructive nastiness of the indulgent reverie. Jonson's exuberant comedy has a mordant, satiric edge.

In passage 4, the speaker is the tempter, Comus, in John Milton's masque *Comus* (1634), lines 710–19. He (rather like Volpone in passage 2) is attempting to seduce a virtuous lady, and he is using the argument that Nature is so surcharged with riches that our duty is to use those riches up – and therefore, by implication, the lady should surrender her virtue and chastity. The devil has the best tunes, and in *Comus* the villain has the best descriptive passages. Milton's audience would not have missed the point that it is because he is the villain that Comus can indulge in such sensuous rhapsodies.

In Keats's poetry, these traditional Christian and ascetic elements have largely faded away; now, if he has misgivings about the sensuous, they are to the effect that the pleasures are ephemeral and may lead to some kind of hangover: 'a heart high-sorrowful and cloy'd,/A burning forehead, and a parching tongue' ('Ode on a Grecian Urn', lines 29–30).

Passage 5 is the opening of Gerard Manley Hopkins' famous sonnet, 'The Windhover' (1877). Hopkins admired Keats and attempted to subscribe to Keats's advice to Shelley – ' "load every rift" of your subject with ore' (R II, 322). Seeking ever greater expressiveness, he carried deliberately sensuous sound-patterning to an extreme. He was influenced by his knowledge of Welsh, of Middle English alliterative poetry, and by the linguistic nationalism of F. J. Furnivall, R. C. Trench and William Barnes, who sought to restore to the English language the concreteness of Anglo-Saxon, which they felt had been displaced by the bloodless abstractions of the Latin tradition.

The passage displays an obvious danger. In striving for greater expressiveness, Hopkins may be defeating his own ends by making the linguistic surface of the poem distractingly opaque: though the poetry is a pleasure to chant, the reader may be conscious that an effort akin to translation is sometimes needed in order to grasp the paraphrasable meaning. Furthermore, this very muscular, contorted diction is relatively appropriate for some subjects (scenes of conflict, storm and stress, like the shipwreck in 'The Wreck of the Deutschland'), but relatively inappropriate for others in which calm lucidity seems desirable (for example, 'Ash-boughs' and 'Tom's Garland'). In the latter cases, the opacity of diction may unfortunately resemble that of a tongue-twister.

Passage 6 is from Dylan Thomas's 'Author's Prologue' to *Collected Poems* (1952). Thomas was influenced by Keats and Hopkins, and from time to time strongly recalls both. At his best, in 'Do Not Go Gentle into That Dark Night' and 'Fern Hill', he controlled his facility for sound-patterning by sufficient reference to the needs of the subject-matter. Example 6 shows, however, that sensuous diction can be self-defeating when it is used constantly and predictably: here the alliterative sequences are too obvious and insistent, and the effect is of a heavily accentuated thudding incantation: though there is sound and fury, the language's ability to express significance tends to diminish rather than increase.

We see, therefore, that the effectiveness of sensuous verse depends largely on the balance between aural opacity (or density) and logical and visual transparency (or lucidity). What makes the relationship problematic is that as the reader becomes familiar with the conventions of such verse, the sound-patterning may lose their force. (The formalist critic, Victor Shklovsky, said that habitual perception kills vivid awareness, but the artist strives to restore vividness – to 'make the stone stony'.) The poet may then respond in various ways. One way, that of Hopkins and Dylan Thomas, is to shift the balance strongly towards aural opacity. Another way is that of contextual contrast. The greater the relative transparency of surrounding passages, the greater by contrast the density of the sensuous passage will seem. The formal devices of poetry often tend to give language a greater richness than it customarily possesses in prose or speech, somewhat as the physical procedures of lovers often tend to give bodily textures a greater palpability than they usually possess.

Comparison with the other poets draws attention to what John Barnard has termed 'Keats's tactile vision': 'a peculiar and richly tactile kind of "seeing"'. Examples include: 'taste/ The pleasant sun-rise' ('To the Nile', lines 12–13), 'To taste the luxury of sunny beams' ('I Stood Tip-Toe', line 74), and 'taste the music of that vision pale' ('Isabella', line 392), in which 'taste' has far greater immediacy than a word like 'experience' and presses the diction towards synaesthesia, a deliberate fusing of alternative kinds of sense-experience. When Shakespeare's Troilus considers how the palate 'tastes indeed/ Love's thrice repurèd nectar' there is a sustained analogy between experiencing sexual bliss and savouring honey; Keats's 'taste the music of that vision pale' jumps more rapidly between different sense-areas. A related tendency to synaesthesia is illustrated by: 'Through bowers of fragrant and enwreathèd light' (*Hyperion*, Book I, line 219) and

> Touch has a memory. O say, Love, say,
> What can I do to kill it and be free......?
>
> ('What can I do.....', lines 4–5)

Of the 'Ode to Psyche', with its final blending of ideas of love and poetic creation, John Barnard says:

> We do not *feel* a painting: and strictly we neither feel nor see through a poem – we experience words. In the 'Ode to Psyche' Keats entangles the senses so as to create a very particular mode of vision – tactile vision is perhaps the best description – which matches his (and indeed Hazlitt's) belief that poetic and artistic truth are intuited through sensation.
>
> ('Keats's Tactile Vision': *Keats-Shelley Memorial Bulletin* XXXIII, 1982, p. 24)

Related to the impulse towards synaesthesia is Keats's use of unusual or newly-minted adjectives and adverbs – a feature which the early reviewers often derided. His adjectives include such compounds as 'cool-rooted', 'crumple-leaved', 'gentlier-mightiest', 'milder-mooned', 'rosy-warm', 'sea-foamy,' 'incense-pillow'd' and 'rain-scented'; while the adverbs include 'cooingly', 'airily', 'dazzlingly', 'hoveringly', 'drowsingly', 'dancingly', 'eye-earnestly', 'slantingly', 'silverly', 'spangly', 'beamily', 'staringly', 'bluely', and even 'tremulous-dazzlingly'. This creation of new verbal and sensuous threshold-experiences is part of Keats's larger preoccupation with the description and enactment of threshold-states.

## Keats's imaginative nexus: the liminal imperative

A nexus is a knot, bond or linkage-point. One of the features which gives a distinctive character to the work of a particular poet is the presence of an imaginative nexus: a preoccupation with certain states of being which acts as a recurrent imperative (perhaps seldom recognised fully by the artist's conscious intelligence) during the creative process.

Keats's work is obviously identifiable through its predilection for combinations of sensuous subject-matter with sensuous diction. What I term a nexus, however, is something deeper and initially less obvious, though it constantly generates small, medium and large effects in his writings. Keats's imaginative nexus is the liminal imperative: the urge to depict a *limen* or threshold; a concern with transition-states – moments or phases of transition from one mode of being to another; and a concomitant feature is the ambiguous status of the modes of being on each side of this threshold.

Once we perceive this nexus, we perceive a remarkable principle of living unity moving within his diversity of subjects and effects. In the works of other poets, either the transition-states are not so diversely prominent, or the modes of being before and after them are less ambiguous and thus generate a much stronger impression of change for the better or the worse. Keats places more emphasis on crucial but equivocal change; and we see why he studied with such evident interest Ovid's *Metamorphoses*, the Latin poem which anthologises ambiguous, legendary transformations. If we look for an equivalent nexus in Shelley, the poet whose preoccupations often closely resemble Keats's, we find a different emphasis: on a transitional cycle which tends to be progressive, in that whether it be in nature or mankind, the poet strongly suggests the value of the rebirth – perhaps into springtime, perhaps into a new and far better era for humans, or perhaps into both combined, as in the triumphant conclusion of *Prometheus Unbound* and the exhortations of 'Ode to the West Wind'.

I begin this survey with small-scale examples of the liminal imperative. There are hundreds of possible instances of Keats's interest in capturing threshold-states. The reader will soon recall how often the most memorable parts of the poems offer them:

> Joy, whose hand is ever at his lips
> Bidding adieu . . . . .
>
> ('Ode on Melancholy', lines 22–3)

> magic casements, opening on the foam
> Of perilous seas, in faery lands forlorn.
>
> Forlorn! the very word is like a bell
> To toll me back from thee to my sole self!
>
> ('Ode to a Nightingale', lines 69–72)

> Hedge-crickets sing; and now with treble soft
> The red-breast whistles from a garden-croft;
> And gathering swallows twitter in the skies.
>
> ('To Autumn', lines 31–3)

In each of these instances there is a threshold; in each case an ambiguous transitional-state. 'Joy', in the first example, is at once going and staying: bidding adieu, but 'ever' in that posture. In the second example, 'casements, opening' is liminal, and the very word 'forlorn' becomes a threshold: its liminal ambiguity occasions the transition-phase from reverie to apparent awakening, just as the later movement of the nightingale away across the threshold of audibility prompts the final questioning of the status of the nightingale-reverie. The third example is about transition from summer to winter; but the emphasis is not the predictable emphasis on movement from a pleasant to an unpleasant state: rather, it falls on the complex natural music of the transition-phase itself.

If we consider effects which are larger in scale, we see that the best odes are markedly liminal, centrally concerned with the capturing of ambiguous phases of transition. The 'Ode on a Grecian Urn' is the most complex example, as the changes (from warm to cold, animate to inanimate, audible to inaudible, mobile to immobile, ephemeral to durable, and mortal to eternal) are adroitly interlinked and boldly confused by the narrator; indeed, the urn itself is a liminal object, the threshold of the permanent and impermanent, just as its words about beauty and truth themselves constitute a liminal statement, at the threshold of revelation and enigma, and these in turn are analogous to the ode as a whole, the threshold of enduring definition and receding flux. What was distinctive about the ode 'To Autumn' can now be seen as consistent, too. It is not a set description of one seasonal landscape but a virtuosic rendering of transitional states within the greater transition between summer and winter: everywhere there is the enactment of change, of mobility of state; from the bending of trees, the filling of fruit, the budding of late flowers, the brimming of cells; from winnowing, fume-drowsed reaping, brook-crossing, and oozing of apple-pulp towards cyder; to the soft dying of day, the rising and falling of gnats in varying wind, the mingling of music and the gathering of swallows; and all my gerunds, these verbal nouns ending in 'ing', are merely an amplifying echo to those of Keats, for his gerunds, whether verbal, nounal, adjectival or implicit, proliferate aptly in this poem of changings.

If we turn to the longest poems, we see again the liminal preoccupation. In *Endymion*, the hero exists for most of the time in a limbo of prolonged transition: a quester seeking the Cynthia of his vision, herself goddess of the very planet of constant change, the moon, and who herself appears in fleeting visions; a man tantalised by the conflicting claims of the ideal and the real, who effects metamorphoses in others (the transformation of doomed lovers), who is aptly rewarded by the metamorphosis of Indian Maid into Cynthia, and whose quest ends, inevitably, in further transition: 'They vanish'd far away!' In *Hyperion*, the poem seems doubly trapped at the transition-point: as a Keatsian experiment, trapped at the threshold of scene-setting and purposeful story; as a narrative, trapped at the transition from the old Saturnian to the new Olympian era. Keats's very Titans, struggling to emerge from the stupor of their fall, resemble Michelangelo's titanic Boboline captives, struggling to emerge from the formlessness of rock – each one an image for the half-emerged epic which is the liminal *Hyperion*. As for Keats's subsequent attempt, *The Fall of Hyperion*: this is even more strongly bound in the nexus: for this version introduces another dimension of transitional-phase by introducing the narrator as an uncertain transitional figure, between death and life, between despair and hope, between the destinies of mere dreamer and true poet; and literally he struggles on the threshold, that of Moneta's temple. Personal threshold within symbolic threshold, on the inaugural threshold of an epic. Furthermore, the epic of Hyperion, as Keats left it to us, is multiply transitional: the incomplete *Hyperion* hovers in an incomplete process of change to the incomplete *Fall of Hyperion*.

If we turn to the poems of intermediate length, we see that these, too, on a variety of scales, express the liminal nexus.

To begin with a detail: In 'Isabella; or, The Pot of Basil' there occurs the most famous literary example of a proleptic epithet: the word 'murder'd' in

> So the two brothers and their murder'd man
> Rode past fair Florence. . . . .

(lines 209–10)

The very phrasing is true to the nexus, because, by superimposing the murdered Lorenzo of the future upon the living Lorenzo of the present, it generates a conceptually transitional state within a passage which already concerns the transition of Lorenzo from life to death. And this poem as a whole has a characteristic preoccupation with related transition-states. When the dead Lorenzo speaks to Isabella, he does so in her dream; and the state he describes is a complex limbo, intermediate between humanity and the grave's oblivion, between rage and gladness:

> 'I am a shadow now, alas! alas!
>    Upon the skirts of human-nature dwelling
> Alone: I chant alone the holy mass,
>    While little sounds of life are round me knelling,
> And glossy bees at noon do fieldward pass,
>    And many a chapel bell the hour is telling,
> Paining me through: those sounds grow strange to me,
> And thou art distant in Humanity.

> 'I know what was, I feel full well what is,

And I should rage, if spirits could go mad;
Though I forget the taste of earthly bliss,
That paleness warms my grave, as though I had
A Seraph chosen from the bright abyss
To be my spouse: thy paleness makes me glad;
Thy beauty grows upon me, and I feel
A greater love through all my essence steal.'

(lines 305–20)

(Though effective enough in their narrative context, these stanzas contain nothing as vividly unexpected as the following stanza's minor liminal reference to times when, sleepless at night,

We put our eyes into a pillowy cleft,
And see the spangly gloom froth up and boil.

Keats's imagination often evades the restraints of a narrative by these semi-digressive sense-notations that spring adjectives like that fine 'spangly'.) The poem's central image, the 'pot of Basil' itself, though deriving from Boccaccio's tale and influenced in treatment by the taste for grisly charnel-house imagery in popular Romantic poems and novels (particularly such Gothic novels as M. G. Lewis's *The Monk*), is developed by Keats in a manner that emphasises the grotesque paradox of the transitional state it represents:

And so she ever fed it with thin tears,
Whence thick, and green, and beautiful it grew,.....
for it drew
Nurture besides, and life, from human fears,
From the fast mouldering head there shut from view.....

(lines 425–6, 428–30)

Tears and fears metamorphosing to beauty; mouldering death metamorphosing to green life; and from the strange copulation of heads – the weeping head of Isabella above and the rotting head of Lorenzo below – is bred the aromatic herb.

Another famous poem which centrally concerns an ambiguous transition-state is 'La Belle Dame sans Merci'. Keats's inner fascination by such states largely explains his decision to offer his own version of this archetypal legend which has so many literary manifestations. (An 'archetypal' legend offers a simple but strangely resonant story with aspects of dream, myth, religion and common experience; it is protean in variants and meanings, and consequently has a *déjà vu* quality – it seems to remind one of itself.) An excellent traditional version is the ballad 'Thomas the Rymer'; and like the best such ballads, Keats's poem combines the specific and the enigmatic. Against the specificity of, for example, the girl's sidelong posture and the 'kisses four' ('an even number that both eyes might

153

have fair play', Keats explained), are the enigmas: who is the girl? what does she represent? and what is the meaning of the story? Robert Graves, in *The White Goddess* (London: Faber and Faber, 1952, p. 431), suggests that 'the Belle Dame represented Love, Death by Consumption (the modern leprosy) and Poetry all at once'. A useful commentary on this ballad is implicit in the inferior and more overtly autobiographical poem, 'What can I do to drive away/Remembrance from my eyes?', in which Keats dramatises characteristically ambivalent judgements of his love for Fanny Brawne: a love which, the poet suggests, offers a heaven and a hell, a release but also a servitude which thwarts poetic ambition ('Those moulted feathers'); a region of brilliant light yet also, as in 'La Belle Dame sans Merci', a waste-land where no birds sing. (The same sequence from intoxication to hangover, from visionary ecstasy to a blighted world, had been explored by Keats in *Endymion*, Book I, lines 566–705; and a connection between Fanny and the tantalising 'enchanting Lady' of an oriental source-tale of 'La Belle Dame' was made by him in a letter of 1819 [R II, 130].) The knight-at-arms of 'La Belle Dame' inhabits his own memorable limbo: possessing neither the joys of the girl nor the finality of death, existing neither in the dream nor in active life, he is 'Alone and palely loitering', a haggard figure in a desolate landscape.

Another markedly liminal poem is 'Lamia', based on a tale in Robert Burton's *The Anatomy of Melancholy*. Here Lamia herself is a strongly ambiguous figure, one central question being whether she is woman or snake, victim or seductress. The poem initially presents her as a snake, though if she speaks truly to Hermes she was formerly a 'nymph'. As 'nymph' after her transformation by Hermes, she tells Lycius first, and tauntingly, that she is a heavenly immortal, and secondly that she is a woman who had long watched and admired him at Corinth; neither claim tallying with what we have seen of her before. She fears Apollonius, who is presented both as a hostile, harsh, cynical figure and as an austere truth-seeking sage concerned to guard Lycius. When he denounces her as a Lamia (a snake-cum-enchantress), Apollonius resembles an exorcist dispelling dangerous illusion (though the narrator upbraids him as a damaging intruder); that his exorcism appears effectual seems to validate his claim about Lamia; but the text does not specify that his words reduce her to a snakehood that is her true nature – we are told simply 'she vanished'. So Lamia remains a largely-unresolved transitionary figure. Apollonius, as we have seen, is ambiguous; although, as one who caused the death of the person he thought to save, the poem's verdict is finally against him. Beneath the poem's ambiguities lie Keats's sense of a conflict between sexual love and intellectual ambition and, more deeply, his sense of the conflict between the poetic imagination and empirical reality. That he had ambitions both intellectual and poetic made these relationships even more recessively problematic. One reason for the power of his imagination's liminal nexus is that he was strongly attracted not only by the morphean pleasures of poetry but also by a sceptical recognition that the world seen as unromantically factual might, after all, be the true world. Apollonius, if he sees the truth, sees a blighting one; Lycius, if deluded, has had ecstatic delusions. As Keats had said in 'Sleep and Poetry':

> A sense of real things comes doubly strong,
> And, like a muddy stream, would bear along
> My soul to nothingness: but I will strive
> Against all doubtings.....
>
> (lines 157–60)

Hazlitt, lecturing on poetry, had stated: 'It cannot be concealed ..... that the progress of knowledge and refinement has a tendency to circumscribe the limits of the imagination, and to clip the wings of poetry' (Lecture I). At Haydon's 'Immortal Dinner', as we have noted, Keats had agreed with Lamb that Sir Isaac Newton had 'destroyed all the poetry of the rainbow by reducing it to the prismatic colours'; and the thought is echoed in 'Lamia':

> Do not all charms fly
> At the mere touch of cold philosophy?
> There was an awful rainbow once in heaven:
> We know her woof, her texture; she is given
> In the dull catalogue of common things.
> Philosophy will clip an Angel's wings,
> Conquer all mysteries by rule and line,
> Empty the haunted air, and gnomèd mine –
> Unweave a rainbow, as it erewhile made
> The tender-person'd Lamia melt into a shade.
>
> (Part II, lines 229–38)

What complicated Keats's judgement, and contributed eventually to the intelligent balance of the greatest odes, was his stubborn recognition of the conflicting claim for the superiority of philosophy over poetic imagination:

> our reasoning[s] ..... though erroneous ..... may be fine –
> This is the very thing in which consists poetry; and if so it is not
> so fine a thing as philosophy – For the same reason that an eagle
> is not so fine a thing as a truth.....
>
> (R II, 80–81)

If Keats thought of himself as 'a sick eagle looking at the sky', it was sometimes because his sceptical reasoning threatened to clip the wings of his aspiring imagination. Should he travel on 'feathers & wings' or on 'patient sublunary legs' (R II, 128)? At the heart of his work was his own transitional state: one of constant to-and-fro between fancy and fact, transcendent yearning and mundane knowledge, vital illusion and mortal empiricism. The great odes made the land of transition his final, resolved homeland, just as the monument to the conflicts and confusions of a disputed frontier is often the enduring castle which arises from them.

Of the narrative poems which illustrate the transition-nexus, the richest, most effectively varied and aptly organised is 'The Eve of St. Agnes'. This is the most cinematic of Keats's poems in its pictorial contrasts, colour-range, pace and tracking, and even – literally – in its 'dissolves'. In cinema techniques, a 'dissolve' is the gradual blending of one scene or frame with the next. The most memorable series of dissolves in the poem lies at its narrative centre. Madeline has been dreaming of her lover, Porphyro. He awakens her; she at first laments the change; but then dream and reality blend.

> 'Ah, Porphyro!' said she, 'but even now
> Thy voice was at sweet tremble in mine ear,
> Made tuneable with every sweetest vow;
> And those sad eyes were spiritual and clear:
> How chang'd thou art! how pallid, chill, and drear!
> Give me that voice again, my Porphyro,
> Those looks immortal, those complainings dear!
> Oh leave me not in this eternal woe,
> For if thou diest, my love, I know not where to go.'
>
> Beyond a mortal man impassion'd far
> At these voluptuous accents, he arose,
> Ethereal, flush'd, and like a throbbing star

*Arthur Hughes: 'The Eve of St. Agnes' (1856).*

*'Hughes's interpretation adopts a triptych, and uses that quintessentially holy format to relate the most successful abduction in English literature. There are three scenes from the poem, Porphyro's stealthy approach to the castle, his awakening of Madeline in her bed-chamber, and as in Hunt's painting, their escape, tiptoeing carefully over the drunken porter.' (Timothy Hilton:* The Pre-Raphaelites, *1970, p. 114.)*

*Although a small black-and-white reproduction cannot convey the rich colour and subtle lighting of the original, this further instance of Keats's influence on the Pre-Raphaelites may serve as a mnemonic of his preoccupation with threshold-states; and the triptychal form graphically indicates the ambiguous appeal (partly religious, partly secular) of Romanticism.*

They told her how, upon St. Agnes' Eve,
Young virgins might have visions of delight,
And soft adorings from their loves receive
Upon the honey'd middle of the night,
If ceremonies due they did aright;
As, supperless to bed they must retire,
And couch supine their beauties, lily white;
Nor look behind, nor sideways, but require
Of Heaven with upward eyes for all that they desire.

Seen mid the sapphire heaven's deep repose;
Into her dream he melted, as the rose
Blendeth its odour with the violet, –
Solution sweet: meantime the frost-wind blows
Like Love's alarum pattering the sharp sleet
Against the window-panes; St. Agnes' moon hath set.

(lines 307–24)

The dialogue is derivative and stagey, but the subsequent description is more interesting. 'Into her dream he melted' effectively suggests a sexual fusion which is simultaneously the fusion of reality with dream. 'Solution sweet', indeed: 'solution' meaning 'dissolving and blending together', suggesting not just the embrace but the merging of lovers; hinting delicately at the erotic, bodily liquefaction (ooze of the female interfused with semen of the male), but sublimating the carnal by an evocation of floral perfumes. And 'solution' means also, here, the solution to the problem that Madeline had set Porphyro, that of reconciling the idealised Porphyro of the dream with the actual Porphyro of the chamber. For Keats, the sexual bliss of lovers could sometimes be the apotheosis of the transitional state.

One early comment on these stanzas came from Keats's offended publisher, Taylor: 'I will not be accessory . . . . . towards publishing any thing which can only be read by Men, since even on their Minds a bad Effect must follow the Encouragement of those Thoughts which cannot be raised without Impropriety' (R II, 182). For us, a more resonant comment on this section of 'The Eve of St. Agnes' is implicit in Keats's words: 'The Imagination may be compared to Adam's dream – he awoke and found it truth' (R I, 185). In its presentation of the transitional state, however, the poem is more complex than this reference to Adam's dream might suggest, and it is typical of the poem's energetic patterning of contrasts (youth versus age, bright colour versus grey darkness, vigour versus decay, softness versus hardness, warmth versus cold, joy versus woe, the sensuous versus the austere) that even as the lovers blend voluptuously,

meantime the frost-wind blows
Like Love's alarum pattering the sharp sleet
Against the window-panes. . . . .

At the conclusion of 'The Eve of St. Agnes' there is a double transition. The fleeing lovers open the groaning bolted door of the castle

And they are gone: ay, ages long ago
These lovers fled away into the storm.

Outward into the storm – and across the threshold into the

158

unknowable, for there is no proof that they reached their home 'o'er the southern moors'; outward into the storm – and across the threshold into the past, the legendary past, and the dark backward and abysm of time.

THE NEXUS AND KEATS'S LETTERS. The concern with liminal states manifests itself in many of the most characteristic reflective passages in the letters. In his speculations on life as 'the vale of soul-making' (R II, 100–104), life itself is seen as transitional: a place in which one's identity is gradually, constantly, being formed. The letter does imply the possible eventual achievement of a defined soul, but typically the theory is offered only as tentative, itself transitional: he says 'I can scarcely express what I but dimly perceive', just as, earlier, he had been merely 'straining at particles in the midst of a wide darkness'; and its premise of the soul's immortality is one which, he indicates, he has adopted for the sake of argument and not necessarily as accepted fact ('human nature admitting it to be immortal which I will here take for granted for the purpose of showing a thought which has struck me concerning it').

Another well-known letter, on life as 'A Mansion of Many Apartments' (R I, 280–83), characteristically makes each chamber seem but a large threshold, a place of transition. He postulates first 'the infant or thoughtless Chamber' where, although 'we do not think', we are at length impelled by the awakening of 'the thinking principle' towards the adjacent second room, 'the Chamber of Maiden Thought', in which we gain knowledge of the world's woes, 'whereby This Chamber of Maiden Thought becomes gradually darken'd and at the same time on all sides of it many doors are set open – but all dark – all leading to dark passages – We see not the ballance of good and evil. We are in a mist'. (Our very bodies, science told Keats, were transitional: 'Our bodies every seven years are completely fresh-material'd – seven years ago it was not this hand that clench'd itself against Hammond' [R II, 208].)

Finally, as we have seen, Keats's most famous 'doctrine' or notion, that of 'Negative Capability', had the supreme practical value for Keats of making the liminal state into the ideal state: the sense of radical uncertainty, attributed to Shakespeare, thus became transformed into the enabling idea of artistic liberty, 'when man is capable of being in uncertainties, Mysteries, doubts, without any irritable reaching after fact & reason'.

One central dilemma of the English Romantic poets, and indeed of many poets in the Romantic tradition from ancient times to the present, was that they were divided between quasi-religious aspirations and sceptical awareness. The combination of these hardy perennials and Keats's unique biochemistry generated

Keats's imaginative nexus, which I have surveyed here.

## Keats's letters

THE COLLABORATIVE MASTERPIECE. Some authors have left disappointing sequences of letters (Jane Austen's and Henry James's come to mind); other authors have left sequences which are full of life, interest and wisdom: Byron's, Conrad's and D. H. Lawrence's are outstanding.

As we have seen, Keats's letters offer an intimate, vivid, engaging account of his personality and aspirations. They can at times be embarrassing, too, in their open gaucheness: we may feel that he is attempting to lift himself by his bootstraps into the realms of genius; he is self-conscious, aware that his correspondence may be read by posterity as 'letters of the artist', and sometimes there is too conspicuous an endeavour to write something that will appear clever, witty or profound. Occasionally, when he attempts to be wittily amusing, the result is a prattling facetiousness (as in the letter of 4 June 1818 [R I, 289–91], though it doubtless entertained the girls who received it); and at other times, as in that much-quoted 'Chamber of Maiden Thought' passage (R I, 280–81), his attempt to be philosophical seems to result rather in the elaborate development of basically simple and familiar ideas.

Nevertheless, his letters give a richly diversified picture of his rapid evolution and of the many aspects of his lively personality. There is plenty of humour (as in the account of the journey through Scotland, or in cameos like that of Brown with voice trebled 'by making love in the draught of a door way'); pathos, bitterness and yearning, in the letters to Fanny Brawne; and repeatedly a thin-skinned vivacity of response – to nature, people, places and language itself – which quickens one's own apprehension. I have suggested earlier that an unrecognised Keatsian masterpiece is the account of the last year of his life: a collective masterpiece consisting partly of his own letters and partly of correspondence (and even pictures) by his friends and acquaintances. A great artistic achievement need not be the work of a single person: successful operas, classic jazz improvisations and memorable stage productions provide evidence to the contrary; and prior intention is supererogatory, since we judge by results. This Keatsian masterpiece has its narrative structure, provided by his illness, the voyage, and the Italian months during which Keats declined towards death; and it has the irony that the intended journey to the sun and health took him through storm and tempest to a wretched end in Rome ('by this journey his life has been shortened – and rendered more painful', said the doctor). It is in some ways a conventionally Romantic story – the suffering and premature death of the young artist. What makes it unconventional is the intensive presentation of so full a range of experience: sea-spray and vomit, blood and diarrhoea, the tedium of delay, the ludicrously-crowded cabin, the oppressive days of quarantine, the worrries about money and health-regulations, fruit-trees in blossom, Brown's puns and anagrams (*'Thanks Joe!'* for 'John Keats'), the doctor's clinical diagnoses, and Severn trembling 'through every vein' while concealing his tears from Keats's 'staring glassy eyes'. The discordant medley of beauty and farce, nobility and squalor, aspiration and pettiness, sensitivity and filth, challenges by contrast the selectivities of the orthodox Romantic artefacts. We sense what may be the greatest irony of Keats's career: that the very illness which seemed to destroy his hopes of artistic fulfilment may itself have occasioned an achievement which in its range, richness and intensity surpasses his fondest plans.

TWO INFLUENCES. In his correspondence as well as in his poetry, Keats was an adept pupil of a great variety of literary mentors, and their dean was Shakespeare. The energetic rhetoric of Shakespeare's comic prose re-echoes in the letters. Here is Falstaff, extolling 'sherris-sack' (dry sherry):

> A good sherris-sack hath a twofold operation in it. It ascends me into the brain, drives me there all the foolish and dull and crudy vapours which environ it, makes it apprehensive, quick, forgetive, full of nimble, fiery, and delectable shapes, which delivered o'er to the voice, the tongue, which is the birth, becomes excellent wit. The second property of your excellent sherris is the warming of the blood, which before, cold and settled, left the liver white and pale, which is the badge of pusillanimity and cowardice; but the sherris warms it, and makes it course from the inwards to the parts' extremes. It illumineth the face, which, as a beacon, gives warning to all the rest of this little kingdom, man, to arm.....
>
> (*2 Henry IV*, Act IV, scene iii, lines 94–108; Arden)

And here is John Keats, extolling claret in a letter to his brother George and his wife:

> I like Claret..... If you could make some wine like Claret to d[r]ink on summer evenings in an arbour! For really 't is so fine – it fills the mouth one's mouth with gushing freshness – then goes down cool and feverless – then you do not feel it quarrelling with your liver – no it is rather a Peace maker and lies as quiet as it did in the grape – then it is as fragrant as the Queen Bee; and the more ethereal Part of it mounts into the brain, not assaulting the cerebral apartments like a bully in a bad house looking for his trul and hurrying from door to door bouncing against the waistcoat;

but rather walks like Aladin about his own enchanted palace so gently that you do not feel his step – Other wines of a heavy and spirituous nature transform a Man to a Silenus; this makes him a Hermes – and gives a Woman the soul and immortality of Ariadne for whom Bacchus always kept a good cellar of claret.....

(R II, 64)

Keats's reflections are sufficiently similar to Falstaff's to make us feel that there is a debt, possibly subconscious; but his development of the idea is original and distinctive, with its own kind of liveliness, while the likening of claret in the brain to Aladdin walking 'gently' in 'his own enchanted palace' betrays a characteristic Keatsian modulation towards the dreamily escapist.

Another important influence on the letters was the work of the eighteenth-century novelist Laurence Sterne, particularly *Tristram Shandy*. (Keats once described the wit of his friend Thomas Richards as 'Shandean': R II, 245.) Sterne specialised in 'writing to the moment' – in a rapid, nervously sensitive response to the immediate, often coupled with a keen eye for the absurdity of the world around and of his own place in it. Keats's letters, in their nimble rapidity, frequently emulate the fidgety hop-skip-and-jump of the Sternian prose. Again, Sterne's Tristram had said that when his thoughts are slow to rise as he writes, his remedy is to shave, change his shirt and coat, 'and in a word, dress myself from one end to the other of me, after my best fashion'; and then he can resume the writing (Vol. IX, Chapter 13). Keats says, similarly,

> Whenever I find myself growing vapourish, I rouse myself, wash and put on a clean shirt, brush my hair and clothes, tie my shoestrings neatly and in fact adonize as I were going out – then all clean and comfortable I sit down to write.

(R II, 186)

Sterne is fond of elaborate, mock-pedantically precise descriptions of pose, stance and gesture. Corporal Trim, for example, when reading a sermon (in *Tristram Shandy*, Vol. II, Chapter 17),

> stood before them with his body swayed, and bent forwards just so far, as to make an angle of 85 degrees and a half upon the plain of the horizon; – which sound orators, to whom I address this, know very well, to be the true persuasive angle of incidence.....

And Uncle Toby (Vol. I, Chapter 21)

> was sitting on the opposite side of the fire, smoking his social pipe all the time, in mute contemplation of a new pair of black-plush-breeches which he had got on.....

162

*Severn: Miniature of Keats.*

Keats, with equivalent attentiveness to posture, writes to George and his wife:

> the fire is at its last click – I am sitting with my back to it with one foot rather askew upon the rug and the other with the heel a little elevated from the carpet – I am writing this on the Maid's tragedy which I have read since tea with Great pleasure – Besides this volume of Beaumont & Fletcher – there are on the tabl[e] two volumes of chaucer . . . . . These are trifles – but I require nothing so much of you as that you will give me a like description of yourselves, however it may be when you are writing to me – Could I see the same thing done of any great Man long since dead it would be a great delight: as to know in what position Shakespeare sat when he began 'To be or not to be' – such thing[s] become interesting from distance of time or place. . . . .
>
> (R II, 73)

He was right; and perhaps it was Sterne's prompting which resulted in this memorable verbal sketch of John Keats by the fireside on 12 March 1819.

Though there were important differences between the two men (not for Sterne the Romantic transcendent yearnings of Keats), both writers were invalids, keenly aware of death's tightening grip on the lungs; and this may partly account for their impatient eagerness to relish and record, with thin-skinned sensitivity, the ephemeral flux of passing life. As Keats said:

> I scarcely remember counting upon any Happiness – I look not for it if it be not in the present hour – nothing startles me beyond the Moment. The setting sun will always set me to rights – or if a Sparrow come before my Window I take part in its existence and pick about the gravel.
>
> (R I, 186)

No series of letters is better than Keats's at recording the moment-by-moment responsiveness to life of an eager, mercurial and generous young nature, learning and growing, erring and hoping; one prematurely silenced by death, but setting an enduring example of vitality. As Keats well knew, the dead open the eyes of the living.

# Part Three
*Reference Section*

# Glossary of classical names

Of the numerous classical names in Keats's poems, I have selected those which have greatest prominence or significance. The main source of this glossary is John Lemprière's *Biobliotheca Classica; or, A Classical Dictionary* (cited as L): the reference-book frequently consulted by Keats. Another of his sources cited here is *The Pantheon*, by 'Edward Baldwin' (William Godwin).

ALPHEUS: the god of the River Alpheus which rises in Arcadia. Alpheus pursued the nymph Arethusa, who eluded him when she was transformed into a fountain by Diana. (Godwin reports the legend that eventually the two streams merged.)

AMPHION: the son of Zeus (or Jupiter). 'When Amphion grew up, he cultivated poetry, and made such an uncommon progress in music, that he is said to have been the inventor of it, and to have built the walls of Thebes at the sound of his lyre' (L): his music moved the very stones.

ANDROMEDA: the daughter of King Cepheus; she was chained to a rock as a sacrifice to a sea-monster, but was rescued by Perseus, who married her.

APOLLO (Phoebus): the Greek god of poetry, music, eloquence and medicine; the patron of shepherds; often regarded as a sun-god. 'He is always represented as a tall beardless young man with a handsome shape, holding in his hand a bow, and sometimes a lyre; his head is generally surrounded with beams of light' (L).

APOLLONIUS: 'A Pythagorean philosopher, well skilled in the secret arts of magic' (L).

ARGUS: a man with a hundred eyes, whom Juno set to keep watch on Io; but Mercury, at Jupiter's command, lulled him to sleep by playing the lyre, so that Jupiter could gain access to Io. The hundred eyes were subsequently transferred to the tail of the peacock.

ARIADNE: the daughter of King Minos; she loved Theseus but was forsaken by him; subsequently Bacchus loved her and gave her a diadem of seven stars.

ASIA: the deity of the Asian continent. Keats ascribes her parentage to Tellus (Earth) and Caf (Kaf or Caucasus).

ATLAS: the Titan who is said to have borne the world (or the heavens) on his shoulders.

AURORA: the goddess of dawn.

BACCHUS (Dionysus): god of the vine, and therefore of intoxication, ecstasy and the wildly irrational; often accompanied by a throng of singing Bacchantes. 'The leader was drawn in a chariot by a lion and a tiger, and was accompanied by Pan and Silenus, and all the Satyrs'; 'As he was the god of vintage, of wine, and of drinkers, he is generally represented crowned with vine and ivy leaves, with a thyrsus in his hand'; 'He often appears naked, and riding upon the shoulders of Pan, or in the arms of Silenus, who was his foster-father' (L). Keats knew Titian's painting, 'Bacchus and Ariadne'.

BAIAE: Italian city founded by Baius and famed for its pleasant situation on the shores of the Mediterranean. 'Baiae's bay' is finely commended in Shelley's 'Ode to the West Wind'.

CERES: goddess of corn and harvests; mother of Proserpine, who was snatched away to the underworld by Pluto (Dis). Keats admired the 'very extraordinary' beauty of *Paradise Lost*, Book IV, lines 268–72:

> Not that fair field
> Of Enna, where Proserpin gath'ring flowers
> (Herself a fairer Flower) by gloomy Dis
> Was gather'd, which cost Ceres all that pain
> To seek her through the World.....

CIRCE: the voluptuous enchantress who transformed Ulysses' men into swine.

CLIO: the daughter of Jupiter and Mnemosyne (Memory); the first of the Muses, she presides over history.

COMUS: 'the god of revelry, feasting, and nocturnal entertainments' (L); the eponymous sensual tempter in Milton's masque.

CUPID: son of Venus and god of love; 'represented as a winged infant, naked, armed with a bow and a quiver full of arrows'; 'Sometimes he appears driving a hoop, throwing a quoit, playing with a nymph, catching a butterfly, or trying to burn it with a torch' (L); the secret lover of the nymph Psyche.

CYBELE: known as the Mother of the Gods; representative of the earth's fertility and of feminine procreation; 'she had an intrigue with Atys, a beautiful youth, whom her father mutilated' (L).

CYNTHIA: 'a surname of Diana, from mount Cynthus, where she was born' (L). Goddess of the moon; represented as a huntress, tall and athletic. 'Though she was the patroness of chastity, yet she forgot her dignity to enjoy the company of Endymion' (L).

DEUCALION: son of Prometheus. When Jupiter sent a deluge to

destroy mankind, Deucalion and his wife Pyrrha survived it in their boat.

DIANA: *see* Cynthia.

DIDO: the Queen of Carthage who committed suicide when her lover, Aeneas, left her.

ECHO: deprived of speech by Juno as a punishment for loquacity, she could only echo the questions put to her; she fell in love with Narcissus, 'and on being despised by him, she pined away, and was changed into a stone' (L). Godwin's version is that she 'wasted to nothing but a voice' after being repulsed by Narcissus.

ENCELADUS: 'the most powerful of all the giants who conspired against Jupiter'. 'He was struck with Jupiter's thunders, and overwhelmed under mount Ætna' (L).

ENDYMION: an ever-young and somnolent shepherd. 'Diana saw him naked as he slept on mount Latmos [in Caria], and was so struck with his beauty that she came down from heaven every night to enjoy his company..... The fable of Endymion's amours with Diana, or the moon, arises from his knowledge of astronomy, and as he passed the night on some high mountain, to observe the heavenly bodies, it has been reported that he was courted by the moon' (L).

FLORA: 'the goddess of flowers and gardens among the Romans..... She was represented as crowned with flowers, and holding in her hand the horn of plenty' (L).

GLAUCUS: a fisherman who sought to emulate fish: 'he leaped into the water, and was made a sea deity by Oceanus and Tethys, at the request of the gods. After this transformation, he became enamoured of the Nereid Scylla, whose ingratitude was severely punished by Circe' (L).

HEBE: the daughter of Jupiter and Juno, and wife of Hercules; the personification of youth, and able to re-invigorate men and gods.

HECATE: 'She was called Luna in heaven, Diana on earth, and Hecate or Proserpine in hell..... She was supposed to preside over magic and enchantments' (L). Keats also knew her as the sinister commander of the Weird Sisters in *Macbeth*.

HERMES (Mercury): the messenger of the gods, with winged cap and ankles, who lulled Argus to sleep.

HERO: 'a beautiful priestess of Venus at Sestos, greatly enamoured of Leander, a youth of Abydos'. Each night, Leander swam across the Hellespont to meet her. 'After many interviews of mutual affection and tenderness, Leander was drowned in a tempestuous

168

night as he attempted his usual course, and Hero in despair threw herself down from her tower and perished in the sea' (L). Keats knew the story from the versions in Ovid's *Metamorphoses*, Book V, and in *Hero and Leander* by Marlowe and Chapman; he re-tells it in 'On a Leander' and *Endymion*.

HESPERUS: the planet Venus: the evening star, which reappears as Phosphorus or Lucifer, the morning star.

HIPPOCRENE: a fountain, sacred to the Muses and Apollo, near Mount Helicon; produced by the stamping of Pegasus's hoof. Its waters were 'violet-coloured' (Godwin).

HYACINTH: a youth loved by Apollo. Zephyrus, who was jealous, blew a quoit thrown by Apollo so that it struck and killed Hyacinth; but Hyacinth's blood was transformed into the flower which now bears his name, and his body was 'placed . . . . . among the constellations' (L).

HYACINTHIA: 'an annual solemnity at Amyclæ, in Laconia, in honour of Hyacinthus and Apollo . . . . . Youths, with their garments girt about them, entertained the spectators, by playing sometimes upon the flute, or upon the harp, and by singing anapestic songs, in loud, echoing voices, in honour of Apollo[;] . . . . . choirs of young men came upon the stage singing their uncouth rustic songs, and accompanied by persons who danced . . . . . The city began then to be filled with joy, and immense numbers of victims were offered on the altars of Apollo . . . . . During this latter part of the festivity, all were eager to be present at the games, and the city was almost left without inhabitants.' This entry in Lemprière was (as B. H. Kemball-Cook suggests) one of the sources of 'Ode on a Grecian Urn'.

HYPERION: 'a son of Cœlus and Terra, who married Thea, by whom he had Aurora, the sun, and moon. Hyperion is often taken by the poets for the sun itself' (L). Keats follows Godwin's *Pantheon* in presenting Hyperion as a sun-god dethroned and superseded by Apollo at the time when Saturn and the Titans were defeated by Jupiter, Neptune and Pluto: 'Hyperion one of the Titans having been according to some accounts the God of the sun before that province was conferred upon Apollo.'

JASON: the hero, warrior and voyager who, with his Argonauts, sailed to Colchis and won the Golden Fleece.

JUPITER (Jove): the most powerful of the ancient gods; he overthrew his father, Saturn. 'Jupiter, now become the sole master of the empire of the world, divided it with his brothers. He reserved for himself the kingdom of heaven, and gave the empire of the sea to

169

Neptune, and that of the infernal regions to Pluto' (L). *Endymion* refers to the legend that Jupiter, as a boy, had been fed with goat's milk by Amalthea.

LAMIA: Robert Burton's *The Anatomy of Melancholy* (Part III, Section 2, Member 1, Subsection 1) provided Keats with the ancient legend of 'a phantasm in the habit of a fair gentlewoman' who solicited and enchanted a young Corinthian. To their wedding feast, 'amongst other guests, came Apollonius, who, by some probable conjectures, found her out to be a serpent, a lamia': he denounced her, and she promptly disappeared. (In Greek and Roman mythology, a lamia is a blood-sucking serpent-witch, analogous to the vampire.) Keats, in 'Lamia', adapted the story so as to make it an allegory of the power of philosophy, or rationalism, to blight natural beauty and the poetic imagination by providing reductively empirical explanations of them. Other important sources were Coleridge's 'Christabel' (1816) and Peacock's *Rhododaphne* (1818).

LEANDER: *see* Hero.

LEDA: the wife of King Tyndarus. Jupiter, in the guise of a swan, copulated with her; subsequently she 'brought forth two eggs, of one of which sprang Pollux and Helena, and of the other Castor and Clytemnestra' (L).

LETHE: 'one of the rivers of hell, whose waters the souls of the dead drank after they had been confined for a certain space of time in Tartarus. It had the power of making them forget whatever they had done, seen, or heard before, as the name implies, λήθη, *oblivion*' (L).

LYCIDAS: John Milton's name for Edward King, whose death by drowning he commemorated in the elegy 'Lycidas'.

MAIA: 'a daughter of Atlas and Pleione, mother of Mercury by Jupiter' (L); she gives her name to the month of May.

MERCURY: messenger of the gods, conductor of the dead, and father of eloquence.

MINOS: the King of Crete who, after his death, became 'supreme and absolute judge in the infernal regions' (L).

MNEMOSYNE: 'a daughter of Cœlus and Terra, mother of the nine Muses, by Jupiter, who assumed the form of a shepherd to enjoy her company. The word *Mnemosyne* signifies *memory*, and therefore the poets have rightly called memory the mother of the muses, because it is to that mental endowment that mankind is indebted for the progress in science [that is, knowledge, wisdom]' (L). Keats follows Hesiod (and Godwin) in regarding her as a Titan.

MOMUS: the son of Nox (Night) and god of mirth, mockery and satire.

MONETA: another name for Mnemosyne, the mother of the Muses (according to Hyginus's *Fabulae*, which Keats consulted). She was sometimes associated with Minerva, the goddess of wisdom. *Moneta* is Latin for 'the reminder' or 'the admonisher' (and 'money'). Keats's characterisation of Moneta in *The Fall of Hyperion* draws on Lemprière's description of the goddess Isis: 'The word *Isis*, according to some, signifies *antient*, and, on that account, the inscriptions on the statues of the goddess were in these words: *I am all that has been, that shall be, and none among mortals has hitherto taken off my veil*'. (Other sources were the Virgil and Beatrice of Dante's *Divine Comedy*.)

NARCISSUS: a beautiful youth who fell in love with his reflection in a pool, thinking it to be a nymph; in his consequent frustration, he pined away, and was transformed into the flower which now bears his name.

NEPTUNE: the sea-god, son of Saturn and Ops, and brother to Jupiter, Pluto and Juno.

NIOBE: the mourning mother, wife of Amphion. She was too proud of her numerous children, so they were slain by Artemis (Diana) and Apollo.

OPS (Opis): wife of Saturn and mother of Jupiter.

ORPHEUS: 'He received a lyre from Apollo, or, according to some, from Mercury, upon which he played with such a masterly hand that even the most rapid rivers ceased to flow, the savage beasts of the forest forgot their wildness, and the mountains moved to listen to his song. All nature seemed charmed and animated' (L). He loved Eurydice, who died and was carried to the Underworld; thither he followed her, and by his sorrow and lyre-playing persuaded Pluto and Proserpine to release her; but on the journey home, contrary to a promise he had made, he looked back at Eurydice, and she was therefore irrevocably snatched down to the Underworld.

PAN: the son of Mercury, and 'the god of shepherds, of huntsmen, and of all the inhabitants of the country . . . . . [H]e had two small horns on his head, his complexion was ruddy, his nose flat, and his legs, thighs, tail, and feet, were those of a goat . . . . . He invented the flute with seven reeds, which he called *Syrinx*, in honor of a beautiful nymph of the same name, to whom he attempted to offer violence, and who was changed into a reed' (L).

PEGASUS: the winged horse loved by the Muses; his hoof created the fountain, Hippocrene.

PEONA: the sister of the hero in *Endymion*, and apparently Keats's invention. She may have been suggested by Leander's sister in *Hero and Leander*, the amatory poem by Marlowe and Chapman. As Peona has healing powers, her name may derive from that of the peony, the flower which is used in medicine and therefore is named after Pæon, physician to the gods; or Keats may have derived it directly from that of the same Pæon, 'a celebrated physician who cured the wounds which the gods received during the Trojan war' (L). Pæon appears in Ovid's *Metamorphoses*, XV.

PLUTO: the son of Saturn; he became ruler of the underworld when Saturn was overthrown by Jupiter. His other names include Dis and Hades. He abducted Proserpine when she was gathering flowers; she became the queen of his gloomy kingdom but was periodically allowed to return to the upper world in springtime.

POMONA: 'a nymph at Rome who was supposed to preside over gardens, and to be the goddess of all sorts of fruit-trees' (L).

PROSERPINE: the daughter of Ceres by Jupiter; associated with flowers and springtime, but also with death. That she spends part of the year in the underworld with Pluto and part in the upper world with Ceres suggests that she is a goddess of vegetation and particularly seed-corn, which 'die' in the cold months and rise from the ground in the warm months. (Godwin remarks: 'Proserpine is said to represent the seed, and Ceres the fertility, of the earth'.) Keats knew the vividly poignant references to her abduction in Shakespeare's *Winter's Tale* (Act IV, scene iv) and in Milton's *Paradise Lost* (Book IV, lines 268–72; quoted previously in the 'Ceres' reference). Proserpine in sometimes identified with Hecate (one of Diana's names).

PSYCHE: 'a nymph whom Cupid married and carried into a place of bliss, where he long enjoyed her company' (L). The Greek word *psyche* (φῡχή) means, in addition to 'breath' and 'desire', both 'soul' and 'butterfly': a linkage probably deriving from the butterfly's ability to arise beautifully from apparent death (after the caterpillar has 'died' as a chrysalis). 'Psyche is generally represented with the wings of a butterfly to imitate the lightness of the soul, of which the butterfly is the symbol, and on that account, among the ancients, when a man had just expired, a butterfly appeared floating above, as if rising from the mouth of the deceased' (L). Keats recalled this duality in *Endymion* and the 'Ode on Melancholy' (as did Joseph Conrad later, in *Lord Jim*, Chapter 20). The nymph's union with Cupid is pictured in 'Ode to Psyche'. Coleridge's *Biographia Literaria* (1817), I, p. 82, said: 'The poetic PSYCHE, in its process to full development, undergoes as many changes as its Greek name-sake, the butterfly'.

SATURN: 'a son of Cœlus, or Uranus, by Terra' (L). He castrated his father and became ruler of the gods. When overthrown by his son Jupiter (in alliance with Neptune and Pluto), he went to Italy to share the kingdom with Janus, and '[h]is reign there was so mild and popular, so beneficent and virtuous, that mankind have called it the *golden age*' (L). In *Hyperion*, Keats changes the legend to make the relationship between Cœlus and Saturn an affectionate one; and, like Ovid in *Metamorphoses*, he associates the Golden Age with Saturn's reign in heaven.

SILENUS: 'a demi-god, who became the nurse, the preceptor, and attendant of the god Bacchus..... Silenus is generally represented as a fat and jolly old man, riding on an ass, crowned with flowers, and always intoxicated' (L).

TEMPE: a beautiful valley in Thessaly, beneath Mount Olympus.

THEA: 'a daughter of Uranus and Terra. She married her brother Hyperion, by whom she had the sun, the moon, Aurora, &c.' (L).

THEMIS: one of the Titans; 'a daughter of Cœlus and Terra' (L).

TITANS: the gigantic sons of Cœlus and Terra. Lemprière and Godwin list their names as Saturn, Hyperion, Oceanus, Japetus, Cottus, Briareus, Typhœus, Mimas, Porphyrion, Rhœtus, Enceladus, Cœus, Creus and Gyges; of whom Hyperion was married to Thea, Oceanus to Tethys, Japetus to Clymene and Cœus to Phœbe. Hesiod adds Themis; she 'married Jupiter against her own inclinations' (L). Keats adds 'Dolor'.

URANIA: 'one of the Muses, daughter of Jupiter and Mnemosyne, who presided over astronomy' (L). 'Urania' was also another name of Venus: whereas 'Pandemian Venus' denoted love in its sensual aspects, 'Uranian Venus' denoted love in its virtuous, spiritual and intellectual aspects. Milton invokes her in *Paradise Lost*, Books I and VII, as does Shelley in *Adonais*.

URANUS (alias Ouranus and Cœlus): the god of the skies: 'the most ancient of all the gods. He married Tithea, or the Earth', whose offspring were 'called from their mother Titans' (L).

VENUS: 'the goddess of beauty, the mother of love, the queen of laughter, the mistress of the graces and of pleasures, and the patroness of courtezans'. 'Venus spr[a]ng from the froth of the sea, after the mutilated part of the body of Uranus had been thrown there by Saturn' (L). Married to Vulcan, she copulated with Mars, Mercury, Bacchus, Neptune, etc., and was the mother of Cupid, Priapus and Eryx. She particularly loved Adonis, the young hunter who was killed by a boar.

The planet Venus is the evening star, which Keats (perhaps recalling Endymion's love for the moon-goddess Cynthia) associated with Fanny Brawne: 'I will imagine you Venus tonight and pray, pray, pray to your star like a Hethen' (R II, 133).

# Biographical list

RICHARD ABBEY. Tea-broker and City business-man who became guardian to the Keats children in 1810; he died in 1837, and later endured a literary purgatory in Keatsian biographies and in E. M. Forster's tale 'Mr. and Mrs. Abbey's Difficulties'.

BENJAMIN BAILEY (1791–1853). In 1817 Keats was his guest at Oxford, where Bailey was reading for holy orders, and there Book III of *Endymion* was composed. Bailey, who himself had poetic aspirations, subsequently became an archdeacon in Colombo.

GIOVANNI BOCCACCIO (1313–75). The story of Lorenzo and Isabella in Boccaccio's *Decameron* was the main source of Keats's narrative poem of 'wormy circumstance', 'Isabella; or, The Pot of Basil'.

FANNY BRAWNE (1800–1865). She met Keats in 1818 and they apparently became engaged in October 1819 (G, 361). Though his emotions towards her were sometimes jealous and tortured, she seems to have been admirably affectionate and loyal to him. Keats addressed to her the sonnet 'Bright star, would I were steadfast as thou art'. She did not marry until more than twelve years after his death.

CHARLES BROWN (1787–1842). Freed from business by an inheritance, he gave time to literary pursuits. His comic opera *Narensky* was produced at Drury Lane in 1814. He was introduced to Keats in 1817 and together the two men rambled through England and Scotland in the following year. They collaborated on *Otho the Great*.

ROBERT BURNS (1759–96). Keats enjoyed his lyrical and light-hearted poems in Scots dialect. In July 1818 Keats wrote: 'One of the pleasantest bouts we have had was our walk to Burns's Cottage, over the Doon and past Kirk Alloway'. In commemoration of the visit he wrote a weak sonnet, 'This mortal body', and the better poem, 'Lines Written in the Highlands after a Visit to Burns's Country'. A related sonnet is 'On Visiting the Tomb of Burns'.

LORD BYRON (1788–1824). Keats referred to him and Scott as the two 'literary kings' of the time, addressed a sonnet to him, and attempted to emulate the topical satire of *Don Juan* in 'The Cap and Bells; or, The Jealousies'. Byron was annoyed by Keats's attack on the Augustans, and disliked *Endymion*: he referred to Keats as 'Jack Ketch' (the hangman) and said 'his is the Onanism of Poetry'. However, on hearing of Keats's death, he nobly wrote to his publisher: 'as he is dead, omit *all* that is said *about him* in any MSS of mine, or publication. His *Hyperion* is a fine monument.....'

THOMAS CHATTERTON (1752–70). The prolific young poet from Bristol who committed suicide in London. Keats, like other Romantics, admired his pseudo-Mediaeval poetry, particularly that of the drama *Ælla*. *Endymion* was dedicated to Chatterton.

GEOFFREY CHAUCER (1340?–1400). Keats admired his *Troilus and Criseyde* and *The Canterbury Tales* (though later he preferred the diction of Chatterton's *Rowley*); in 1817 he said that at Canterbury 'the Remembrance of Chaucer will set me forward like a Billiard-Ball' (R I, 147).

CHARLES COWDEN CLARKE (1787–1877). The son of the headmaster at the Enfield school which Keats attended; a close boyhood friend whose poetic encouragement is commemorated in the verse letter 'To Charles Cowden Clarke'. In 1817 he moved to Ramsgate with his parents. He helped with the proof-sheets of *Endymion* in 1818 but thereafter lost contact with Keats. His own poems, *Carmina Minima*, were published in 1859.

CLAUDE (CLAUDE LORRAIN, 1600–1682). The painter whose 'Romanticised Classicism' (legendary figures seen amid enchanted landscapes) had great influence on the Romantic artists and their precursors. Keats wrote to Reynolds: 'You know, I am sure, Claude's Enchanted Castle and I wish you may be pleased with my remembrance of it' (R I, 263). The 'remembrance' occurs in the verse-letter 'To J. H. Reynolds'.

SAMUEL TAYLOR COLERIDGE (1772–1834). The poet and critic who discussed nightingales, metaphysics and nightmares with Keats during their walk in April 1819. His 'Christabel' influenced Keats's 'The Eve of St. Agnes' and 'Lamia'.

DANTE (DANTE ALIGHIERI, 1265–1321). Keats studied his *Divina Commedia* in Cary's translation (published by Taylor and Hessey in 1814). The presentation of the poet as pupil of an immortal female mentor (Beatrice) influenced the transformation of *Hyperion* into *The Fall of Hyperion*, while the legend of Paolo and Francesca (*Inferno*, Canto V) helped to engender 'As Hermes once'.

CHARLES WENTWORTH DILKE (1789–1864). He worked at the Navy Pay Office but was also a literary scholar: eventually he became owner and editor of *The Athenæum*. In 1818 Keats wrote: 'I am a good deal with Dilke and Brown – we are very thick – they are very kind to me' (R I, 237).

WILLIAM HASLAM (1795 or 1798 to 1851). The solicitor who was a loyal friend and advisor to Keats, lending him money and helping to arrange the voyage to Italy. Fanny Brawne said 'his kindness cannot be described' (R I, 75).

BENJAMIN HAYDON (1786–1846). He painted portraits and topical scenes, but his keenest enthusiasm was reserved for the grandiose canvases on religious and historical subjects (for example, 'Christ's Entry into Jerusalem' and 'The Judgement of Solomon'). For a while, his lofty ambitions helped to arouse Keats's, though Haydon's subsequent financial straits led to an estrangement. Long afterwards, in poverty and despair, Haydon killed himself. His most original painting is probably the unconventionally-posed 'Waiting for *The Times*'; and his most vital work is certainly the autobiographical Journal.

WILLIAM HAZLITT (1778–1830). Keats met him socially, attended his lectures, and read his critical works on Shakespeare and the English poets. His ideas (for example, that Shakespeare was 'nothing in himself') influenced Keats's notions of 'Negative Capability' and the poet's character. Keats owned a copy of Hazlitt's *Essay on the Principles of Human Action*, which emphasised the value of sympathetic identification with other beings.

JAMES HENRY LEIGH HUNT (1784–1859). The poet, critic and essayist who was the most important early patron and friend of Keats, publishing his work and extolling it in the *Examiner*. Both the content and the versification of Hunt's 'The Story of Rimini' influenced Keats's earlier poetry, as did his taste for the 'luxuries' of imaginative hedonism. He was fiercely attacked in *Blackwood's* as an immoral writer. Though Keats came to regard him as vain and patronising, Hunt maintained a life-long admiration of Keats's work and character. Both men were potent influences on the Pre-Raphaelite artists: Keats through his poetry, Hunt partly through his seminal enthusiasm for the Camposanto frescoes at Pisa. If Hunt resembles an Aesthete living many years ahead of his appropriate time (the era of Pater and Wilde), this is partly because he helped to engender that later era: Hunt is an underestimated deflector of certain Romantic energies towards Aestheticism.

ISABELLA JONES. Keats met her at Hastings in 1817 and subsequently in London; 'warmed with her . . . . . and kissed her' (R I, 403). She is probably the 'Isabel' of his love-poem 'Hush, hush, tread softly'. Keats's words have warmed her from cold oblivion into literary history, though she was 'an enigma' to him and remains so to his biographers.

EDMUND KEAN (1787–1833). John Keats admired his energetically-expressive acting, and wrote *Otho* in the hope that Kean might play Ludolph. The actor would have made a better subject for a play, as was later demonstrated by Jean-Paul Sartre (in *Kean, ou Désordre et génie*, 1954) and by Raymund FitzSimons.

TADEUSZ KOŚCIUSZKO (1746–1817). The Polish patriot who fought as a volunteer in the American War of Independence and subsequently led his countrymen in their uprising against the Russians (1791–4). Both Hunt and Keats celebrated him in sonnets.

JOHN MILTON (1608–74). The Puritan poet whose epic, *Paradise Lost*, exerted a profound influence on the Romantics. Keats attempted to emulate him in *Hyperion*. Numerous echoes, not only of *Paradise Lost* but also of 'L'Allegro', 'Il Penseroso', 'Lycidas' and particularly *Comus*, can be found in Keats's poems; and Keats resurrected Milton's Lycidas in 'On Visiting Staffa'.

JOHN HAMILTON REYNOLDS (1794–1852). Author, critic and lawyer who befriended Keats in 1816 and introduced him to Brown, Dilke, Taylor, Hessey and others. He favourably reviewed the *Poems* of 1817 in the *Champion*, discussed poetry with Keats and encouraged him to write 'Isabella', originally planned as a joint venture.

JOSEPH SEVERN (1793–1879). The engraver and painter who bravely accompanied the dying Keats to Rome; he subsequently became Consul there from 1861 to 1872. His tombstone says: 'To the Memory of / Joseph Severn / Devoted friend and death-bed companion / of / John Keats / whom he lived to see numbered among / The Immortal Poets of England.....'

WILLIAM SHAKESPEARE (1564–1616). Among those works of Shakespeare which exerted a potent influence on Keats are *Hamlet*, *King Lear*, *Troilus and Cressida*, *A Midsummer Night's Dream*, *The Tempest* and *The Sonnets*. Keats's major odes, earlier pieces like 'When I have fears', and his letters, variously and intermittently recall Shakespearian scenes and phrases. He praises Shakespeare in the sonnet 'On Sitting Down to Read *King Lear* Once Again'. Keats used a seal-ring bearing a picture of Shakespeare; a bust of Shakespeare ornamented his ink-tray; and a portrait hung on the wall.

PERCY BYSSHE SHELLEY (1792–1822). The noble poet of atheistic and anarchistic views whose work marks the lyrical extreme of Romantic verse. Keats's *Endymion* is partly a response to Shelley's *Alastor*. Shelley commemorates Keats in *Adonais*, a pastoral elegy.

EDMUND SPENSER (1552–99). The Puritan poet whose *Faerie Queene* was greatly admired by Keats. Among Keats's earliest work is the 'Imitation of Spenser', and 'The Eve of St. Agnes' also employs the Spenserian stanza (eight lines in pentameter followed by an Alexandrine, and rhyming ABABBCBCC).

RICHARD WOODHOUSE (1788–1834). The kindly lawyer who loaned Keats books and magazines, aided and advised him, and strove to advance his fame.

# Gazetteer

The most important shrine for Keatsian pilgrims is without doubt the Keats House at Hampstead: Wentworth Place, in Keats Grove, London NW3 2RR, a few minutes' walk downhill from Hampstead Underground Station. Now owned and maintained by the Borough of Camden, this attractive house is open to the public and has an important collection of manuscripts and memorabilia. It was built as a double dwelling in 1815–16 by Charles Dilke and Charles Brown, who subsequently became friends of Keats. Brown shared his half of the house with the young poet, while Mrs Brawne later rented Dilke's half, so that Keats and Fanny Brawne lived in adjacent homes and shared the garden – the very garden in which the 'Ode to a Nightingale' was composed. The old plum tree has been replaced, but in the front lawn stands the Stuart mulberry tree that the poet knew well. The manuscripts include letters from Keats to Dilke, Mrs Brawne and Fanny, and the collection of books includes his copies of *Paradise Lost*, Ovid's *Metamorphoses*, Lemprière's *Classical Dictionary*, and an edition of Shakespeare inscribed with the 'Bright star' sonnet. Other items include the almandine engagement ring, locks of his brown hair, and the poem of tribute by Thomas Hardy, 'At a House in Hampstead' (1920), which concludes:

> Pleasanter now it is to hold
> That here, where sang he, more of him
> Remains than where he, tuneless, cold,
>     Passed to the dim.

Although based in London, Keats travelled so widely in the British Isles that a remarkably large number of places have Keatsian associations. In 1817, for example, he visited the Isle of Wight, lodging at Carisbrooke; then Margate, Canterbury, Bo-Peep, Oxford and Stratford-upon-Avon; in 1818 he visited Exeter, Teignmouth and Dawlish, and set out on the Northern walking tour with Brown which took him to Liverpool, Kendal, Ambleside and Grasmere, to Carlisle and Kirkcudbright, across the sea to Belfast, and back to Ballantrae, Ayr, Glasgow, Iona and Staffa. At the end of the year he stayed at Chichester. In 1819 he spent the summer at Shanklin, Isle of Wight, and later moved to Winchester. Then in 1820 he sailed from Gravesend for Italy. The house at Rome in which he died, 26 Piazza di Spagna, beside the Spanish Steps, remains intact; it is now the Keats-Shelley Memorial House, and holds numerous manuscripts, rare books and pictures. Further afield, an important collection of manuscripts is housed in the Houghton Library at Harvard University.

The Keats Memorial Library, housed in the Public Library next to Wentworth Place, holds microfilm copies of much of the Harvard collection and of the documents at the Roman Memorial House.

The old Swan and Hoop at Moorfields was demolished by 1875. Clarke's school-house at Enfield has also gone, though part of its upper storey has been preserved at the Victoria and Albert Museum. The Elgin Marbles, the subject of two early sonnets, can still be seen at the British Museum. Keats's visit to Oxford resulted in the comic poem, 'The Gothic looks solemn', while the Devon journey produced 'For there's Bishop Teign', 'Where be ye going, you Devon Maid.....?' and 'Over the hill and over the dale'. Poems of the Scottish journey include 'On Visiting the Tomb of Burns', 'Ah! ken ye what I met the day', 'To Ailsa Rock', 'Lines Written in the Highlands' and 'Read me a lesson, Muse' (a sonnet written at the peak of Ben Nevis).

Keats wrote the ode 'To Autumn' at Winchester, where he liked to stroll through the meadows by the River Itchen. For those who wish to follow his footsteps he has left very clear directions:

> Now the time is beautiful. I take a walk every day for an hour before dinner and this is generally my walk – I go out at the back gate across one street, into the Cathcdral yard, which is always interesting; then I pass under the trees along a paved path, pass the beautiful front of the Cathedral, turn to the left under a stone door way – then I am on the other side of the building – which leaving behind me I pass on through two college-like squares seemingly built for the dwelling place of Deans and Prebendaries – garnished with grass and shaded with trees. Then I pass through one of the old city gates and then you are in one College-Street through which I pass and at the end thereof crossing some meadows and at last a country alley of gardens I arrive, that is, my worship arrives at the foundation of Saint Cross, which is a very interesting old place, both for its gothic tower and alms-square and for the appropriation of its rich rents to a relation of the Bishop of Winchester – Then I pass across St Cross meadows till you come to the most beautifully clear river – now this is only one mile of my walk.....

> (R II, 209–10)

# Further reading

BIBLIOGRAPHY   *Keats: A Bibliography and Reference Guide,* edited by
J. R. McGillivray. Toronto: University of Toronto Press, 1949.

CONCORDANCES   *A Concordance to the Poems of John Keats,* edited by
D. L. Baldwin *et al.* Washington: Carnegie Institute, 1917;
reprinted, 1963.
*A Concordance to the Poems of John Keats,* edited by M. G. Becker, R. J.
Dilligan and T. K. Bender. New York: Garland Publishing, 1981.

THE POEMS   *The Poetical Works of John Keats,* edited by H. W. Garrod.
Oxford University Press, 1939; revised, 1958. This became the
standard scholarly edition.
*The Poems of John Keats,* edited by Miriam Allott. London: Longman,
1970; paperback, 1972. Provides admirably full annotation.
Although the quotations have occasional inaccuracies, the range of
cited source-materials is vast and illuminating.
*John Keats: The Complete Poems,* edited by John Barnard.
Harmondsworth: Penguin, 1973. Provides detailed explanatory
comments.
*The Poems of John Keats,* edited by Jack Stillinger. London:
Heinemann, 1978. A scholarly edition of the texts which in various
ways (e.g. the range of variants) superseded Garrod's.

THE LETTERS   *The Letters of John Keats,* 2 Volumes, edited by Hyder
Edward Rollins. Cambridge University Press, 1958. The standard
scholarly edition.

BIOGRAPHY   *The Keats Circle: Letters and Papers 1816–1878,* 2
Volumes, edited by H. E. Rollins. Cambridge, Mass.: Harvard
University Press, 1948; 2nd edition, 1965. Essential biographical
documents.
Walter Jackson Bate: *John Keats.* Oxford University Press, 1967.
(Previously, Cambridge, Mass.: Harvard University Press, 1963.)
An admirable critical biography.
Robert Gittings: *John Keats.* London: Heinemann, 1968. This gives
more biographical minutiae than Bate, who often gives fuller critical
discussion of the poems.
Timothy Hilton: *Keats and His World.* London: Thames and Hudson,
1971. A concise introduction with an interesting range of pictures.
Anthony Burgess: *ABBA ABBA.* London: Faber and Faber, 1977.
The novelist's brief fictional biography of Keats's last months in
Rome. Quirky and acute, sympathetic and provocative.

CRITICISM  *Keats: The Critical Heritage,* edited by G. M. Matthews. London: Routledge and Kegan Paul, 1971. A large selection of nineteenth-century criticism. Historically, the most admirable critic of Keats is Leigh Hunt, who is represented alongside the notoriously hostile early reviewers.

A. C. Bradley: *Oxford Lectures on Poetry.* London: Macmillan, 1907. Gradually, various Romantic assumptions became critical orthodoxies. These discussions of Keats's letters and poems mark an academic completion of the process.

D. H. Lawrence: 'The Nightingale': a polemical essay of 1927 reprinted in *Phoenix.* London: Heinemann, 1936.

F. R. Leavis: *Revaluation: Tradition and Development in English Poetry.* London: Chatto and Windus, 1936. The assessment of Keats in Chapter 7 was very influential.

Cleanth Brooks: *The Well Wrought Urn.* London: Methuen, 1968. (Previously, New York: Reynel and Hitchcock, 1947.) Chapter 8 analyses the 'Ode on a Grecian Urn'.

Earl Wasserman: *The Finer Tone: Keats's Major Poems.* Baltimore: Johns Hopkins, 1953. A sophisticated discussion.

Ian Jack: *Keats and the Mirror of Art.* Oxford University Press, 1967. A speculative survey of putative connections between various paintings and Keats's poetry.

William Empson: *The Structure of Complex Words.* London: Chatto and Windus, 1969. Contains a bold and lively discussion of 'Ode on a Grecian Urn'.

John Jones: *John Keats's Dream of Truth.* London: Chatto and Windus, 1969. A vigorously responsive and sensitive study.

*John Keats: The Odes: A Casebook,* edited by G. S. Fraser. London: Macmillan, 1971. A useful collection of critical material.

Christopher Ricks: *Keats and Embarrassment.* Oxford University Press, 1974. A preoccupation with embarrassment is the pretext of a clever discussion.

William Walsh: *Introduction to Keats.* London: Methuen, 1981. A concise critical survey.

David Morse: *Romanticism: A Structural Analysis.* London: Macmillan, 1982. A brief but provocative analysis of Keats forms part of this general appraisal of Romanticism.

DISCUSSION ON TAPE AND CASSETTE  Robert Gittings and Roger Sharrock: *Keats.* Wakefield: Educational Productions, 1975.

LITERARY SOCIETIES  The Keats-Shelley Memorial Association. Secretarial Address: Keats House, Keats Grove, London NW3 2RR. The Association holds occasional meetings, publishes an annual *Bulletin,* and helps to maintain the house in Rome where Keats died. The Keats-Shelley Association of America, Inc.

# General Index